Microfinance and Poverty Alleviation

About the Author

Dr. A. Rajmani Singha currently working as head, in the Department of Commerce Manipur University. His area of interest is finance and accounting and teaching financial management and securities analysis and portfolio management to the students of Commerce. He has conducted several national seminar, training programme and workshop in the areas of commerce education, financial management, accounting package with TALLY and financial inclusion. He has been participating in national and international conferences and seminar as paper presenter, discussant, rapporteur and organizer. Dr. Singha is also the author/co-author of ten books, 25 chapters in books, 24 research papers in journal and 12 articles published. Commerce Education in North East India, Financial Inclusion for Inclusive Growth, Tourism Industry in India, Microfinance: A boon or Bane and Youth, Peace and Development are among the books of worth mentioning. He is the editor of the journal of business studies "The Kangleipak Business Review".

Microfinance and Poverty Alleviation

A. Rajmani Singha

CONCEPT PUBLISHING COMPANY PVT. LTD.
NEW DELHI-110059

ISBN-13 : 978-93-5125-139-2

First Published 2015

Published and Printed by

Concept Publishing Company Pvt. Ltd.
A/15-16, Commercial Block, Mohan Garden
New Delhi-110059 (India)
T: 25351460, 25351794, *F*: 091-11-25357109
E: publishing@conceptpub.com, W: www.conceptpub.com
Editorial Office: H-13, Bali Nagar, New Delhi-110 015, India.

Cataloging in Publication Data—*Courtesy:* D.K. Agencies (P) Ltd. <docinfo@dkagencies.com>

Singha, A. Rajmani , author.
Microfinance and poverty alleviation / A. Rajmani Singha.
pages cm
Includes bibliographical references (pages) and index.
ISBN 9789351251392

1. Microfinance—India—Manipur. 2. Self-help groups—India—Manipur. 3. Poverty--Government policy—India—Manipur. 4. Women—Employment—Government policy--India—Manipur. I. Title.

DDC 332.095417 23

Dedicated
to
My Grandfather
Late A. Tomal Singha

Preface

Women form a vital part of the Indian economy, which constitute 1/3rd of the labour force, and primary members contributing in the survival of the family. Women are the backbone of the agricultural sector, comprising the majority of agricultural labourers in India. In order to alleviate the rural poverty, easy access to micro credit and micro loan for development and promotion of micro enterprises and economic activities is imperative. Considering the significance of it, SHG based micro financing programmes and projects have implemented in India in the later part of the 19th century. In India, micro credit has received attention both from the government and the formal banking sector. In fact, over 80 per cent of micro credit outreach has been through banks. In order to address issues of development, a large number of women focused schemes have been promoted in the country. Swarna Jayanti Gram Swarozgar Yojana (SJGSY) and Micro financing schemes of Rashtriya Mahila Kosh (RMK), SHG formation under NABARD were launched by the Government of India to address issues of women's socio-economic empowerment.

Women empowerment through SHG based microfinance, micro credit, micro loan and micro insurance have been given more focus for development of rural and semi-urban India. Government has also paid special attention to women's empowerment through more involvement in economic oriented activities. Women empowerment enhances their status in social, political, cultural and economic condition of the people living in the rural and semi-urban areas in particular and also in urban areas in general. SHG based microfinance programme have greater impact on women's empowerment in comparison with other women development programmes. Further, it is also notice that microfinance has linked up with various areas of social issues such as financial inclusion, micro insurance, women empowerment, sustainable development, social interventions, poverty alleviation, health, housing, education and so on. Microfinance has saved millions and millions of lives of poor Indian who are living below poverty line, funded entrepreneurial spirit of poor and reduced income inequalities by making capital accessible to low income groups and encourage to undertake economic oriented activities by establishing micro enterprises. Today, after thirty years of existence, Microfinance Institutions are believed to have reached more than 100 million clients, which is a remarkable achievement world-wide. But as per the World Bank statistics, this remarkable achievement is believed to meet only 4 per cent of the total world demand for such funds. Against this view point, the present book has been undertaken by the author to see the impact of microfinance to poor people of work has divided into nine different broad chapters. The first chapter is delves on the introduction of Microfinance which provides a brief sketch of microfinance evolution, its growth and development in the global and in Asian continent. The second chapter is deals on the development of microfinance such as microfinance institution, microfinance and microcredit, microfinance and financial institution, microfinance and micro-enterprise and microfinance and micro-insurance, etc. Third chapter is highlighting on the Microfinance in India on current status, recent trends, regulation, microfinance institutions and role of government for microfinance development. Fourth chapter provides on the microfinance in north eastern states of India. Fifth chapter covered on the research methodology and sixth chapter discuss on microfinance in Manipur. Chapter seven is all about the impact of microfinance on micro-enterprise development in Manipur. Data analysis is the title of the 8th chapter and Chapter 9th is concluding remarks where it provide main findings and policy recommendations for further improvement.

The present study is the outcome of inspiration, encouragement, cooperation, help and supports extended from officials, experts and practitioners in the field of microfinance. It is indeed great pleasure from my part to acknowledge with gratitude to the officials of the University Grants Commission (UGC) New Delhi and also officials of the Manipur University for getting moral and physical support. The financial assistance and grants supported by the University Grants Commission, Government of India, New Delhi has enabled us to pursue the present study at state level. We place on record the sincere appreciation of concerned officials of the Microfinance Institutions and NGOs at the national, regional and state level, district level who extended all kind of support for smooth conduct of field survey and make available of desired information.

It is indebted to Prof. H.N.K. Sarma Vice Chancellor, Manipur University Prof. E. Bijoy Kumar Singh, Dean, School of Social Science and Prof. N. Lokendra Singh Registrar, Manipur University for giving not only the financial support but also the moral and physical support in the process of bringing out this volume. I am also thankful to all the faculty members, staff and students of the department for their encouragement and support in completion of this project.

I would like to record the appreciation of Dr. Th. Surjit Singh and K. Suraj Sharma research scholars and the respondents especially the microfinance institutions, SHGs and Micro entrepreneurs for providing their support in successful completion of the study.

I am thankful to Mr. A.K. Mittal, Nitin Mittal and other members of Concept Publishing Company Pvt. Ltd., New Delhi for taking pain in conversion of manuscripts to the present volume of the book in short period of time.

Last but not least, I am grateful to my wife Mrs. A. Sulochana Devi, Suraj Aheibam, Lanchenba Aheibam, my mom, uncle, aunty and all the family members for their full support in bringing out this volume.

Finally, the Almighty GOD, whose benevolence and blessings shower to complete this effort within this stipulated time.

A. Rajmani Singha
Imphal

Contents

List of Tables

List of Figures

Abbreviations

ACCION	Americans for Community Cooperation in Other Nations
ADB	Asian Development Bank
APPBO	Average Population per Bank Office
APRACA	Asia Pacific Rural and Agricultural Credit Association
ARD	Association for Rural Development
ASA	Association for Social Advancement
ASCAs	Accumulating Savings and Credit Associations
ATMs	Automatic Machines
BASIX	Bhartiya Samruddhi Investments and Consulting Services
BC	Business Correspondents
BF	Business Facilitators
BIRD	Bankers Institute of Rural Development
BPL	Below Poverty Line
BPR	The Bank Perkreditan Rakyat
BRAC	Bangladesh Rural Advancement Committee
BRI	Bank Rakyat Indonesia
BTSWA	Baite Tribal Social Welfare Association
CAGR	Compounded Annual Growth Rate
CBOs	Community Based Organizations
CCACN	Central de Coop de Ahorroy Credito Financieras de Nicaragua
CDF	Community Development Foundation
CDPOs	Child Development Project Officers
CENVAT	Central Value Added Tax
CGAP	Consultative Group to Assist the Poor
CIC	Cooperative Insurance Company

CLUSA	Cooperative League of the USA
CML	Centre for Microfinance and Livelihood
CWWS	Chakhesang Women Welfare Society
DCCB	District Cooperative Credit Bank
DMFC	District Microfinance Committees
EMP	European Microfinance Programme
EBS	Equity Building Society
EZE	Evangelische Zentarlstelle
FINCA	Foundation for International Community Assistance
FFAs	Formal Financial Agencies
FFT's	Formal Financial Institutions
FWWB-I	Friends of Women's World Banking–India
GDRC	Global Development Research Centre
GSPCL	Grameen Silk Producer's Company Ltd
GTZ	German Technical Cooperation
IASC	Indian Association of Savings and Credit
IBPs	Individual Banking Programmes
ICDS	Integrated Child Development Services
ICICI	Industrial Credit and Investment Corporation of India Ltd.
IFAD	International Fund for Agricultural Development
IIBM	Indian Institute of Bank Management
IIP	Indices of Industrial Production
ILO	International Labour Organization
IMAGE	Intervention with Microfinance for AIDS and Gender Equity
IRDP	Integrated Rural Development Programmes
IRnet	International Remittance Network
IRV	Individual Rural Volunteers
JLG	Joint Liability Group
KYC	Know Your Customer
LAB	Local Area Bank
LBP	Loyalam Bank Project
LSS	Lok Seva Samity
MABS	Microenterprise Access to Banking Services
MACS	Mutually Aided Cooperative Societies Act

MASK	Mahila Shakti Kendra
MBB	Micro Banking Bulletin
MCI	Micro Credit Institutions
MDGs	Millennium Development Goals
MD&EF	Micro Finance Development and Equity Fund
MFC	Micro Finance Centre
MFIs	Micro Finance Institutions
MFMI	Microfinance Management Institution
MFN	Microfinance Network
MFO	Micro Finance Organization
MFP	Micro Finance Programme
MIS	Management Information System
MIX	Microfinance Information Exchange
MRB	Manipur Rural Bank
MSCB	Manipur State Cooperative Bank
MSEs	Micro and Small Enterprises
MSME	Micro, Small and Medium Enterprises
MSMED	Micro, Small and Medium Enterprises Development
MVK	Mahila Vikas Kendra
MYRADA	Mysore Resettlement and Development Agency
NABARD	National Bank for Agriculture and Rural Development
NBC	National Bank of Commerce
NBFCs	Non-Banking Financial Companies
NCAER	National Council of Applied Economic Research
NEDFI	North Eastern Development Finance Corporation Ltd.
NEIIPP	North East Industrial and Investment Promotion Policy
NER	North-Eastern Region
NGOs	Non-Governmental Organizations
NGO-MF	NGO-Microfinance Programme
NGO-SP	NGO-Support Programme
NMB	National Microfinance Bank in Tanzania
NPA	Non-Performing Assets
NRM	National Rural Mission
ORI	Organization for Rural Improvement
OSI	Open Society Institute
PACS	Primary Agricultural Cooperative Credit Societies
PAD	People Action for Development
PDA	Personal Digital Assistants
POS	Point of Sale
PRI	Panchayati Raj Institution
PRF	Portfolio Risk Fund

RAID	Rural Agricultural and Industrial Development
RBA	Rongmei Baptist Association
RBI	Reserve Bank of India
RDO	Rural Development Organization
RFA	Revolving Fund Assistance
RGVN	Rashtiya Gramin Vikas Nidhi
RGVN-CSP	RGVN-Credit and Savings Programme
RMK	Rashtriya Mahila Kosh
RoSCAs	Rotating Saving and Credit Associations
RRB	Regional Rural Bank
SBI	State Bank of India
SEDO	Social Economic Development Organization
SEEP Network	Small Enterprise Education and Promotion Network
SEWA	Self-Employed Women's Association
SGSY	Swaranajayanti Gram Swarozgar Yojana
SHARE	Society for Helping Awakening Rural Poor through Education
SHG	Self-Help Group
SHPIs	Self-Help Group Promotion Institutions
SIDBI	Small Industries Development Bank of India
SLBC's	State Level Bankers Committee
SMBK	Suraj Mukhi Banijyik Kendra
SME	Small Micro Enterprise
SMI	Student Microfinance Initiative
SPM	Social Performance Management
SSI	Small Scale Industry
TSWT	Tata Social Welfare Trust
UBI	United Bank of India
UNCDF	United Nations Capital Development Fund
VO	Voluntary Organisation
VVD	Volunteers for Village Development
WSDS	Weaker Sections Development Society
WOCCU	The World Council of Credit Unions
WSHG's	Women Self-Help Groups
YVU	Youth Volunteers' Union

One

Introduction to Microfinance

> "Micro credit is a critical anti-poverty tool and a wise investment in human capital. Now that the nations of the world have committed themselves to reduce to half by the year 2015 the number of people living on less than $1 a day, we must look even more seriously at the pivotal role that sustainable microfinance can play and is playing in reaching this Millennium Development Goal."
>
> —*Kofi Annan*

Introduction

Microfinance has gradually developed to be a world-wide movement, no longer being a subject matter of microfinance practitioners alone. Governments, NGOs, donors, rural development agencies, banks, financial institutions, foundations, corporations, business communities, civil societies, researchers, universities, consultants, philanthropists and others are taking an increasing interest on it. Further, it is no longer confine to any discipline of study. It has wide interdisciplinary relevance in Commerce, Finance, Management, Economics, Mathematics, Psychology and Rural Development.

In recent past many semi-government financial institutions are also actively involved in the promotion and development of microfinance activities where private sector plays the important role in few years back. Many scholars have continuously working in the field over the last few decades and still continuing for better strategies and techniques for upliftment of people those who are living below poverty line in one side and mitigation of alarming growth of unemployment problems of the country on the other side. The increasing level of acceptance of microfinance among the various groups of stakeholders worldwide presents the following questions: Is microfinance becoming popular because it is a good business to make money? Or Is it because microfinance a potential tool to fight poverty? Or is it good area for serving the society? Or both?

Since the inception of the Grameen Bank, microfinance has spread to cover five continents of the world and penetrated in rural, semi-urban and urban markets. They have achieved success with a variety of credit products and collection mechanisms in numerous countries. The Grameen Bank system has been adopted in Bolivia, Chile, China, Ethiopia, Honduras, India, Malaysia, Mali, Philippines, Sri Lanka, Tanzania, Thailand, United States of America and Vietnam. Many other countries of the world also adopted different system of microfinance to meet their socio-economic status.

The Microfinance Information Exchange (MIX) estimates range from 1,000 to 2,500 MFIs serving some 67.6 million clients all over the world. Of these total clients, more than half of them come from the bottom 50 per cent of people living below poverty line. That is some 41.6 million of the poorest people of the world have been reached by Microfinance Institutions. As MFIs have become more efficient and increased their client base, they have begun to expand their services through different product offerings such as micro-savings, micro and flexible loan repayment schemes, micro insurance, etc. Some MFIs have also begun to seek out public and international financing, further increasing their amount of working capital and expanding the scope of their operations.

Again, the World Bank has called South Asia is the "*Cradle of Microfinance*". Statistics indicate that some 45 per cent of all the people in the world who use microfinance services are living in South Asia. However, the overall percentage of the poor and vulnerable people with access to financial services remains very small, amounting to less than 20 per cent of poor households in India. The World Bank estimates that more than 87 per cent of India's poor cannot access credit from the formal sources of finance and therefore, they are not borrowing at all or have to depend on local moneylenders who charged them at a higher interest rates ranging from 48 to 120 per cent per annum and sometimes much higher than these rates.

A study by the Institute for Financial Management and Research in India estimates that the registered chit fund industry could be as large as 10 to 50 per cent of all lending to priority sectors; the unregistered chit fund market could be as large as 15 times the registered market (Linder, 2010).

This demonstrates that there are large volumes of potential clients for microfinance services in India, as well as in Asia region depending on the level of demand for financial services, from those poor who are unable to access. The provision of such services, if done correctly and proper direction could have been a significant impact on the poor.

Today, it is commonly accepted that, microfinance plays a major role in the development of many African, Asian and Latin American underdeveloping nations. Its impact is substantial enough to have warranted acknowledgement by the United Nations who declared 2005 "*The international year of microfinance*", reminding millions of people that worldwide benefit from microfinance activities. This declaration marked the long journey of microfinance from an obscure experiment in the mid-1970s to the status of a worldwide movement. In the international arena, governments, non-profit organisations, community and development agencies have targeted microfinance development by viewing it as one of the most sustainable paths to local economic growth, employment generation and poverty reduction. (Eversole, 2003)

Historical Context of Microfinance and Its Evolution

The concept of microfinance is not new. Savings and credit groups that have operated for centuries together include the "merry-go-rounds" Kenya "susus" of Ghana, "chit funds" and "Marup" in India, "tandas" in Mexico, "arisan" in Indonesia, "Kibati" in Tanzania, "cheetu" in Sri Lanka, "tontines" in West Africa, and "pasanaku" in Bolivia, "Stockvel" in South Africa, "esusu" in Nigeria as well as numerous savings clubs and burial societies found all over the world. Despite of introducing and implementing the modern microfinance, they are still popularly using in different parts of the world.

Formal credit and savings institutions for the poor have also been around for decades, providing customers who were traditionally neglected by commercial banks a way to obtain financial services through cooperatives and development finance institutions. One of the earlier and longer-lived micro credit organizations providing small loans to rural poor with no collateral was the Irish Loan Fund system, initiated in the early 1700s by the author and nationalist Jonathan Swift. Swift's idea began slowly but by the 1840s it had become a widespread institution of about 300 funds all over Ireland. Their principal objective was making small loans with interest for short duration. At their peak they were making loans to 20 per cent of all Irish households annually.

In 1800s, various types of larger and more formal savings and credit institutions began to emerge in Europe, organized primarily among the rural and urban poor. These institutions were known as People's Banks, Credit Unions, and Savings and Credit Co-operatives Societies.

The concept of the credit union was developed by F.W. Raiffeisen and his group of supporters. Their altruistic action was motivated by concern to assist the rural population to break out of their dependence on scrupulous moneylenders and to improve their welfare. From 1870, the unions expanded rapidly over a large sector of the Rhine Province and other religions of the German states. The cooperative movement quickly spread to other countries in the Europe and North America, and eventually, supported by the cooperative movement in developed countries and donors, also even to developing countries.

In Indonesia, the Indonesian People's Credit Banks or The Bank Perkreditan Rakyat (BPR) opened in 1895. The BPR became the largest microfinance system in Indonesia with close to 9,000 units.

In the early 1900s, various adaptations of these models began to appear in different parts of rural Latin America. While the goal of such rural finance interventions was usually defined in terms of modernizing the agricultural sector, they usually had two specific objectives, increased commercialization of the rural sector, by mobilizing "idle" savings and increasing investment through credit, and reducing oppressive feudal relations that were enforced through indebtedness. In most cases, these new banks for the poor were not owned by the poor themselves, as they had been in Europe, but by government agencies or private banks. Over the years, these institutions became inefficient and at times, abusive too.

Between the 1950s and 1970s, governments and donors focused on providing agricultural credit to small and marginal farmers, with the hopes of raising productivity and incomes. These efforts to expand access to agricultural credit emphasized supply-led government interventions in the form of targeted credit through state-owned development finance institutions or farmers' cooperatives in some cases, that received concessional loans and on-lento customers at below-market interest rates.

Meanwhile, starting in the 1970s, experimental programmes in Bangladesh, Brazil, and a few other countries extended tiny loans to groups of poor women to invest in micro-businesses. This type of micro-enterprises credit was based on solidarity group lending in which every member of a group guaranteed the repayment of all members. These "microenterprise lending" programmes had an almost exclusive focus on credit for income generating activities targeting very poor borrowers.

Americans for Community Cooperation in Other Nations (ACCION) International was founded by a law student, Joshep Blatchford, to address poverty in Latin America's cities. Begun as a student-run volunteer effort in the shanty towns of Caracas with $90,000 raised from private companies, ACCION today is one of the premier microfinance organizations in the world, with a network of lending partners that spans Latin America, United States and Africa.

In 1972 the Self-Employed Women's Association (SEWA) was registered as a trade union in Gujarat (India), with the main objective of "strengthening its members' bargaining power to improve income, employment and access to social security." In 1974, to address their lack of access to financial services, the members of SEWA decided to found "a bank of their own". 4,000 women contributed a share capital of ₹ 10 each to establish the Mahila SEWA Co-operative Bank. Since, then it has been providing banking services to poor, illiterate, self-employed women and has become a viable financial venture with around 93,000 active clients.

In Bangladesh, Professor Muhammad Yunus addressed the banking problem faced by the poor through a programme of action-research. With his graduate students in Chittagong University in

1976, he designed an experimental credit programme to serve them. It spread rapidly to hundreds of villages. Through a special relationship with rural banks, he disbursed and recovered thousands of loans, but the bankers refused to take over the project at the end of the pilot phase. They feared it was too expensive and risky in spite of his success. Eventually, through the support of donors, the Grameen Bank was founded in 1983 and now serves more than 4 million borrowers. The initial success of Grameen Bank also stimulated the establishment of several other giant microfinance institutions like BRAC, ASA, Proshika, etc in Bangladesh.

Meanwhile, microcredit programmes throughout the world improved upon the original methodologies and defied conventional wisdom about financing the poor. They are:

- First, they showed that poor people, especially women, had excellent repayment rates among the better programmes rates that were better than the formal financial sectors of most of the developing countries.
- Second, the poor were willing and able to pay interest rates that allowed microfinance institutions (MFIs) to cover their costs.

Another flagship of the microfinance movement is the village banking unit system of the Bank Raky ndonesia (BRI), the largest microfinance institution in developing countries. This state-owned bank serves about 22 million micro savers with autonomously managed micro banks. The micro banks of BRI are the product of a successful transformation by state-owned agricultural bank during the mid-1980s.

The 1990s saw a growing enthusiasm for promoting microfinance as a strategy for poverty alleviation through financing economic oriented activities. The microfinance sector started operating in many countries, lending to multiple financial services firms, serving the needs of micro entrepreneurs and poor households. These gains, however, tended to concentrated in urban and densely populated rural areas.

It was not until the mid-1990s that the term "microcredit" began to be replaced by a new term that included not only credit, but also savings and other financial services. "Microfinance" emerged as the term of choice to refer to a range of financial services to the poor, that included not only credit, but also savings and other services such as insurance and money transfers.

ACCION helped in formation of BancoSol in 1992, the first commercial bank in the world dedicated solely to microfinance. Today, BancoSol offers its more than 70,000 clients an impressive range of financial services including savings accounts, credit cards and housing loans-products that just five years ago were only accessible to Bolivia's upper classes. BancoSol is no longer unique: more than 15 ACCION-affiliated organizations are now regulated financial institutions.

Today, practitioners and donors are increasingly focusing on expanded financial services to the poor in frontier markets and on the integration of microfinance in financial systems development. The recent introduction by some donors of the financial systems approach in microfinance which emphasizes favourable policy environment and institution-building-approach has improved the overall effectiveness of microfinance interventions. But numerous challenges remain, especially in rural and agricultural finance and other frontier markets. Today, the microfinance industry and the greater development community share the view that permanent poverty reduction requires addressing the multiple dimensions of poverty. For the international community, this means reaching specific Millennium Development Goals (MDGs) in education, women's empowerment, and health, among others. For microfinance, this means viewing microfinance as an essential element in any country's financial system.

Recent Innovations in Financial Services for the Poor

Following are some of the recent innovation in financial services for the poor developed globally.

1. *Central de Cooperatives de Ahorroy Credito Financieras de Nicaragua (CCACN)* is marketing its "Agriculture Salary" savings product to farmers. The goal of the product is to smooth the flow of income from the proceeds of an annual or semi-annual harvest. Each credit union works with its farmers to identify their individual expenses and determine a monthly "Salary" to be withdrawn from the credit union. In its infancy stage, the credit unions have noted an interest from agriculture-based clients in such a savings management programme.

2. *Caja Los Andes in Bolivia* offers four loan repayment options that fit the cash flow of various agricultural activities, including an end-of-term payment for both principal and interest that fits single crop activities, and unequal payments harvesting periods. Flexibility is also provided in loan disbursements, and farmers can receive the sanctioned loan amount in as many as three instalments.

3. *Prodem in Bolivia* has introduced a combination of biometric fingerprint and smart cards to deliver financial services to its clients. Biometric technology measures an individual's unique physical or behavioural characteristics, such as fingerprints, facial characteristics, voice pattern, and gait, to recognize and confirm identity. Prodem's fingerprint verification has reduced fraud, and repudiation of transactions.

4. *International Remittance Network (IRnet)*: In late 1990, WOCCU, in partnership with Vigo, a money transfer firm, launched IRnet. As of June 2003, 173 credit unions in Central America offer IRnet, expanding the possibilities for sending remittances through 800 US credit union points of service. The Central America credit unions distribute remittances primarily to rural clients. The distributing credit unions help to integrate remittance recipients into the formal financial sector through trained staff who cross-self services. When a non-member enters a credit union to pick up a remittance, a staff person encourages this person to become a credit union member and save a portion of the remittance in an interest- bearing voluntary savings account.

5. *Unibanka (Latvia)*: Prior to introducing credit scoring, Unibanka, a commercial bank, viewed microfinance loans as too costly to deliver. With the assistance of Bannock Consulting, Unibanka instituted a credit-scoring system based on qualitative client data because sufficient quantitative data was not available to develop a statistical model. Branch staff now uses score cards to evaluate microfinance loan applications quickly, which has reduced the cost of review and made microfinance lending profitable for Unibanka.

6. *Managed ASCAs*: A number of local organizations in the Nyeri District of Kenya provide management services to group-based loan funds. The groups operate as Accumulating Savings and Credit Associations (ASCAs) and receive management services provided by ASCA Management Agencies (AMAs). The AMA model serves a wider client base than the mainstream donor

funded MFIs who tend to focus their attention on micro and small entrepreneurs. The clientele of AMAs are also drawn from other socio-economic strata, including salaried workers such as nurses, teachers and civil servants as well as subsistence and semi-commercial farmers. Hence their reach into the rural areas is much greater than the MFIs.

7. *ICICI Bank (India)*: Two state banks in India (Corporation and Canara) partnered with an NGO to provide salaried low-income workers with access to savings. The project uses the already established Automatic Teller Machines (ATMs) in the factories to offer a recurring savings product, along with education on personal finance.

8. *Microenterprise Access to Banking Services (MABS) in Philippines* nurtures the expanded use of the credit bureau by rural banks, which was started in 2001 to minimize client over indebtedness and defaults. MABS has helped to integrate the rural banks' microenterprise loan clients into an existing national credit bureau, by creating an e-mail encryption programme that allows rural banks to share information electronically at a low cost.

9. *Bhartiya Samruddhi Investments and Consulting Services (BASIX)* in India reduced transportation and transaction costs for its clients and decreased staff expenses by establishing tellers in manned phone booths operating in India. The company receives a service fee and phone booth operators are being trained in basic collection operations and accounting. BASIX is currently redesigning the project after the pilot and preparing it for re-launching.

10. *Credit, life and funeral insurance*: A World Council of Credit Unions (WOCCU) study on savings and credit cooperatives (SACCOs) in Kenya indicates that HIV/AIDS poses high levels of risk to rural finance institution soundness. The Cooperative Insurance Company (CIC), a professional insurance provider, insures over half of Kenya's more than one million credit union members who subscribe to policies through their credit unions.

11. *The National Microfinance Bank in Tanzania (NMB)* was created to retain the extensive rural branch network of the National Bank of Commerce (NBC) when it was privatized in 1997. The key to making it commercially viable has been rigorous control of costs through drastic simplification of the business model and tight managerial oversight. Key initiatives have been correct pricing of products, particularly payments and remittance

services, which had traditionally been cross-subsidized by other product lines and the development of microfinance products, mainly small (average US $400) individual loans.

12. *ADOPEM (Dominican Republic)* thoroughly evaluated its PDA (Personal Digital Assistants) programme and recorded dramatic improvements. Client retention improved significantly, and the number of days between application and disbursement dropped from five days to two days. Expenses for paper work dropped by 60 per cent and data entry expense dropped by 50 per cent. Loan officer cash loads and other productivity measures increased by about 35 per cent.

13. *The International NGO Techno Serve* has developed in inventory credit scheme in Ghana that enables farmers' group to obtain higher value for their crops by providing post-harvest credit through linkage with a rural financial institution. Instead of selling their entire crop at harvest–when prices are lowest–in order to meet cash needs, small scale farmers in the scheme store their crop in a cooperatively-managed warehouse and receive a loan of about 75-80 per cent of the value of the stored crop, which serves as collateral. This loan permits them to clear their accumulated debts and satisfy immediate cash requirements.

14. *Savings-based, Agriculture-oriented Rural Credit Unions–SICREDI-Brazil* specializes in agricultural lending; primarily for the production of rice, wheat, beef, fodder, fish, and vegetables and for agricultural equipment. Loan approvals are based upon the members' savings history and credit record, with the size limited to 50 per cent of production costs and dependent up to the potential return of crop sale at harvest as well as household income and debt obligations. The borrower makes monthly interest payments and then a balloon payment of the principal at the harvest time.

15. *Producer Associations as Clients of a Financial Institution (GAPI and CLUSA in Mozambique)* GAPI offers investment and working capital loans to associations) of small farmers and small and micro-enterprises. GAPI collaborates with CLUSA to set-up and register these fora. Loans are secured through a solidarity group-like guarantee between the participating fora. Each forum on-lends to its member associations, who collect the produce from their individual members and other area farmers and deliver it to the forum in return for the loan. About 80 per cent of the profits

from the sale of produce are handed back to the associations-the remaining 20 per cent of the profits are kept by the forum as interest payments.

16. *In South Africa, a network of 8,000 armoured* trucks equipped with thumb print recognition and smart-card technology deliver pension payments of about $60 each month to 4.5 million South Africans. The potential of this vast infrastructure to offer pensioners other kinds of financial services is tremendous.

17. *Banco Postal in Brazil,* a joint venture between the Post Office and the largest private bank (Bradesco) has offered banking (and payment) services through its network of postal branches in remote and poor areas of the country since March 2002. The performance of the Postal Bank has benefited directly and indirectly to the Brazilian population as to offer financial services to people without access to the banking system.

18. *Equity Building Society (EBS) in Kenya* has emerged as one of Kenya's leading microfinance institutions, with over 1,55,000 savings clients and 41,000 borrowers. Once insolvent, EBS transformed itself into a profitable financial service provider by rigorously focusing on the needs of its clients in particular by developing a wide range of market based financial products including a mobile banking service.

On the basis of recent innovation in financial services and more importantly in the microfinance segments, one must be eager to know the concept of microfinance. How it is operating? What are different forms of microfinance? Why it is essential for socio economic development of poor? The following paragraph will define what microfinance is?

What is Microfinance?

To most, microfinance means helping very poor families with very small amount of loans (microcredit) to help them engage in productive and economic oriented activities or grow their tiny businesses suitable to their locality. Over time, microfinance has come to include a broader range of services such as credit, savings, insurance and remittance etc. As we have come to realize that the poor and the very poor that lack access to traditional formal financial institutions require a variety of financial products.

Definition of Microfinance

The declaration of the micro-credit summit held in Washington DC in 1997 defined micro-credit programmes as those "extending small loans to poor people for self-employment projects that generate income, allowing them to care for themselves and their families". The declaration also stated that, "in most cases, micro-credit projects offer a combination of services and resources to their clients in addition to credit for self-employment". These often include savings facilities, training networking and peer support.

According to International Labour Organisation (ILO), "microfinance is an economic development approach that involves providing financial services through institutions to low income clients".

NABARD Task Force-2000 and Reserve Bank of India also defined microfinance as "provision of thrift, credit and other financial services and products of very small amounts to the poor in rural, semi-urban or urban areas enabling them to raise their income levels and improve their living standards"

> "A type of banking service that is provided to unemployed or low-income individuals or groups who would otherwise have no other means of gaining financial services. Ultimately, the goal of microfinance is to give low income people an opportunity to become self-sufficient by providing a means of saving money, borrowing money and insurance." —*Investopaedia*

Thus, Microfinance is the provision of a broad range of financial services such as—deposits, loans, payment services, money transfers and insurance products—to the poor and low-income households, for their microenterprises and small businesses, to enable them to raise their income levels and improve their living standards.

Significance of Microfinance

Microfinance has emerged as 'a key policy variable in promoting economic development across the nation with a salubrious impact on the all-round development of women' (NABARD, 2000). The relevance of microfinance as a tool for reducing poverty depends on local circumstances. Generally, the basic causes of poverty are due to low economic growth, high population growth and extremely unequal distribution of resources. To mitigate the unemployment, creation of more jobs is required and to raise productivity and income, investment in human and physical capital is needed. In India, microfinance has got vital significance, because here the age-old adage '*India is a rich country where the poor people live*' still holds good even though there has been considerable decrease in percentage of people below poverty line.

The Grameen Bank experience of Bangladesh has demonstrated the capacity of the poor to generate productive self-employment if the right quantum of working capital on the right terms is provided to them by some intermediary agency like NGO or Microfinance institutions. Microfinance has become one of the most effective tool for poverty alleviation in developing countries like India. It has become a very important tool that can be used effectively to address poverty, empowerment of the socially marginalized poor and strengthen the social fabric (Aban, Amro, 2007).

Principles for Microfinance

For convenient of the study, following principles of microfinance have been developed. They are:

- The poor need a variety of financial services, not just loans
- Microfinance should serve as boon not as bane for poor
- The poor has the capability to repay loans, pay the real cost of loans and generate savings
- Microfinance is a powerful instrument against poverty
- Microfinance institutions must aim to provide financial services to an increasing number of disadvantaged people

Characteristics of Microfinance

Microfinance has different characteristics depend on the geographical location, size and its way of implementation. On the basis of some similarities, following characteristics have been developed by the researcher for the present study on microfinance (Table next page).

Characteristics	Distinguishing Features
Type of client	• Low Income • Employment in informal sector; low wage rate • Lack of physical collateral • Closely interlinked household/business activities
Lending Technology	• Prompt approval and disbursement of micro loans • Lack of extensive loan records • Collateral substitutes; group-based guarantees • Conditional access to further micro-credits • Information-intensive character-based lending linked to cash flow analysis and group-based borrower selection.
Loan Portfolio	• Highly volatile • Risk heavily dependent on portfolio management skills
Organizational Ideology	• Remote form/non-dependent on government • Cost recovery objective vs. profit maximizing.
Institutional Structure	• Decentralized • Insufficient external control and regulation • Capital base is quasi-equity (grants, soft capital)

Source: Notes on Microfinance, www.bsp.gov.ph

- Microfinance can and should be undertaken on a sustainable basis
- Microfinance NGOs and programmes must develop performance standards that will help define and govern the microfinance industry toward greater reach and sustainability.
- Microcredit is not always the answer
- Interest rate ceilings can damage poor people's access to financial services

Who are the Clients of Microfinance

The typical microfinance clients are low-income persons that do not have access to formal financial institutions. Microfinance clients are typically self-employed, often household-based entrepreneurs. All over the globe the women clients is more involve than the male clients in microfinance. In rural areas, they are usually small farmers and other disadvantage people who are engaged in small income-generating activities such as food processing, handloom, handicrafts, animal rearing activities and petty trade business. In urban areas, microfinance activities are more diverse and include shopkeepers, service providers, artisans, street vendors and vegetable vendors etc. Thus, the types of microfinance clients changes as per the suitably of the location and it differ from one segements to other segments.

How does Microfinance Help the Poor?

Experience shows that microfinance can help the poor to increase their income, build viable businesses and reduce their vulnerability to external shocks. It can also be a powerful instrument for self-empowerment by enabling the poor, especially women, to become agents of economic change. Poverty is multi-dimensional. By providing access to financial services, microfinance plays an important role in fighting against the many aspects of poverty. For instance, income generation from a business helps not only the business activity expand but also contributes to household income and its attendant benefits on food security, children's education and overall improves of standard of living. Moreover, for women, who, in many contexts, are secluded from public space, transacting with formal institutions can also build confidence, communication skills, decision-making and empowerment.

Why do MFIs Charge such High Interest Rates to Poor People?

Providing financial services to large size of poor people is quite expensive, especially in relation to the transactions involved. This is one of the most important reasons why formal banks and financial institutions don't make small loans. A ₹ 100 loan, for example, requires the same personnel and resources as a ₹ 2,000 one thus increasing per unit transaction costs. Loan officers must visit the client's home or place of work, evaluate credit worthiness on the basis of interviews with the client's family and references, and in many cases, follow through with visits to reinforce the repayment culture. It can easily cost ₹ 25 to make a microloan. While that might not seem unreasonable in absolute terms, it might represent 25 per cent of the value of the loan amount, and force the institution to charge a "high" rate of interest to cover its cost of loan administration.

The microfinance institution could subsidize the loans to make the credit more "affordable" to the poor. However, the institution then depends on permanent subsidy from the government under rural development scheme. Subsidy-dependent programmes are always fighting to maintain their levels of activity against budget cuts and seldom grow significantly. They simply aren't sustainable, especially if other microcredit operations have shown that they can provide credit and grow on the basis of "high" rates of interest-and along the way serve far greater numbers of clients.

Can Microfinance be Profitable?

Yes it can. Data from the Micro Banking Bulletin reports that 63 of the world's top MFIs had an average rate of return, after adjusting for inflation and after taking out subsidies programmes might have received, of about 2.5 per cent of total assets. This compares favourably with returns in the commercial banking sector and gives credence to the hope of many that microfinance can be sufficiently attractive to mainstream into the retail banking sector. Many feel that once microfinance becomes mainstreamed, massive growth in the numbers of clients can be achieved. Others worry that an excessive concern about profit in microfinance will lead MFIs up-market, to serve better off clients who can absorb larger loan amounts. This is the "crowding out" effect. This may happen; after all, there are a large number of very poor, poor, and vulnerable non-poor who are not able to reach by the banking sector.

What is the Government's Role in Supporting Microfinance?

Governments have a complicated role when it comes to microfinance. Until recently, governments generally felt that it was their responsibility to generate 'development finance', including credit programmes for the disadvantaged people who are living below poverty line. Thirty years of insightful critique of rural credit programmes revealed that governments do a very bad job of lending to the poor. Short term political gain is just too tempting for politically controlled lending organizations; they disburse too quickly and they collect too sporadically. In urban areas, governments never really got into the act and subsidized microenterprise credit is still relatively rare when compared to its rural counterpart.

Now that microfinance has become quite popular, governments are tempted to use savings banks, development banks, postal savings banks, and agricultural banks to move micro credit. This is not generally a good idea, unless the government has a clear acceptance of the need to avoid the pitfalls of the past and a clear means to do so. Many governments have set up apex facilities that channel funds from multilateral agencies to MFIs. Apex facilities can be quite complicated and there are few successful examples in microfinance. Successful apex organizations in microfinance tend to be built on the backs of successful. MFIs, not the other way around. Finally, governments can also get involved in microfinance by concerning themselves with the regulatory framework that impinges in the ability of a wide range of financial actors to offer financial services to the very poor.

Financial Regulator and Development of Microfinance?

Many feel that the most important role of a financial regulator in supporting the development of microfinance is to create an alternative institutional type that allows sound financial NGOs, credit unions and other community-based intermediaries to obtain a license to other deposit services to the general public and obtain funds through apex organizations. In a few countries, this may be an appropriate strategy. In most countries, however, the general level of development of the microfinance industry does not yet warrant the licensing of a separate class of financial institutions to serve the poor. And, in most countries, budgetary restrictions faced by bank regulators make it very unlikely that they will be able to supervise a whole host of small institutions; these institutions' total assists may make up a tiny per cent of the total financial system, but the cost of adequate supervision could eat up between 25 to 50 per cent of the total budget of the agency.

Rather, regulators can work with the nascent microfinance industries of most countries on issues such as modifying usury limits as stated in the commercial code to allow appropriate levels of interest, generating credit information clearinghouses to share information on defaulting borrowers to limit their ability to go from one MFI to another, working with civil authorities to ensure that private loan contracts can be recognized by courts in those transition economies that lack even basis legislative infrastructure,

and reporting requirements that will prepare MFIs to eventually become regulated.

Regulators can also examine the laws, executive decrees, and internal regulations that limit the ability of traditional banking institutions to do microfinance. These regulations include limits on the per cent of a loan portfolio that can be lent on an unsecured basis, limits on group guarantee mechanisms, reporting requirements for the contents of loan files. Not least, banking regulators may need to look at the way in which they would evaluate microloan portfolios within large banks.

Current State of Global Microfinance

Since the inception of the Grameen Bank, microfinance has spread to cover five continents and numerous countries of the world. The Grameen Bank has been replicated in Bolivia, Chile, China, Ethiopia, Honduras, India, Malaysia, Mali, Philippines, Sri Lanka, Tanzania, Thailand, the United States and Vietnam; the microfinance information exchange market (MIX) lists financial information for 973 MFIs in 105 different countries. Some MFIs have also begun to seek out public and international financing, further increasing their amount of working capital and expanding the scope of their operations.

As MFIs have become more efficient and increased their client base, they begun to expand their services through different product offerings such as micro-savings, flexible loan repayment, and insurance. We discuss these three different product offerings below. At the time of their inception, many MFIs included a compulsory savings component that limited a borrower's access to deposited funds. This promoted long-term savings, but ignored the fact that many poor save for the short-term to smooth consumption during seasonal lows of production. As MFIs have applied their innovations in lending to the collection of deposits. One of the leading examples is Safe save, Bangladesh, which uses the idea that frequent small deposits will guard against the temptation of spending excess income.

The original Grameen Bank was one of the first MFIs that incorporated a compulsory savings requirement into their lending structure. Every client was required to make a deposit worth 5 per cent of their given loan, which was placed into a group fund with strict withdrawal rules (generally no withdrawal before three years). In 2001, the Grameen Bank reviewed both its lending and saving policy and reinvented itself as Grameen II. At the heart of this change were more savings options and more flexible loans, which act as a form of insurance. New to Grameen II is a pension fund, which allows clients with loans greater than 8,000 taka ($138) to contribute at least 50 taka ($0.86) per month. The client receives 12 per cent per year in compound interest, earning a 187 per cent return after the mandatory 10 year wait.

Other MFIs have begun experimenting with health insurance and natural disaster insurance. As with lending, agency problems present a dilemma for micro insurance. To this end, some groups such as FINCA Uganda require life insurance of all borrowers, including "risky" and "healthy" alike and thus avoid the adverse selection problem. Other ideas include providing rain insurance to guard against catastrophes. This relies on the assumption that crop yields (and much of the developing economy) are tied to seasonal rain cycles. This innovation eliminates the problem of moral hazard associated with a crop loan. By trying performance to rain cycles, a farmer has no incentive to take crop insurance and then fail to adequately produce a crop during a season of adequate rainfall. A more recent phenomenon in microfinance is the emergence of foreign investment in MFIs. As more and more MFIs establish positive returns, microfinance is being seen by many professional investors as profitable investment avenues. One of the most important developments for the MFIs was the June 2007 release of Standard & Poor's (S&P) report on the rating methodology for MFIs. By applying a common methodology, S&P will be able to send a stronger signal to potential investors about the quality of MFI investment like corporate world.

Microfinance Around the World

As Prof. Yunus and the Grameen Bank began to prove that microfinance is a viable method to alleviate poverty, their methodology and programme began to spread and adopted by most countries of the world. It is difficult to know exactly how many MFIs are there currently working, but Microfinance Information Exchange (MIX) estimates range from 1,000 to 2,500 serving some 67.6 million clients. Of these 67 million, more than half of them come from the bottom 50 per cent of people living below poverty line. That is, some 41.6 million of the poorest people in the world have been reached by MFIs. MFIs have expanded their operations into five different continents and penetrated both rural and urban markets. They have achieved success with a variety of credit products and collection mechanisms.

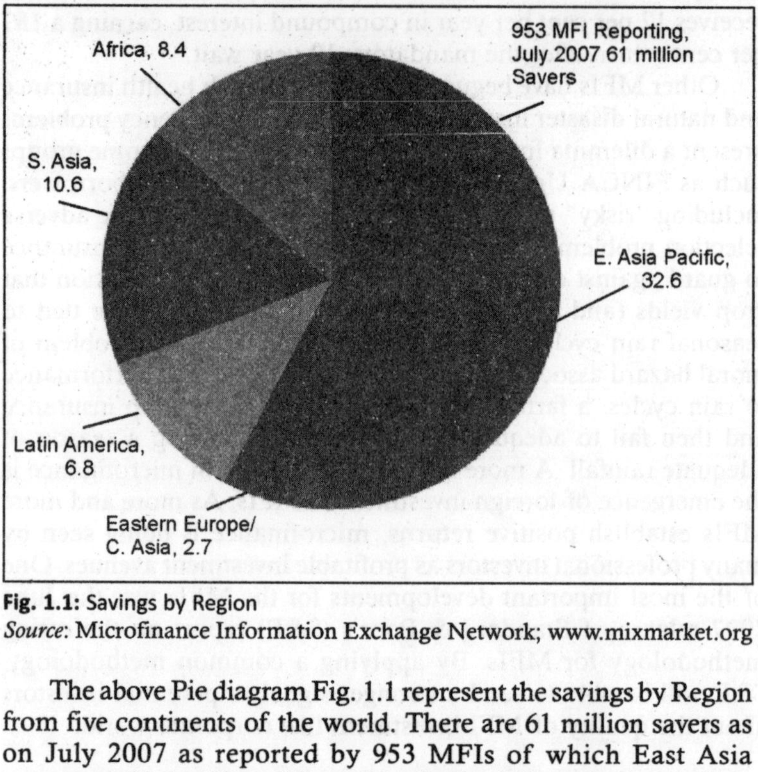

Fig. 1.1: Savings by Region
Source: Microfinance Information Exchange Network; www.mixmarket.org

The above Pie diagram Fig. 1.1 represent the savings by Region from five continents of the world. There are 61 million savers as on July 2007 as reported by 953 MFIs of which East Asia represents 32.6 million followed by South Asia with 10.6 million and Africa with 8.4 million respectively.

Top 20 Microfinance Institutions of the World

Table 1.1 shows the top 20 Microfinance Institutions of the world spreading in five different continents. ASA Bangladesh emerge the top in the rank scoring 14 scale, 83 efficiency level with risk of 56 and returns of 40. Followed by Bandhan (Society and

NBFC) from India in the second rank among the top 20 microfinance institutions of the world. Among the five continents Asia accounts the top having 7 microfinance institutions out of top 20 microfinance institutions representing 4 from India and 3 from Bangladesh.

Forbes' first-ever list of the World's Top 50 Microfinance Institutions were chosen from a field of 641 micro-credit providers. The list was prepared by the Microfinance Information Exchange (www.themix.org) under the direction of *Forbes* magazine. To qualify, the institutions must have made available their audited financials and must have passed review by a *Forbes* panel of advisers.

This sortable Table 1.1 gives the rank (out of 641) for the top institutions according to scale, which is based on the size of their gross loan portfolio; efficiency, which considers operating expense and the cost per borrower as a per cent of the gross national income per capita of their country of operation; risk, which looks at the quality of their loan portfolios, measured as the per cent of the portfolio at risk greater than 30 days; and return, which is measured as a combination of return on equity and return on assets. Each category is equally weighted for an institution's overall ranking.

The four MFI from India are: (i) Bandhan (Society and NBFC) (2nd) (ii) Microcredit Foundation of India (13th) (iii) Saadhana Microfin Society (15th) and (iv) Grameen Koota (19th). The three MFI from Bangladesh are: (i) ASA (1st) (ii) Jagorani Chakra Foundation (16th) and (iii) Grameen Bank (17th) position respectively as per *Forbes*' first-ever list of the World's Top 50 Microfinance Institutions.

Microfinance in Asia

Microfinance institutions in Asia continue to dominate the global microfinance market, building on rapid growth and massive scale to capture a disproportionate share of microfinance clients worldwide. Overall the region remains heavily credit-oriented, with savings often taking the form of compulsory deposits collected as a requirement for membership or access to loans. The picture may soon change as increasingly more countries begin to open the door to voluntary savings mobilization, allowing institutions that meet certain criteria to provide this much needed

Table 1.1: Top 20 Microfinance Institutions in the World in 2007

Rank	Name	Country	Scale	Efficiency	Risk	Return
1.	ASA	Bangladesh	14	83	56	40
2.	Bandhan	India	108	49	42	1
3.	Banco do Norwest	Brazil	46	27	213	25
4.	Fundacion Mundial de la Mujer	Colombia	58	72	193	1
5.	FONDEP Micro Credit	Morocco	119	26	196	1
6.	Amhara Credit and Savings Institution	Ethiopia	56	126	118	42
7.	Banco Compartamos, S.A., Institución de Banca Múltiple	Mexico	15	24	295	11
8.	Association Al Amana for the Promotion of Micro-Enterprises	Morocco	17	212	133	1
9.	Fundación Mundo Mujer Popayán	Colombia	53	181	141	1
10.	Fundación WWB Colombia – Cali	Colombia	27	206	155	4
11.	Consumer Credit Union 'Economic Partnership'	Russia	82	300	19	1
12.	Fondation Banque Populaire pour le Microcrédit	Morocco	59	126	219	1
13.	Microcredit Foundation of India	India	75	142	7	185
14.	EKI	Bosnia and Herzegovina	66	102	242	1
15.	Saadhana Microfin	India	263	79	73	1
16.	Jagorani Chakra Foundation	Bangladesh	136	176	128	1
17.	Grameen Bank	Bangladesh	8	280	100	62
18.	Partner	Bosnia and Herzegovina	64	169	230	1
19.	Grameen Koota	India	209	106	156	1
20.	Caja Municipal de Crédito de Cusco	Peru	48	99	222	119

Among the different countries representing top 20 Microfinance Institutions, Columbia and Morocco represents 3 MFI each and Bosnia and Herzegovina 2 MFIs and Brazil, Ethiopia, Mexico, Russia and Peru with one MFI each respectively.

service and potentially draw even more clients into the folds of microfinance. Many institutions, however, have yet to achieve the financial soundness and operational strength necessary to convince regulators of their ability to manage client savings. Leverage ratios are among the highest in the world, leaving institutions with rather tight equity bases to cover eventual losses. In the absence of a massive infusion of fresh equity capital, institutions will have to shore up their thin profit margins and build up their retained earnings. For some, the challenge will be to reduce costs, while for others the only option may be to raise prices.

Asian microfinance stands unrivalled in scale. Institutions in the region have traditionally employed stepped, group-lending models that have proven to be a successful blueprint for rapid expansion of outreach. Asian MFIs easily master the standard suit of products that are typical of group lending and are able to more quickly roll out services than their counterparts in other regions, exceeding global productivity levels by 12 per cent to reach 125 borrowers each. Building on this high staff productivity, Asian MFIs operating in densely populated areas attain colossal scale, with a handful serving several million clients each. With its concentration of large MFIs, Asian microfinance captures a disproportionate share of global clients. In 2006, Asian MFIs served over 35 million borrowers with US$ 6.97 billion in loans, reaching two-thirds of global borrowers while representing just one-third of institutions sampled. A similar picture emerges on the savings front; with over 47 million depositors, Asian MFIs served three-fourths of voluntary savers at microfinance institutions worldwide.

Despite the stunning scale and growth of Asian micro-finance, and the remarkable depth of outreach attained by MFIs in the region, many potential microfinance clients continue to lack access to basic financial services. Data from 2,207 institutions across the globe suggests that MFIs in Asia have been more successful than their peers in bridging the gap between supply and demand of microfinance services, though penetration rates vary considerably across the region. Bangladeshi MFIs led the charge against exclusion, reaching 35 per cent of potential demand, suggesting that growth will have to accelerate even further it MFIs are to truly break down the barriers to financial services. A number of other sectors barely registered on the top (Afghanistan, China), while others stood at intermediate levels. MFIs in Sri Lanka and Vietnam served one-fourth of the poor in those countries, while Cambodian and Indonesian institutions reached one-tenth of their potential clientele. Asian microfinance has certainly made tremendous achievements over the past, but much work remains ahead, both in scaling up of outreach and diversification of products and services.

Faced with legal limitations on deposit mobilization across the region, the typical Asian MFI sourced just one per cent of its assets from savings. Historically modest profit margins combined with increased competition for donations and the preponderance of NGOs in the sector have moreover curtailed the expansion of the equity base, which at 17 per cent, was the lowest among all regions. More so than its counterparts, the typical Asian MFI has therefore had to turn to borrowings to finance much of its portfolio. For every dollar in capital, Asian MFIs raised four dollars in debt, surpassing runners-up in Latin America that raised less than three. These borrowings were largely sourced at market rates, so that three-fourths of the MFI's portfolio was financed by commercial sources.

Profitable institutions are generally more adapt at breaking down the barriers to financial services, and the Asian region is no exception. Sustainable institutions across the region typically reach more than three times as many borrowers as their loss-making peers and experience stronger growth. The majority of Asian MFIs within the sample have crossed the profitability threshold, and others are close behind. Many, however, suffer heavy losses, and with the full set of MFIs earning a median 0.1 per cent return on assets, the region faces the challenge of consolidating profits and solidifying its position. Globally, institutions in Latin America and Eastern Europe/Central Asia were the only ones that enjoyed healthy profit margins. Despite incurring higher costs and running less efficient operations, these MFIs invested a greater portion of assets in their lending activities while charging more for their loans than their Asian peers, thereby boosting their revenue streams. Across Asia, some markets followed a similar high cost/high revenue pattern while others reinforced the low cost/low revenue curve that characterizes the region, with varying degrees of success.

Microfinance Networks in Asia

What makes microfinance networks in Asia unique? For the most part, networks in Asia face many of the same issues with which other networks contend. There is a range of well-established networks such as those in India, Pakistan, Bangladesh and the Philippines and a number of more nascent networks like those in Lao PDR, Vietnam and China. In terms of their members however, there are a few characteristics that make microfinance in Asia somewhat unique from other parts of the world, particularly in terms of the structure of microfinance in the region. Many lenders in Asia have a strong social orientation coupled with a group based lending approach as opposed to a more financial and individual lending focus in other parts of the world. This kind of approach leads to higher outreach numbers, reduces costs, but limits the number of products which can be offered. With massive populations and high concentrations of borrowers, Asia dominates microfinance around the world in terms of overall outreach.

According to Mix Market, as of 31st January 2008 and reported in 2007 *Mix Asia 100 Ranking of Microfinance Institutions,* the 392 MFIs surveyed were reaching more than 40 million borrowers with 8.4 dollar billion in loans and providing savings mobilization services with over 50 million voluntary deposit accounts totalling more than 6.3 dollar billion. 75 of the top 100 MFIs in Asia surveyed came from South Asia including 29 from India, 26 from Bangladesh and 10 from the Philippines. 13 of the largest MFIs in the world, in terms of number of active borrowers, are located in Asia.

Considering the unique context of the microfinance industry and the fact that the sector has grown rapidly, Networks in Asia have a significant role to play in guiding the future direction of microfinance in the world. In order to meet the changing demands of the market and to respond to competition from a wide variety of players (both commercial and non-profit), microfinance providers in the region will need to look to diversify their products.

Microfinance Resources

Following are some of the selected microfinance resources of the world.

ACCION International: The mission of ACCION International is to give people the tools they need to work their way out of poverty. By providing "micro" loans and business training to poor women and men who start their own businesses, ACCION's partner lending organizations help people work their own way up the economic ladder, with dignity and pride. Available in English, French and Spanish.

Alternative Finance: The Alternative Finance Website is the forum for MFI practitioners and researchers to access otherwise unpublished documents and information on all aspects of alternative and microfinance. They hold a broad and rapidly expanding article database in English and Spanish.

Bankakademie International: Bankakademie International is internationally known for innovative training and consulting services to strengthen the financial sector in transition countries and developing economies. Bankakademie International is part of Bankakademie, the leading bank training and consultancy institute in Germany.

Banking with the Poor: The Banking with the Poor is a network of some 20 national policy institutions, commercial banks and NGOs from eight countries in Asia namely– Bangladesh, India, Indonesia, Malaysia, Pakistan, Philippines, Sri Lanka and Thailand. Its objective is to link microfinance with the financial system.

Consultative Group to Assist the Poor (CGAP): It is a consortium of 33 public and private development agencies working together to expand access to financial services for the poor in developing countries. Multilingual information is available.

Cow Fund: Cow Fund is an Australian non-profit initiative that aims to support the delivery of microcredit projects to developing communities in Asia.

European Microfinance Programme: The European Microfinance Programme (EMP) is the first of its kind in Europe. The EMP is aimed at students who want to complete a specialization in microfinance and acquire expertise by working in a developing country. It provides students with a multidisciplinary approach to the challenges facing the microfinance sector today.

Foundation for International Community Assistance (FINCA): FINCA provides financial services to the world's poorest families so that they can create their own jobs, raise household incomes and improve their standard of living. They deliver the services through a global network of locally managed, self-supporting institutions.

The Global Development Research Centre (GDRC): The Global Development Research Centre is a virtual organization that carries out initiatives in education, research and practices. The Virtual Library on Microcredit is a repository of information on alternative, non-conventional financial systems and microfinance/ microcredit issues. Case Studies and Illustrations on Microcredit are available.

Grameen Bank: Grameen Bank invented the concept and practice of micro-credit, providing working capital to the poorest of the poor without demanding collateral in order to remove poverty from Bangladesh. The bank has been in operation since 1983 and was founded by Professor Muhammad Yunus.

Imp Act (Improving the Impact of Microfinance on Poverty: Action Research Programme): Imp-Act supports microfinance institutions (MFIs) in developing their own Social Performance Management (SPM) systems.

International Network of Alternative Financial Institutions (INAFI): A network of alternative microfinance organizations known for their quality in the presentation and innovation of technical services and development that contributes to the consolidation of microfinance as instruments to improve the quality of life for the poor in Latin America. Available in English and Spanish.

The Journal of Microfinance: The Journal of Microfinance is a forum for the sharing of ideas and information pertaining to the practice of microfinance and microenterprise development. The Journal's purpose is to influence practice by focusing on experiences and lessons learned from the field. This journal requires a paid subscription to view articles.

Mercy Corps: Mercy Corps works amid disasters, conflicts, chronic poverty and instability to unleash the potential of people who can win against impossible odds. Since 1979, Mercy Crops has provided $1 billion in assistance to people in 82 nations of the world. Mercy Corps pursues its mission through emergency relief services that assist people afflicted by conflict or disaster; Sustainable economic development that integrates agriculture, health, housing and infrastructure, economic development, education and environment and local management; and civil society initiatives that promote citizen participation, accountability, conflict management and the rule of law.

The Micro Banking Bulletin: The Micro Banking Bulletin (MBB) is the premier benchmarking source for the microfinance industry. Its benchmarks are widely used by investrs, donors and other service providers to facilitate greater standardization and a better understanding of the development of the microfinance sector. Originally an output of the Micro Banking Standards project, the MBB is one of the principal products offered by the Microfinance Information Exchange (MIX).

Micro Capital: Micro Capital is news and research initiative on international microfinance investment led by David Satterthwaite, housed in Prisma Microfinance, a for-profit microfinance institution (MFI).

Microcredit Summit: The Microcredit Summit Campaign brings together all the microcredit practitioners, advocates, educational institutions, donor agencies, international financial Institutions, non-governmental organizations and others involved with micro-credit to promote best practices in the field, to learn from each other and to work towards reaching their goal.

Microfinance Technical Support Website: The purpose of this website is to provide support services to users of CGAP's Business Planning and Financial Modelling Handbook, including the Microfin projection model.

The Microfinance Centre (MFC) for Central and Eastern Europe and the New Independent States: The MFC is an international, grass-root network of over 90 microfinance institutions from the region. MFC's mission is to contribute to poverty reduction and human potential development by promoting a socially oriented and sustainable microfinance sector that provides adequate financial and non-financial services to a large number of poor families and micro-entrepreneurs.

The Microfinance Gateway: With over 5,300 documents in their virtual library, the Microfinance Gateway is the most comprehensive source of information for and about the microfinance industry. It includes research and publications, discussion groups, specialized resource centres, organization and consultant profiles and the latest news, events, and job opportunities in microfinance.

Microfinance Management Institute: The mission of the Microfinance Management Institute (MFMI) is to advance capacity in microfinance management worldwide. The MFMI was co-founded in July 2003 by the Consultative Group to Assist the Poor (CGAP), a secretariat of the World Bank, and the Open Society Institute (OSI), New York.

The Microfinance Network: The Microfinance Network (MFN) is a global association of leading microfinance institutions committed to improving the quality of life of the poor through the provision of credit, savings, and other financial services. Network members believe in applying a commercial approach to the establishment of sustainable financial institutions that reach large volumes of clients who are not served by traditional financial institutions.

Micro LINKS: Micro LINKS is a dynamic knowledge-sharing website designed to improve the impact of USAID-funded microenterprise programmes and activities. Created through USAID's Accelerated Microenterprise Advancement Project, micro LINKS allows the Micro-enterprise Development and financial services practitioners.

Micro-Save: Micro-Save is a unique project that promotes the development of savings and other more client- responsive financial services among microfinance institutions (MFIs).

Micro-Vest: Created as a capital-mobilizing intermediary for microfinance institutions (MFIs) Micro-Vest offers investors the opportunity to invest directly in an instrument that facilitates the growth of microfinance institutions while maintaining focus on the return of principal and fiduciary responsibility. Micro-Vest One's global investments reach viable, proven MFIs seeking capital to continue their growth, Instruments include debt, subordinated debt, loȧn guarantees, equity (with an exit strategy), and quasi-equity sub-debt.

The MIX Market: The MIX Market™ is a global, web-based, microfinance information platform. It provides information to sector actors and the public at large on microfinance institutions (MFIs) worldwide, public and private funds that invest in microfinance, MFI networks, ratters/external evaluators, advisory firms, and governmental regulatory agencies. The MIX Market seeks to develop a transparent information market to link MFIs worldwide with Investors and Donors and promote greater investment and information flows.

Oikocredit: Started as a pioneer in the field of development financing, Oikocredit is one of the largest financiers of the microfinance sector worldwide. Oikocredit is one of the few ethical investment funds, which finances development projects in the South benefiting disadvantaged and marginalized people. Privately owned, Oikocredit is a unique cooperative society, which encourages investors to invest their funds in a socially responsible manner.

PlaNet Finance: PlaNet finance's ambition is to become a platform for bringing together those involved in the microfinance sector, while developing practical tools with the potential for furthering the aims of microfinance.

ProMis: ProMis (Promotion of the Microfinance Sector) is a comprehensive cooperation programme implemented by the Ministry of Finance, Sri Lanka in collaboration with German Technical Cooperation (GTZ). The overall goal of ProMis is to enhance and improve in a sustainable manner, the services offered by selected microfinance institutions (MFIs) to the poorer sections of society and to micro and small enterprises.

Rural Finance Learning Centre: Rural Finance is about providing financial services for people living in rural areas. This Learning Centre aims to assist organizations in developing countries to build their capacity to deliver improved financial services which meet the needs of rural households.

SEEP Network: The SEEP Network is an organization of more than 50 international private and voluntary organizations that support micro and small business and microfinance institutions in the developing world.

Student Microfinance Initiative (SMI): The Student Microfinance Initiative (SMI) is an international student network dedicated to the promotion of microfinance around the world. SMI works with students in the United States and abroad developing educational and outreach programmes focusing on maximizing impact at a reasonable cost.

Tufts University: The Fletcher School Provides information about working in the field of microfinance, as well as providing links to various industry leaders, both governmental and non-governmental. The site also lists databases and listings for jobs in microfinance.

United Nations Capital Development Fund (UNCDF): Microfinance Matters online newsletter published by the UNCDF.

UNITUS Global Microfinance Accelerator: Unitus accelerates the growth of carefully selected, highest-potential small and mid-sized microfinance institutions (MFIs) through significant investments in capital and active involvement in capacity-building, allowing millions of poor people to improve their standard of living by gaining access to microfinance products and services.

Summary

Thus, microfinance has long history since time immemorial especially in underdeveloped and developing countries of the world. However, the nature of its operation differs from one country to another country and even within the country with one region to another region. Despite of its different, the basic aim of providing microfinance is to help the people those who are living below poverty line through financial assistance and other assistance for undertaking economic oriented activities. Among the different regions of the world, Asia continent emerged as top in the field of microfinance services for upliftment of poor people. World's top microfinance institutions are operating in this region to fulfill the needs of the poor.

Two
Development Stages of Microfinance

"Give a man a fish, he'll eat for a day. Give a woman microcredit, she, her husband, her children and her extended family will eat for a lifetime."

— *Bono*

Introduction

The failure of the formal banking institutions in delivering credit to the poor, particularly the rural poor, has resulted in the emergence of a new, innovative, helping hand, sensitive and viable institutional structure commonly known as Microfinance. This structure, seeks to reach the unreach and address all types of financial needs of the poor, who hitherto were not able to access credit from banking institutions due to non-possession of collateral, lengthy process and high cost transaction. The approach of microfinance is supposed to overcome these problems while at the same time improving recovery of loans, a problem that has plagued the rural banking institutions and affected their profitability.

An important feature of most of the microfinance programmes is the use of group approach to deliver financial services particularly micro credit to the poor. It is the key for success of microfinance worldwide. The popularity and acceptance of microfinance as a development tool for fighting against poverty is due to pioneering work of Muhammad Yunus who established the Grameen Bank model in the early 1980s.

It is prerequisite to know the concept of Self-Help Groups (SHGs) before knowing the microfinance concept clearly. SHGs are the key strategies for making successful of microfinance activities. Establishment of SHGs having a group of 5 to 15 members setting up of peer pressure at the time of repayment, empowering themselves in active involve in group economic oriented activities brings the effective strategies for successful of microfinance.

Genesis of SHGs

Self-Help in essence is forgoing 'collaborative' ties between individuals who need each other's co-operation in solving their day-to-day crisis. Lawson & Anderson (1996) have defined collaboration "as a process of pooling resources, linking and allying with one another to develop innovative, new responses for tackling social problems including poverty. Bailey & Koney (1996), Weil (1996) and Paesloe (1990) have pointed out that collaboration is necessary to address social issues that require multi-agency approach to alleviate them. SHGs are one such medium to achieve social collaboration. Graham & Barter (1999) have described collaboration as a relational system in which two or more stake holder's pool together resources in order to meet objectives that neither could meet individually. 'collaboration' differs from 'co-operation' in the sense that cooperation facilitates support and assistance for meeting the goals that are specific to an individual stake holder, whereas collaboration insists on goals that are mutually agreed upon based on an established value base to which all stakeholder shave a commitment. According to Hord (1986) collaboration proposes joints sharing and decision-making in the interest of change, as well as changes in relationships to facilitate these ends. He has also indicated that motivation to engage or refrained collaboration is necessarily influenced by differences among stake holders in expertise, status, empowerment and access to external and internal resources.

Conceptualization of SHG's Bank

The Self-Help Groups are voluntary associations of people formed to achieve both social and economic goals. The concept of micro financing rural poor for self-employment was started by Prof.

Muhammad Yunus of Bangladesh and is now being followed in more than 52 countries around the globe. Many international NGO's such as, Foundation for International Community Assistance (FINCA), Americans for Community Cooperation in Other Nations (ACCION), Women's World Banking (WWB), Freedom from Hunger, etc. are executing various projects, through their partners mostly in developing countries. The concept of SHG mainly revolves around the reasons that may lead to the genesis of self-help stretegies as a way to mitigate the problems faced by the people specially those who are living below poverty line.

A study conducted by the World Bank (1991) has also conclusively revealed that lack of people's participation in developmental activities do not foster entrepreneurial abilities, which results in low take off of developmental projects. The growing realization among the rural poor to collectively pool their small savings so as to create a corpus of funds cater to their emerging credit needs underlined the emergence of SHG's and other group related saving and credit activities in many developing countries such as Bangladesh, Indonesia, Bolivia and India.

Formation and Development of SHGs

According to Rao *et al.* (1999) a systematic approach in the formation of SHGs is of paramount importance to the long-term sustainability of these informal community based organizations. It has been observed by Fernandes (1992) that SHGs formed and promoted for limited purposes of availing subsidy, bank loans, grants and other materialistic benefit generally disintegrate, while according to Srinivasan & Rao (1996) the SHGs developed for genuine purpose of self-help in the wake of needs had much better chances of long term sustainability.

SHGs like any other type of groups have distinct phases through which they pass over a period of time. According to Johnson & Johnson (1994) there have been well over 100 theories to describe the development staged of groups. Hills & Gruner (1973) have opined that most of these theories are based on 'Sequential Stage Theory' while others are best described as in the 'Recurring Phase Theory'. Theories based on sequential stage of group development are based on the identification of definite phases in the lifecycle of group. The most famous of these theories has been proposed by Tuckman (1965) and Tuckman & Jensen (1997).

Tuckman studied a number of groups of varying nature and objectives such as therapy, training, and focus groups and identified four distinct development stages, viz. *Forming, Storming, Norming and Performing*. These distinct stages are characterized by the specific focus attributed by the groups during each stage and the related consequences on the behaviour of the members.

- *Forming stage* is marked with initial attraction towards each other in a group. The stage is characterized by initial euphoria of coming together, chaos and uncertainty. Kruger & King (1998) have indicated that during forming stage each member tries to figure out his/her own role in the group and gets indulged in evaluating his likely individual gains *vis-a-vis* group objectives. Lingering suspicion and anxiety prevail among the group members during these stages.
- *Storming stage* is earmarked by the expression of varying thoughts by the individual members, which reflects the prevailing conflict and confusion in the group. Kruger & King have indicated that this stage is completed with the evolution of leadership and decision-making capabilities within the group.
- *Norming stage* is reached when the group under the chosen leader/starts evolving group norms and the group's solidarity comes into force. The group becomes more cohesive and development oriented as gradually the individualistic tendencies are replaced by the collectivism.
- *Performing stage* is the state of readiness to act. Leadership is established, role clarity is developed and the group behaves in a unified manner so as to achieve its mission with the help of collective action.

Gerber (1994) as quoted by Harper (1995) has also identified the above four stages in the development as prospective membership stage like:

- new member stage,
- full member stage,

- marginal member stage, and
- ex-member stage.

Similarly Worchel *et al.*, (1992) have also identified six sequential stages of group development, which have been identified on the basis of prevailing 'feelings' in the members. These are:

- discontent stage,
- participative stage,
- identifying with the group stage,
- involvement in the group activities stage,
- proactive involvement stage, and
- disintegration stage.

Based on Tuckman's theory, Johnson & Johnson (1997) have identified seven stages in the development of co-operative learning groups. These are:

- defining and structuring procedures and becoming oriented,
- conforming to procedures and getting acquainted,
- recognizing mutuality and building trust,
- rebelling and differentiating,
- committing to and take ownership of the goals, procedures, and other members,
- functioning maturely and productively, and
- terminating.

Thus, from the above discussion on various stages of SHGs developed by different experts on microfinance reveals that SHGs can be formed in different ways, considering the needs and suitably of the areas.

SHG Linkages—The Indian Experience

The Indian experience of SHG linkage programme is unique in some respects. RBI and NABARD have tried to promote 'relationship banking' i.e. improving the existing relationship between the poor and bankers with the social intermediation by

NGOs. The Indian model is predominantly "linkage model", which draws upon the strengths of various partners—NGOs (who are the best in mobilizing and capacity building of poor) and bankers (whose strength is financing). Thus, as compared to other countries, where "parallel" model of lending to poor (i.e. NGOs acting as financial intermediaries) is predominant, the Indian linkage banking tries to use the existing formal financial network to increase the outreach to the poor while ensuring necessary flexibility of operations for both the bankers and the poor. Thus in a nutshell, the SHG linkage programme offers a win-win situation for the credit delivery system comprising banks of all types.

The SHG movement in India is basically aimed at utilizing the SHG's as an 'intermediary' between the banks and the rural poor to help drastically reduce transaction costs for both the banks and the rural clients. NABARD with its headquarters at Mumbai is an Apex Development Bank in India for financing and promoting agriculture, small scale industries, cottage and village industries, handicrafts and other rural crafts so as to promote integrated rural development.

In wake of banking sector reforms invoked in early 1990's the role of commercial banks in providing credit to rural poor came under intensive debate *vis-a-vis* the sustainability of entire banking operation for providing banking services–both in terms of savings and credit to the rural poor. Sheokand (1998) has indicted that as the rural poor's state in availing formal sector credit got further marginalized, NABARD, in 1992 launched the SHG-Bank linkage programme with the policy back up of the Reserve Bank of India. According to Shanmugam (1998) the SHG-Bank linkage programme initiated by NABARD, in active collaboration with Non-Governmental Organisations (NGOs), aimed at enhancing the coverage of rural poor under institutional credit thereby focusing on poverty alleviation and empowerment. Prior to this, NABARD's initiative in promoting active partnership between banks and SHG's was encouraged by the findings of a study conducted in 1988-89 by NABARD in collaboration with member institutions of Asia Pacific Rural and Agricultural Credit Association (APRACA), Manila. The study covered 43 NGOs involved in promoting savings and credit SHGs in 11 states of the country.

As per a NABARD report (1995) the scheme on SHG's was made applicable to RRB's and co-operative banks of the country in 1993 and in April 1996, RBI advised the banks that lending to SHG's should be considered as an additional segment under priority sector advances and it be integrated with mainstream normal credit operation. Rao & Das Gupta (1999) has commented that the SHG-Bank Linkage Programme has gained considerable movement in southern region of the country, though the northern states too are also now catching up fast growth. Since, the inceptions of NABARD promoted SHG linkage programme there has been an appreciable increase both in formation of SHG and their linkage with the banks. The concept and importance of SHGs has been accepted and adopted by policy makers and it now forms the backbone of rural poverty alleviation strategies, implemented by the Government of India.

Functioning of SHG's and their Impact

Self-Help Group based microfinancing in India has become a major tool for development and empowerment of poor. Group systems for micro financing services evolved in Bangladesh and Latin America have promoted micro credit to the poor. However, effective functioning of SHGs is to be ensured in order to initiate and sustain income-generating activities for economic growth and development.

Impact of SHG's on Women Empowerment

Microfinance interventions are well-recognized world over, as an effective tool for poverty alleviation and improving socio-economic conditions of the poor. In India too, microfinance is making headway in its efforts for reducing poverty and empowering women in particular. The impact of micro finance programme through Self-Help Groups has been effective in making positive social change to all members, irrespective of direct borrowers of the micro credit. Importantly, in the rural context, the SHGs have facilitated the poor; especially the women to overcome the existing constraints grappling the formal credit institutions. These groups provide considerable social protection and income opportunities to the members. The SHGs have acquired a prominent status in maximizing social and financial returns. The promotion of income generating activities for the poor rural women is perceived as a powerful medium to resolve several socio-economic problems such as reduction in poverty, provision of goods and services appropriate to local needs, redistribution of income and opportunities in the communities, etc.

Microfinance Institutions (MFIs)

Microfinance institutions are organisations involved in the delivery of financial services to the population segment that is otherwise considered un-bankable. They may range from benign and socially responsible NGOs to profit oriented NBFCs. There has been an explosive growth in MFI activity in India over the past decade as a plethora of NGOs and private organisations have converged into this field, some having the genuine intention of socio-economic advancement, while others cashing in on the fortune at the bottom of the pyramid.

Quite simply, a microfinance institution is an organization that offers financial services to low income populations. Almost all of these offer micro-credit and only take back small amount of savings from their own borrowers, not from the general public. Within the microfinance industry, the term microfinance institution has come to refer to a wide range of organizations dedicated to providing these services.

The image most of us have when we refer to MFIs is of a "financial NGO", an NGO that is fully and virtually exclusively dedicated to offering financial services; in most cases micro-credit NGOs are not allowed to capture savings deposits from the general public. This group of a few hundred NGOs have led the development of micro-credit, and subsequently microfinance, the world over. Most of these constitute a group that is commonly referred to as "best practice" organizations, ones that employ the reach down far into poor sectors of the economy on a sustainable basis.

A great many NGOs that offer micro-credit, perhaps even a majority, do many other non- financial development activities and would bristle at the suggestion that they are essentially financial institutions. Yet, from an industry perspective, since they are engaged in supplying financial services to the poor, we call them MFIs. The same sort of situation exists with a small number of commercial banks that offer microfinance services. For our purposes, we refer to them as MFIs, even though only a small portion of their assets may actually be tied up in financial services for the poor. In both cases, when people in the industry refer to MFIs, they are referring only to that part of the institutions that offers microfinance.

There are other institutions, however, that consider themselves to be in the business of microfinance and that will certainly play a role in a reshaped and deepened financial sector. These are community-based financial intermediaries. Some are membership based such as credit unions and cooperative housing societies. Others are owned and managed by local entrepreneurs or municipalities. These institutions tend to have a broader client base than the financial NGOs and already consider them to be part of the formal financial sector. It varies from country to country, but many poor people do have some access to these types of institutions, although they tend not to reach down market as far as the financial NGOs.

Evidence shows that clients willingly pay the higher interest rates necessary to assure long-term access to credit. They recognize that their alternatives—even higher interest rates in the informal finance sector (money-lenders, etc.) or simply no access to credit-are much less attractive for them. Interest rates in the informal sector can be as high as 20 per cent per day among some urban market vendors. Many of the economic activities in which the poor engage are relatively low return on labour, and access to liquidity and capital can enable the poor to obtain higher returns, or to take advantage of economic opportunities. The return received on such investments may well be many times greater than the interest rate charged.

Moreover, the interest rate is only a small part of their overall transaction cost of credit, and if microfinance institutions offer credit on a more accessible basis, substantial costs in terms of time, travel, paperwork, etc. can be reduced, thus benefiting the poor. A long series of studies has shown that many programmes that charge subsidized interest rates end up using rationing mechanisms to distribute credit in response to excess demand. These mechanisms cause the borrower to have to "jump through hoops"; increasing the time and money s/he must put out to get the loan. In fact, these transactions costs are frequently higher than the interest costs, which take away the advantage to the

Table 2.1: Main Features of the Global Microfinance Models

Operational Features	*Grameen Bank Model*	*BC Model in Brazil*	*ACCION's Service Company Model*	*South Africa Teba Bank Model*
Basis	Group and Social collateral	Technology e.g., POS, Kiosk	Bank Partnership	Technology e.g., POS, Kiosk
Linkage with Commercial Bank	No linkage with commercial bank	Linkage with commercial banks as BCs are appointed Banks	Linkage between bank and service co. as partners	Service is provided as a wing of bank
Service focus	Credit	Full Banking services	Credit	Full Banking services
Appropriate client	Clients from rural or urban area and usually women from low income groups pursuing income generating activates	People having no access to banking services/bank branch including both poor and non-poor	Mostly urban including both men and women having small and medium incomes	Poor people in rural and small towns both employed and self-employed
Group	Group	Individual	Group	Individual
Repayment	Group responsibility	Joint between Bank and the retails outlets	Bank responsibility	Bank responsibility

Source: Notes on Microfinance, www.bsp.gov.ph

borrower of the interest rate subsidy. However, while increased access to credit for poor on a long-term and sustainable basis can bring significant benefits, MFIs must continue to work to improve efficiency levels and the benefits transferred to the poor in terms of improving loan products, better access to loans, and lower borrowing costs.

Microfinance Models at International Context

Globally there are number of microfinance model adopted by different countries differently. However, on the basis of their similarities, following models of microfinance have been developed for the present study.

1. *Grameen Bank Model*: It was developed in "Bangladesh in 1976 by Prof. Yunus which is well-known and the most admired model in the world. In this model the centres of around five to seven such groups were formed. The group members make regular savings with the Micro Finance Organization (MFO) as per affixed compulsory amount and take regular loans.

2. *Teba Bank of South Africa Model*: Originally Teba Bank started its operations in mining industry. The bank previously operated as the Teba Savings Fund, and provided basic banking services as entry level player mine workers on gold and platinum mines since 1976. Thereafter, it started to target low income households in urban and rural areas as a wing of the bank. In 2000 it was granted license to operate as a microfinance bank. It is a niche bank, aiming to provide affordable microfinance services to the under-banked in non-metropolitan South Africa. Here, bank provides financial services to the low-income households in small town and rural areas through agents who uses mobile Point of Sale (POS) devices in the form of hand held mobile phone. The customer uses their debit card at the terminal to deposit and withdraw cash, make balance inquiry and transfer funds. In this system agents can accept cash from the clients and disburse cash physically. Typical agents here are the neighbourhood grocery stores and their accounts at the bank are instantaneously debited and credited as per case.

3. *Banking Correspondent Model in Brazil*: Brazil as a country has several similarities with India mainly huge demographic areas. Even six years before, 1700 municipalities out of 5500 municipalities were lacking a single branch of bank. The rural people had no option to deposit their money, no access to credit except informal sources say family and no chances of building their credit history. In 1997, Banking Correspondents (BC) which are small outlets with extended working hours offered basic banking services (RBI, 2005) BCs are full service retail channel that Brazil's Banks have developed using technology and business

arrangements with grocery stores, medical stores, post offices, lottery outlets and other retail shops. The BC offer many services including deposits, withdrawals, fund transfer, bill payments, new account opening, insurance, etc. BC model is highly technology intensive wherein a combination of devices like EFTROS device, a bar scanner, POS, PC and sort of teller machine is used at retail stores, post offices or other retail outlets. The retail outlets provide a staff person to man the device and handle the transactions for clients. Clients are given bank cards which in some cases are debit card. POS device is connected by VSAT to the central server that store account information. In the case of post office the post offices themselves identify retail outlets and handle all equipment, training, contracting, etc. These banks use the services of management companies for managing the BCs. These companies manage the BCs on behalf of banks.

4. *ACCION's Service Company Model*: In Latin America the commercial banks have been a significant player in providing microfinance services during last few years. Entry of commercial bank is said to be good as customers would get full range of services and as a whole it would be a very cost effective system for microfinance as it has a strong base of physical, financial and human resources. In the light of specific potential that a commercial bank has, ACCION international (a microfinance resource institution based in USA and working in American continent) has developed relationship with some commercial banks to start and expand microfinance operations. In this respect ACCION and its partners are using an approach known as service company model. A microfinance service company is a non-financial company that provides the loan origination and credit management services to the bank. The service company does all the work of promoting, evaluating, appraising, tracking and collecting loans but loan sit in the books of the bank and not of the service company. In return of these services the company gets a fee. The service company employs the loan officer and microfinance programme staff while the bank furnishes services to the service company. This could include human resource, teller support or information technology support. The service company can be a wholly owned subsidiary of bank or it can involve other institution.

Microfinance Model in Indian Context

In addition to the international microfinance model adopted by different countries, they also have adopted their own model of microfinance keeping in view the geographical variations, environment and implementation. On the basis of suitably, necessity and accepted, following models are adopted in India:

1. SHG-Bank Linkage Model

It is the oldest and most popular model practice in India and on the basis of the modes of formation, nurturing, monitoring of groups and credit linkages with organization SHGs can be basically categorized into three groups and they have been briefly discussed as follows:

Model-I: SHGs Formed and Financed by Bank: Under this model, the bank themselves act as SHPIs in forming and nurturing groups, opening their savings accounts and providing them with bank credit.

Model-II: SHGs Formed by NGOs, and Formal Agencies but Directly Financed by Banks: This is called as NGO facilitated SHGs. This appears to be the most popular model amongst bankers. Under this model, NGOs and formal agencies working in the field of micro-finance act as facilitators. They propagate the message, organize groups, train them in thrift and credit management and nurture them over a period. Banks in due course, link these groups by directly providing loans to them. More than 70 per cent of the SHGs are linked through this model.

Model-III: SHGs Financed by Banks Using NGOs as Financial Intermediaries: In this model, NGOs take on the dual role as facilitators and also financial intermediaries. They help in formation of SHGs, nurturing them, training them in thrift and credit management. Eventually, the NGOs approach banks for bulk loan assistance for on lending to these SHGs.

2. NGO Guided But Self-Supported SHGs

This category of SHGs are entirely formed and supported by the group members, neither getting any assistance/support from the bank nor from NGOs. By observing the group formed in the neighbourhood areas, these groups have initiated themselves and function as others models mentioned above.

3. Completely Self-Supported SHGs

Yet another category of SHGs formed and initiated by the NGOs, guided by them on the rules and regulations, accounts to be maintained, etc. But no financial support either directly or through the linkage with banks is arranged but only the savings of the members is used for internal lending as well as for starting an enterprise. Of all the four groups mentioned above this group seems to be different, self-dependent and accordingly may be encouraged. However, by not getting any external support, the size of the enterprise initiated may be too small and also expansion is not possible.

4. Grameen Bank Model

The Grameen Bank model of Bangladesh has been replicated in India by some two dozen MFIs. Its features and methodology has been discussed in the earlier section on international models. In India the major MFIs which are using this replicated model are SHARE in Andhra Pradesh, ASA in Tamil Nadu, CASHPOR in Eastern Uttar Pradesh and Loyalam Bank Project under RDO in Manipur.

5. Individual Banking Programmes (IBPs) Model

In this model microfinance services are provided by MFIs to individual who do not belong to any group but sometimes they may be associated with a particular group like SHG, Joint Liability Group (JLG) or cooperative society group. This method is popular in the case of microfinance through cooperatives and commercial banks and basically suitable for larger clients in urban areas who are engaged in their own enterprise or running such enterprises that provide self-employment to other poor.

6. ICICI-Bank Partnership Model

This model has been used and polarized by the private bank and said to pioneer by ICICI bank. In this model the MFI originates the loan, evaluates, recommends, tracks and collects the loan but the loan appear in the books of the Bank and not of the MFIs books. For the credit management services that the MFI provides to the bank MFI charges a service fee from the borrowers. With this partnership structure ICICI is working with more than 30 MFIs in India accounting for loans outstanding of approximately 55 $ million in December 2004.

7. IFAD Model

International Fund for Agricultural Development (IFAD) Rome is a specialised agency of the United Nations dedicated to combating rural poverty in the most disadvantaged regions of the world. Microfinance is one the activities undertaken by them in different forms in different parts of the world such as a cooperative bank in Armenia, financial service associations in Benin and Haiti, rural bank in Ghana, credit and savings associations in Kenya and Tanzania. However, in India, Self-Help Groups are being developed and linked to commercial banks with IFAD support.

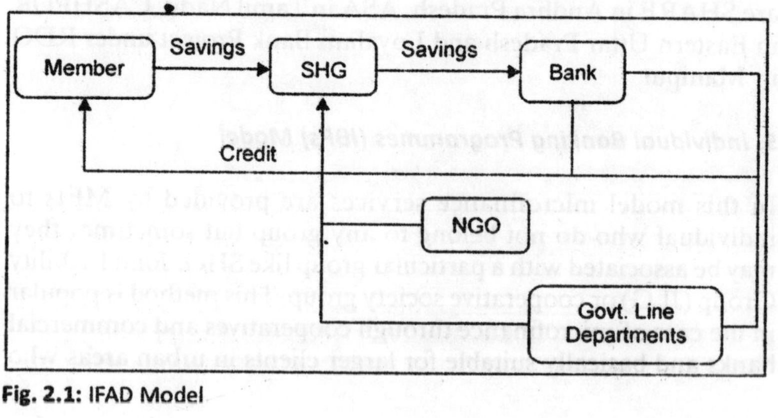

Fig. 2.1: IFAD Model

8. Mix Model

Some MFIs uses mixed model wherein the elements of grameen model and SHG bank are mixed. The number of such type of MFIs is relatively less but their numbers are growing. Another prominent example of this model is SPANDANA in the Guntur region of Andhra Pradesh which has larger JLGs of around 10 members. Another examples are Cashpoor, a Varanasi based MFI, Indian Association of Savings and Credit (IASC) a section 25 company promoted by the HDFC bank gives individual as well as group loans.

9. Business Facilitator/Business Correspondent Model

In 2006, RBI permitted banks to appoint business facilitator (BF) and business correspondents (BC). While the former can merely promote the business of the bank, the latter can take on a larger scope of activities, such as disbursal of small value credits, collection of small value deposits, sale of microinsurance, pension and other third party products as well as receipt and delivery of small value remittance and other payment instruments.

Microfinance and Other Areas of Poverty Alleviation Programmes

Microfinance is considering and accepting as one of the most effective tool for poverty alleviation in the recent past globally. It has directly and indirectly helping to those poor people who are living below poverty line through small financial assistance for setting up of micro enterprises and other economic oriented activities. In this process, quite a good number of new areas have emerged and microfinance have directly related with them and also differentiated from them. Few of important areas have been highlighting in the following paragraphs, they are–

(a) Microfinance and Micro-credit

The concept of micro finance and micro-credit are usually used interchangeably. But micro-credit is always dovetailed with thrift and hence microfinance is a more appropriate expression rather than credit. It includes the whole gamut of financial services like thrift, credit, insurance, leasing of equipment, remittance, etc. required by the poor. Micro-credit is the credits of meagre amount of money which plays an important role while enhance the human life which should be used in proper way to achieve income generation, removal of poverty, create employment, etc.

Thus, Microfinance refers to loans, savings, insurance, transfer services and other financial products targeted at low-income clients. Micro-credit refers to a small loan to a client made by a bank or other institution. Micro-credit can be offered, often without collateral, to an individual or through group lending.

Table 2.2: Differences Between Micro-Credit and Microfinance

Characteristics of Loan	*Micro-Credit*	*Microfinance*
1. Size of Loan	Small	Small
2. Repayment Period	Short	Short
3. Sources of Mobilization	External	Both external and internal
4. Repayment	Definite obligation to Repay	Obligation if source External
5. Collateral	May or may not be needed	Not needed
6. Purpose of use	Mostly fixed; limited scope for deviation	Flexible; consumption, income generation, any other
7. Scope of operation	Usually individual loans though group loans too	Mostly group loans trickling down to individuals.

Source: Society for Development Studies, series of policy Research Studies.

(b) Microfinance and Financial Inclusion

Financial inclusion has been defined as the "provision of affordable financial services" (RBI, 2006a) to those who have been left unattended or under-attended by formal agencies of the financial system. These financial services include "payments and remittance facilities, savings loan and insurance services". Microfinance has been looked upon as an important means of financial inclusion in India. As already discussed, the Indian concept of microfinance encourages access of SHGs to banks both as means of savings and providers of loan services. However, going a step further, we can say that microfinance has to act proactively not just as a means of financial inclusion and also has to work towards reducing dependence of poor borrowers on various informal sources of credit that are often notorious for the onerous terms at which they offer credit. An effective financial inclusion is possible only with the accomplishment of effective microfinance scheme.

(c) Microfinance and Micro-insurance

Members of microfinance programmes typically have low and often irregular, incomes. By building their savings and by access to credit, they are able to avail of lump sums of money that they need from time to time. The savings and loan products of most microfinance programmes are better suited to address the 'certain' financial needs of its clients. There are financial needs of an individual, however, that arise out of situations that cannot be predicted with any certainty. For instance, sickness, disability due to accident, loss of life-due to natural or unnatural causes, damage to business assets due to fire, theft and such other reasons, damage to house due to fire, flood, cyclone are all situations that cannot be anticipated with certainty. These situations can make survival very difficult for the poor given their low incomes and thus the low capacity to recoup financially. Insurance is a financial service that is designed to meet these uncertain needs of individuals.

(d) Microfinance and Micro-enterprise

In many developing counties micro-enterprise in its various forms is the major source of livelihood in rural as well as urban areas. It contributes to a large proportion of employment generation in developing as well as developed countries. Micro-enterprises are considered to be the source of equitable distribution. Otero and Rhyne (1994) stated that "For increasing number of poor people, micro-enterprise is a source of income and employment where no other alternatives are available. In urban areas, a growing per centage of the working population—sometimes as high as 50 per-cent is engaged in micro-enterprise activity. In rural settings, most families combine micro-enterprise with the farming and many depend on it as the main source of family income". Otero and Rhyne have assumed that the "new world of micro-enterprise" finance has the potential to do in "finance what the green revolution has done in agriculture: provide access on a massive scale to the poor".

Mentioning the importance of MSEs in India, Awasthi stated that "Micro and Small Enterprises (MSEs) constitute an important segment of the Indian economy. Besides providing employment to nearly 25 million persons, mostly belonging to the lower rungof socio-economic strata in the society, the sector helps the process of economic diversification, utilization of otherwise dormant resources, balanced regional development, production of and demand for wage goods, equitable distribution of income, and widening the base of entrepreneurial supply" (Awasthi, 2004).

Describing the potential and importance of micro-enterprise and microfinance Rangarajan stated that "If a serious impact on the economic conditions of the rural poor has to be made, a much larger flow of credit to support a much broader production base is required. It is in this direction the movement has to travel. Self-Help Groups (SHGs) have to graduate into promoting micro-enterprises. Though micro enterprises are not a panacea for the complex problems and chronic unemployment and poverty in rural and urban areas, yet promotion of micro-enterprises is a viable end. Effective strategy for achieving significant gains in income and assets for poor and marginalized people" (Rangarajan, 2005).

This contribution of micro-enterprise is not uniform across the world. It depends on several factors within the country i.e. internal and external environment and their support to these micro-enterprises. Khanka (1990) rightly argued that the role of entrepreneurship in economic development varies from economy to economy and it depends on several factors like availability of material resources, industrial climate and responsiveness of the political system to the entrepreneurial function. India has a good potential to promote micro-enterprise because it has got enough material resources with favourable industrial climate. But there is a need to promote responsiveness of the political system to the entrepreneurial function.

In another study in Nicaragua it was found that "MFIs like CARITAS Matagalpa are making a difference in the lives of thousand. For more than 10,000 clients of CARITAS Matagalpa, microfinance has enabled micro-entrepreneurs the opportunity to start, expand, and develop enterprises with the goal of enhancing their lives" (Pisani & Yoskowitz, 2005).

Other than economic benefit there are some social benefits of micro-enterprise and microfinance development. Singh (2002) mentioned that "The social development approach of micro-finance is based on the premise that people should earn money by investing in viable micro-enterprises. They should earn profit from their enterprises. Major share of the profit should be reinvested in enterprises for their growth. The other share of the profit should be spent on social development that is, health, education, housing, sanitation, etc. by earning profit from the viable micro-enterprises, people will increase their paying ability for services delivered to them". And finally this will lead to the development of the society.

It has been clearly discussed in the above section that micro-enterprise can play an important role in various aspects of social and economic development of the society. Increasing income opportunities and finally leading to empowering the poor is the basic objective of the micro-enterprise. Empowerment of the poor community is the way to development of society.

(e) Sustainable Microfinance for Women's Empowerment

Microfinance programmes is not only give access to savings and credit, but reach millions of people worldwide bringing them together regularly in organised groups. Although no 'magic bullet', they are potentially a very significant contribution to gender equality and women's empowerment, as well as pro-poor development and civil society strengthening. Through their contribution to women's ability to earn an income these programmes have potential to initiate a series of 'virtuous spirals' of economic empowerment, increased well-being for women and their families and wider social and political empowerment. Microfinance services and groups involving men also have potential to question and significantly change men's attitudes and behaviours as an essential component of achieving gender equality.

There is evidence of significant potential for microfinance to enable women to challenge and change gender inequalities at all levels if there is a strategic gender focus. There have also been many important innovations in products and services to enable women to better benefit. Nevertheless benefits cannot be assumed and even financially sustainable microfinance if it is gender blind may seriously disempower women and increase inequality. It is clear that most microfinance programmes have a long way to go before they make their full potential contribution to gender equality and empowerment. Many of the strategies promoted for financial sustainability may exacerbate the negative impacts of debt, because of over rapid expansion, rigid product design inappropriate to women's economic activities, cutting of necessary support services and lack of attention to local economic contexts.

(f) Microfinance and Social Interventions

There are currently a few social interventions that have been combined with microfinancing to increase awareness of HIV/AIDS. Such interventions like the "Intervention with Microfinance for AIDS and Gender Equity" (IMAGE) which incorporates microfinancing with "The Sisters-for-Life" programme a participatory programme that educates on different gender roles, gender-based violence, and HIV/AIDS infections to strengthen the communication skills and leadership of women "The Sisters-for-Life" programme has two phases where phase one consists of ten one-hour training programmes with a facilitator with phase two consisting of identifying a leader amongst the group, train them further, and allow them to implement an Action Plan to their respective centres.

Microfinance has also been combined with business education and with other packages of health interventions. A project undertaken in Peru by Innovations for Poverty Action found that those borrowers randomly selected to receive financial training as part of their borrowing group meetings had higher profits, although there was not a reduction in "the proportion who reported having problems in their business.

(g) Microfinance and Primary Agricultural Credit Societies (PACS)

The share of Primary Agricultural Credit Societies (PACS) in rural credit stood at 18.6 per cent in 1991. A good deal of this amount went to people who were relatively better-off, that is to those who do not belong to the BPL households notwithstanding this, a certain percentage of the credit flow has benefited the poor. **According to the World Bank NCAER study (2004) the share of**

PACS in micro-credit is as high as 30 per cent or one-third. PACS are, as such yet another important channel of microfinance.

(h) Microfinance and Technology

Technology can reduce transaction costs and improve transparency in delivering financial services, both of which can translate into increased access and lower costs for many lower income clients. Streamlined and automated processes allow financial institutions to extend services to harder to reach and more costly clientele by replacing people and branches with point of sale (POS) devices and branchless banking strategies. Technology helps the management information and reporting systems that are essential for efficient financial service delivery.

Despite the appeal of advanced delivery technologies, relatively few financial institutions have successfully deployed them to reach poor and low income clients. Developing a solid management information system still remains one of the most important tasks facing microfinance institutions, particularly those scaling up. Challenges include the high cost and limited availability of existing technological solutions, lack of widely available local technical support to support MIS software, consumer adoption rates of technology, lack of basic communications infrastructure in many countries, and inadequate policy environments.

Information lies at the very heart of microfinance. Whether by hand or by computer, microfinance institutions (MFIs) hold and maintain large amounts of important business data, from basic client information to detailed analyses of portfolio statistics. This data must be stored, processed and clearly presented so that MFI Boards and Managers can make sound decisions. A good information system should do just that: it should act as a conduit through which raw data become useful and useable information.

Technology is consistently cited as one of the greatest challenges faced by MFIs around the world. While efficient use of technology can help reduce costs, improve efficiency, and increase outreach, many MFIs continue to make poor technology investments or simply do not invest in technology thus limiting their ability to grow and respond to demand.

(i) Microfinance and IFAD

International Fund for Agricultural Development (IFAD) is a specialized agency of the United Nations dedicated to combating rural poverty in the most disadvantaged regions of the world. Microfinance is an important part of their activities. Seventy-five per cent of IFAD-funded projects provide financial services to poor rural men and women. They work with poor people and their organizations to develop sustainable innovative and diversified rural finance systems.

Providing financial services in rural areas presents a number of challenges. For instance, loans cost more when they are extended to populations dispersed over large areas. Moreover, incomes in rural areas are often erratic due to their stronger dependence on agriculture-related activities.

(j) Post office Network and Banking Services

The existing extensive formal banking structure is still not sufficient to meet the growing demand of rural credit Lack of Sufficient number of retail outlets of formal banking sector has been a big handicap in reaching the poor. Of the 155,000 post office branches in India reported in March 2008, more than 98 per cent offer some type of savings services. The post office controlled 174.7 million savings accounts (or 40.7 per cent of what banks held), accounting for Rs 3.4 trillion in deposits (more than US$75.6 billion, 42.9 per cent of what banks held). Even more encouraging for financial inclusion is that, unlike banks, 89.8 per cent of all post offices are located in rural areas. (Linder, 2010a).

Post-offices have been already into the business of collecting small deposits from people and been providing services of transferring money. Post-office network could very well be considered for increasing the outreach of banking services, especially in remote and rural areas. One of the important principles of micro-finance is to provide door-step and timely delivery of financial service. The scheme of pigmy deposits pioneered by some banks in the past met these criteria. This experiment, however, failed because of unscrupulous agents who indulged in fraud. The post-offices are also known to have experimented with similar schemes and had a greater measure of success. They have a regular and paid staff and with little training and incentives, their services could be utilised very usefully.

(k) Islamic Microfinance

Islamic microfinance refers to a system of localised finance arrangements set-up as an alternative source of funds for small, low income Islamic clients. Typically, users of Islamic microfinance have little or no collateral, as they do not possess significant assets, and would therefore, be excluded from other forms of financing, including Islamic bank financing. Thus, Islamic microfinance provides a means of accessing funds for those who are unlikely to qualify for other forms of finance, yet are still seeking full compliance with Islamic law and the Islamic way of life.

Islamic microfinance is becoming an increasingly popular mechanism for alleviating poverty, especially in developing countries around the world. The Islamic finance industry as a whole is expected to reach over $2 billion dollars in 2012 and is a continually growing sector due to its ethical principles and prohibition of riba or interest (Tasnim Nazeer).

The concept of Islamic microfinance adheres to the principles of Islam and is forms of socially responsible investing investors who use their wealth for Islamic microfinance projects only involve themselves in halal projects which benefit the community at large. Such projects include *zakat*, which is charity based or trade and industry projects to develop a country's economy.

The mechanism of lending in Islamic microfinance differs from conventional microfinance due to the prohibition of riba. Unlike conventional microfinance offers an interest-free way to give small loans to people who are poor and in need. One key method of lending is through the Islamic financial instrument, qard'l-hasan, which is a loan that has been extended by the lender on a goodwill basis and the borrower is only required to pay the exact amount borrowed without additional charges or interest. The Q-clearly encourages Muslims to provide qard'l-hasan, or benevolent loans, to "those who need them" "who is he that will give Allan qard'l-hasan? For Allah will increase it manifold to his credit."

Many regions around the world have already created tailor-made Islamic microfinance programmes, either through Islamic banks or Islamic microfinance institutions to cater for dealing with poverty. Utilizing Islamic financial instruments such as Murabahah and Musharaka to help in facilitating Islamic microfinance can not only spur the Islamic microfinancial sector but can also increase the options of Islamic finance and make it more accessible to poverty stricken countries.

Thus, Islamic microfinance has been an unprecedented way to combat poverty which may also provide the affected people of Somalia with a form of economic relief and provide a financial solution to developing countries worldwide.

(l) Microfinance and Shopkeepers

Microfinance scheme can also extend to those small shopkeepers who have been starting small shops otherwise unable to growth due to lack of credit. Linkage with bank like linkage of SHG-bank should be undertaken. MFI or SHPI have worked with local banks to provide microfinance for shopkeepers so they can strengthen their businesses, increase their revenues and improve their quality of life. In the last two years, more than 4,000 shopkeepers have benefited from US$6 million made available in micro credit financing.

Summary

To conclude, it has been seen that microfinance has now expanded its scope in different areas and it is no longer confined to specific areas. In its evolution stage, it has shifted from micro credit to microfinance, microfinance to micro-enterprise, micro-insurance, remittance, etc. in the process of expanding its scope various obstacles and hindrances have been facing by the microfinance promoting agencies. From time to time government and policy-makers have to framed various policies and regulation to control the microfinance to bring into proper and right direction for poverty alleviation strategies.

THREE

Microfinance in India

> "My vision for the future? Two things: to make credit a human right so that each individual human being will have the opportunity to take loans and implement his or her ideas so that self-exploration becomes possible. And second: that it will lead to a world where no body has to suffer from poverty—a world completely free from poverty."
>
> — *Muhammad Yunus*

Introduction

Microfinance refers to small amount of financial services for both credits and deposits that are provided to those people who operate small or micro-enterprise where goods are produced, recycled, repaired or traded; provide services; work for wages or commissions; gain income from renting out small amounts of land, vehicles, draft animals or machinery and tools; and to other individuals and local groups in developing countries in both rural and urban areas' (Marguerite S. Robinson.) The Indian Government put stress on providing financial services to the poor and underprivileged since Independence. The commercial banks were nationalized in 1969 and were directed to lend 40 per cent of their loanable funds, at a concessional rate, to the priority sector. The aim was to provide resources to help the poor to attain self-sufficiency.

To supplement these efforts, the credit scheme Integrated Rural Development Programme (IRDP) was launched in 1980. But these supply side programmes (ignoring the demand side of the economy) aided by corruption and leakages, achieved little.

Further, "the share of the formal financial sector in total rural credit was 56.6 per cent compared to informal finance at 39.6 per cent and unspecified sources at 3.8 per cent (RBI, 1992). Not only had formal credit flow been less but also uneven. The collateral and paper work based system shield away from the poor. The vacuum continued to be filled by the village money-lender who charged interest rates of 2 to 3 per cent per month (K.G. Karmakar, 1999). More than 70 per cent of landless/marginal farmers did not have a bank account and 87 per cent had no access to credit from a formal source. (World Bank NCAER, Rural Financial Access Survey, 2003).

While the first decade of the programme was meant to demonstrate the potential of SHGs to organize themselves and be instrumental in managing their own savings and extending emergent micro-credit needs, the second decade laid emphasis on establishing the replicability of the model across the regions, with focus on resource poor regions of the country. This decade also witnessed greater confidence among the financing banks to "own" up the programme as a potential business model thereby extending its outreach to the current level. The development planners including the Government of India and the State Governments also recognised the real potential of the SHG movement in development of the poor and it was made an essential ingredient of all poverty alleviation programmes of the Government. Even the private sector started realising the untapped potential of SHGs for deep penetration to the emerging rural markets. The turbulence witnessed in the microfinance sector in the recent past due to the mushrooming growth of Microfinance Institutions and their questionable ways in which they went ahead in extending their outreach and credit intensification, could not make any significant dent in the popularity of the SHG-Bank Linkage Programme.

The third decade of the programme promises to be one of maturing the linkage programme with livelihoods support, lot more innovations in the product range offered through SHGs and path breaking reforms in leveraging technology to improve efficiency, while extending its outreach to more geographical regions, especially the most resource poor regions of the country. It is widely believed that the SHGs of the poor will be the vehicles leading the march of India's emergence as a super economic power in the next decade. A number of countries, especially the developing countries and international agencies are turning to India to learn from its experiments with microfinance and to explore possibilities of replication of the model in other parts of the globe.

It was in this cheerless background that the Microfinance Revolution occurred worldwide. In India it began in the 1980s with the formation of pockets in informal SHGs engaging in micro activities financed by Microfinance. But India's first Microfinance Institution Shri Mahila SEWA Sahkari Bank was set up as an urban co-operative bank, by the Self-Employed Women's Association (SEWA) soon after the group was formed in 1974. The first official effort materialized under the direction of NABARD. The Mysore Resettlement and Development Agency (MYRADA) sponsored project on "Savings and Credit Management of SHGs was partially financed by NABARD during 1986-87 (P. Satish, 2005).

Addressing poverty is the most significant challenge in this millennium, clearly reflected in the Millennium Development Goals that seeks to halve global poverty by 2015. The concern also forms a component of other global initiatives like the UN Habitat Agenda and campaign for good governance. Development initiatives to empower the poor, in the context of addressing the global challenges of poverty, invariably have a credit component. The rationale is that economic empowerment of the poor through strengthening the income generating capacity, equips the poor to access all the development requirements to get out of the multifaceted dimensions of poverty.

The impact of microfinance has touched the bottom of the development pyramid in the recent past. In 2003, the global outreach of micro-credit extends to 80.9 million people, of which the poorest clients accounted for about 68 per cent. The share of India in the global micro-credit market was 13 per cent of all clients and 16 per cent of the poorest in 2003. The micro-finance movement in India, unleashed around the 1970s, has come a long way from being a tool for welfare, to becoming an effective strategy for poverty alleviation. The movement has gained significant momentum, with 563 district (out of 593) being covered all over India, with around 3,024 NGOs associated with the programme and 560 commercial banks providing direct or indirect credit linkages to SHGs which has emerged as an important part of the delivery and management system. The cumulative disbursement of credit from all these institutions taken together has been estimated at ₹ 5,038 crore (US $ 1132 mn) and the total number of SHGs in India has grown to 1,276,035 as on December 30, 2004 (Government of India, the Economic Survey, 2004-05). However, in terms of the share in the credit of the formal sector institutions, it is estimated to be less than 0.15 per cent of the outstanding loans to the priority sector and 0.51 per cent of the all commercial banks. After 10 years of growth, micro-credit has dropped for the first time 205 million to 195 million beneficiaries from 2010 to 2011 in the global context. This decline is primarily due to the decrease of 14.2 million beneficiaries in India.

In the context of poverty eradication in the developing countries, microfinance is being increasingly used as a mechanism to provide access to credit to the poor and low income household whose access to the commercial banks is limited. In India, the poverty situation continues to be dismal, despite the collective efforts made by the government policies and the NGOs. Official estimates show that during the beginning of the new millennium, 260 million people were living below the poverty line (Tenth Five Year Plan). This is a staggering figure for a country where year after year, resources schemes and funds are mobilized from all quarters, to benefit the lot of the poor.

Apex Microfinance Wholesalers in India

The details of Microfinance wholesalers in India are shown in Table 3.1. The largest coverage of poor has been reported by NABARD with the largest amount cumulative number of SHGs. However, interest rate has been reported significantly higher in case of NABARD as compared to other wholesalers.

Microfinance Distribution Approaches—Retailer Level

Just as MFIs offer a varied combination of products and adopt different pricing techniques, they also differ in the credit delivery mechanism. It is dependent on factors such as nature and demographic profile of the clientele; products mix, pricing technique, legal and procedural requirements and above all, the long-term Micro-Credit are commonly prevalent in India:

Table 3.1 Apex Microfinance Wholesalers in India

Institution	*Year*	*Operations*	*Coverage of Poor*	*Cumulative No. of Groups*	*Interest*	*Repayment Schedule*	*Purpose of Loan*
1. NABARD	1982	1. Direct financing 2. Refinancing 3. Support Grant to NGOs	390 lakh on 31March 2002	79,60,000 SHGs, on 31March, 2012	11 % p.a.	Within 4 years; on quarterly basis	Production/ consumption/Any other
2. FWWB-I	1982	1. Direct financing to NGOs, MFIs 2. Direct financing to SHGs/ Federation 3. Support grants for conducting trainings	N.A.	N.A.	N.A.	N.A	Production only
3. SIDBI	1990	1. Direct MFI Financing 2. Capacity building grand 3. Grant tongs	10.41 lakh on 31 March 2004	192 MFIs on 31 March 2004	9 % p.a.	Within 4 years, on quarterly basis	Production/ Consumption/Any Other
4. RGVN	1990	1. Support forgo Schemes 2. Creation and financing SHGs	26,693 on 31 March 2004	N.A.	10 % p.a.	N.A.	Production/ Consumption/ Housing
5. RMK	1993	1. Refinancing 2. Support for NGOs Schemes 3. Creation of SHGs	4.8 lakh on 31st March 2004	24,030 SHGs on 31st Jan 2004	8 % p.a.	Within 3 years, on quarterly basis	Production/ Housing

Source: SDS Policy Research, *Notes*: NA—Not available

- The Basic Self-Help Group model and its minor variations (PRADAN, NBJK, LEAD and others).
- GRAMEEN Replicator Approach (SHARE, ASA, CASHPOR India).
- Cooperative-Grameen Hybrid Model (Mahila Vikas).
- NBFC Approach (BASIX and SANGHAMITRA).
- Federated SHG approach (DHAN Foundation).
- Rural Industries Promotion (SHG) Framework (MYRADA).
- Urban Cooperative Banking Model (SEWA Bank).
- Multi-State Cooperative Solidarity Group Model (ICNW)
- Enabling Cooperative Networking Framework (CDF AND MACS).

Present Status of Microfinance in India

The term microfinance is defined in the Indian context as "the provision of thrift, credit and other financial services and products of small amounts to the poor in rural, semi-urban and urban areas for enabling them to raise their income levels and improve living standards". Two models of delivery of microfinance have become prominent, the SHG Bank Linkage Model (SHG Model) and the Micro Finance Institution (MFI) Model. The SHG Model was developed by the National Bank for Agriculture and Rural Development (NABARD) in 1991-92. In 1996 it became a normal activity of banks. In 2000, it was indicated that loans up to ₹ 50,000 (₹ 1,25,000 in the case of housing finance) were considered as microfinance. Due to rapid growth NABARD's target of linking one million SHGs was achieved in 2005, three years ahead of the target date. The draft microfinance Bill (2007) reiterated the same definition. The average loan per customer in the Indian microfinance sector however is much smaller and ranges between ₹ 3,500 and ₹ 5,000 for both models (Srinivasan, 2009). While the upper limit of microfinance loans has been specified as ₹ 50,000, the lowest end loans of most commercial banks, namely personal loans, start at ₹ 1,00,000. The definitions pertain to the microcredit aspect, though increasingly microfinance providers are also offering micro-insurance, micro pensions and remittances by tying up with mainstream providers. Though the sector cannot be precisely delineated, as there may be institutions which may be partially or indirectly involved in microfinance, the sector is typically defined in the Indian context as lending by banks to self-help groups (SHGs) and lending by MFIs (Srinivasan, 2009).

By 2008, there were 54 million microfinance customers in India. Of these, 39.9 million customers were served by the SHG model while accounted for 77 per cent of the total outreach, its growth rate of 15 per cent in 2007-08, was lower than that of the MFI model which grew by 40 per cent. Some studies such as the Intellecap study entitled "Inverting the Pyramid" (2007) estimate that the potential market may be 245 million individuals, suggesting there is still a lot of scope for the sector to grow. The growth in microfinance has been exhibited most noticeably by the Southern state of Andhra Pradesh, Tamil Nadu and Karnataka. In case of the SHG model, the share of the Southern states in clients outreach was 48.2 per cent while in the MFI model, it was 52 per cent in March 2008 (Srinivasan, 2009).

The last major event which impacted the financial and banking system in India was the liberalization of India's financial system in the 1990s characterized by a series of structural adjustments and financial policy reforms initiated by the Reserve Bank of India (RBI). These financial liberalization measures then made it possible for NABARD to transform what was then a small research project into a full blown microfinance programme for the whole country. This programme was better known as the 'SHG Bank Linkage' model which has come to be one of the most well-known and widespread microfinance models in India. Since many consider the SHG Bank Linkage model of microfinance to be one of the major successes of microfinance delivery in the country it will provide the most important direct contrast to the delivery of microfinance services by individual MFIs.

The microfinance providers include apex institutions like National Bank for Agriculture and Rural Development (NABARD), Small Industries Development Bank of India (SIDBI), and Rashtriya Mahila Kosh (RMK). At the retail level, Commercial Banks, Regional Rural Banks, and, Cooperative Banks provide microfinance services. Today, there are about 60,000 retail credit outlets of the formal banking sector in the rural areas comprising 12,000 branches of district level co-operative banks, over 14,000 branches of the Regional Rural Banks (RRBs) and over 30,000 rural and semi-urban branches of commercial banks besides almost 90,000 cooperatives credit societies at the village level. On an average, there is at least one retail credit outlet for about 5,000 rural people. This physical reaching out to the far flung areas of the country to provide savings, credit and other banking services to the rural society is an unparalleled achievement of the Indian banking system.

The microfinance sector has also grown impressively in India. According to the Microfinance India State of the Sector Report 2009, there were 76.6 million microfinance accounts in the country as of March, 2009; while the total microfinance sector loans outstanding were ₹ 35,900 crore. The MFIs in India can be broadly sub-divided into three categories organizational forms such as Wholesalers, NGOs supporting SHG Federations and NGOs directly retailing credit borrowers or groups of borrower. The wholesalers will include agencies like NABARD, Rashtriya Mahila Kosh, New Delhi and the Friends of Women's World Banking (FWWB) in Ahmedabad. Few of the NGOs supporting SHG Federations include MYRADA in Bangalore, SEWA in Ahmedabad, PRADAN in Tamil Nadu and Bihar, ADITHI in Patna, SPARC in Mumbai, and ASSEFA in Madras, etc. While few of the NGOs directly retailing credit to Borrowers are SHARE in Hyderabad, ASA in Trichy, and RDO Loyalam Bank in Manipur. While there is no published data on private MFIs operating in the country, the number of MFIs is estimated to be around 800.

Overall Progress under SHG-Bank Linkage for last 4 years

Table 3.2 shows the overall progress of Microfinance under SHG-Bank Linkage for the last 3 years from 2008-09 to 2011-12. The number of SHGs savings with bank as on 31st March has increased from 61.21 lakhs in 2008-09 to 79.60 lakhs with a net increase of 18.39 lakhs SHGs. However, the percentage of women SHGs has reduced an insignificant of 4 lakhs.

SHG Bank Linkages Programme in Cumulative Progress

SHG bank linkages programme in cumulative progress is shown in Table 3.3. There has been significant increase in the number of SHG linked and bank loan starting from 1992-93 till 2011-12. Year-wise, it was only 255 SHGs have been linkage with banks

Table 3.2: Overall Progress under SHG-Bank Linkage for last 4 years

	Particulars	*2008-09*		*2009-10*		*2010-11*		*2011-12*	
		No. of SHGs	*Amount*	*No. of SHGs*	*Amount*	*No. of SHGs*	*Amount*	*No. of SHGs*	*Amount*
SHGs savings with Banks as on 31st March	Total SHGs	61.21	5545.62	69.53	6198.71	74.62	7016.30	79.60	6551.41
		(22.2%)	(46.5%)	(13.6%)	(11.8%)	(7.3%)	(13.2%)	(6.7%)	(-6.7%)
	SGSY group	15.06	1563.38	16.94	1292.62	20.23	1817.12	21.23	1395.25
		(25.1%)	(93.1%)	(12.5%)	(17.3%)	(19.4%)	(40.6%)	(5.0%)	(-23.2%)
	% of SGSY	24.6	28.1	24.4	20.9	27.1	25.9	26.7	21.3
	Women SHGs	48.64	4434.03	53.10	4498.66	60.98	5298.65	62.99	5104.33
		(22.0%)	(42.6%)	(9.18%)	(1.46%)	(14.8%)	(17.8%)	(3.3%)	(-3.7%)
	% of Women SHGs	79.5	80.0	76.4	72.6	81.7	75.5	79.1	77.9
Loans disbursed to SHGs during the year	No of SHGs	16.10	12253.51	15.87	14453.3	11.96	14547.73	11.48	16534.77
		(31.1%)	(38.5%)	(-1.4%)	(17.9%)	(-24.6%)	(0.01%)	(-4%)	(13.7%)
	SGSY Groups	2.65	2015.22	2.67	2198	2.41	2480.37	2.10	2643.56
		(7.3%)	(8.5%)	(1.0%)	(9.1%)	(-9.9%)	(12.8%)	(12.9%)	(6.6%)
	% of SGSY	16.4	16.4	16.9	15.2	20.1	17.0	18.3	16.0
	Women SHGs	13.75	10527.38	12.94	12429.37	10.17	12622.33	9.23	14132.02
		(32.0%)	(40.8%)	(5.8%)	(18.1%)	(-21.4%)	(1.6%)	(-9.2%)	(12.0%)
	% of Women SHGs	85.4	85.9	81.6	86	85	86.8	80.4	85.5
Loan outstanding against SHGs as on 31st March	Total SHGs	42.24	22679.84	48.51	28038.28	47.87	31221.17	43.54	36340.00
		(16.5%)	(33.4%)	(14.8%)	(23.6%)	(-1.3%)	(11.4%)	(-9.0%)	(16.4%)
	SGSY group	9.77	5861.72	12.45	6251.08	12.86	7829.39	12.16	8054.83
		(6.5%)	(21.7%)	(27.5%)	(6.6%)	(3.4%)	(25.2%)	(-5.4%)	(2.9%)
	% of SGSY	23.1	25.8	25.7	22.3	26.9	25.1	27.9	22.2
	Women SHGs	32.77	18583.54	38.98	23030.36	39.84	26123.75	36.49	30465.28
		(12.3%)	(39.4%)	(18.9%)	(23.9%)	(2.2%)	(13.4%)	(-8.4%)	(16.6%)
	% of Women SHGs	77.6	81.9	80.3	82.1	83.2	83.7	83.8	83.8

Source: Status of Microfinance in India 2012, NABARD.

and it rose to 9,23,000 as on March end 2012. Further, it is also seen there is a tremendous growth from 255 in 1992-93 to 79,60,000 in 2011-12. On the other hand the released of bank loan amount also increased from ₹ 0.29 crore in the year 1992-93 to ₹ 16534.77 crore in 2011-12. As on 31st March 2012, a cumulative total of ₹ 84606.42 has been released by the government for the promotion and development of Microfinance in the country.

Region-wise Progress of Microfinance – Savings of SHGs with Banks

Table 3.3 shows the skewed growth of the SHGs across the regions. The Southern region accounts for 46 per cent of the SHGs

Table 3.3: SHG Bank Linkage Programme Cumulative Progress

(Amount in ₹ crore)

Year (end-March)	No. of SHGs linked		Bank loan	
	Current Year	Cumulative Total	Current Year	Cumulative Total
1992-93	255	255	0.29	0.29
1993-94	365	620	0.36	0.65
1994-95	1502	2122	1.79	2.44
1995-96	2635	4757	3.62	6.06
1996-97	3841	8598	5.78	11.84
1997-98	5719	14317	11.92	23.76
1998-99	18678	32995	33.31	57.07
1999-00	81780	114775	135.91	192.98
2000-01	149050	263825	287.89	480.87
2001-02	197653	461478	545.47	1026.34
2002-03	255882	717360	1022.33	2048.67
2003-04	361731	1079091	1855.53	3904.20
2004-05	539365	1618456	2994.26	6898.46
2005-06	620109	2238565	4499.00	11397.46
2006-07	1105749	4160584 (3344314)	6570.39	17967.85
2007-08	1227770	5009794 (4572084)	8849.26	26817.11
2008-09	1609586	6121147 (6181670)	12253.51	39070.62
2009-10	1586822	6953000 (7768492)	14453.30	53523.92
2010-2011	1196134	7462000 (8964626)	14547.73	68071.65
2011-2012	923000	7960000 (9887626)	16534.77	84606.42

Source: NABARD;
Note: *figures in the parentheses are calculated figure.

and 51 per cent of the SHG credit during 2009-10. Further, it is also seen that the same 46 per cent of the SHG and slightly increased to 56 per cent of SHG credit in 2011-12. This is mainly because of presence of large number of NGOs there. The poorer regions like North-Eastern, and Northern, which are credit starved, account for only 4.2 per cent and 5.0 per cent respectively in 2009-10. Further, it is slightly increase to 4.6 per cent and 5.1 per cent of SHG credit respectively in the year 2011-12.

Table 3.4: Progress under Microfinance – Savings of SHGs with Banks Region-wise position as on 31 March 2012

(Amount ₹ lakh)

Sl. No	Region	2009-10		2010-11		2011-12	
		No. of SHGs	Savings Amount	No. of SHGs	Savings Amount	No. of SHGs	Savings Amount
1.	Northern	351801	34207.31	372772	32857.16	409326	25276.88
2.	North East	292188	12167.09	324739	13104.6	366718	15251.75
3.	Eastern	1374242	112014.60	1527618	140837.61	1625714	94726.20
4.	Central	765965	51363.57	786436	60338.01	812767	61358.23
5.	Western	945620	92667.48	960921	82901.13	1062087	87193.68
6.	Southern	3223434	317450.84	3489460	371591.77	3683737	371334.70
	Total	6953250	619870.89	7461946	701630.28	7960349	655141.45

Source: Status of Microfinance in India 2012, NABARD.

Southern states are leading over the northern states as far as spread of SHGs is concerned. The bank linkages of SHGs also show that a large number of SHGs linked with banks where in southern region followed by eastern and central regions. Cumulative bank loan has also been reported significantly high in southern region.

Progress under Microfinance during 2011-12

An update on microfinance as at the end of March 2012 is being presented in 3 different sections. The Progress under Microfinance-Savings of SHGs with Banks Region-wise/State-wise/Agency-wise position as on 31st March 2012 has been covered in the first part, while the activities of MFIs has been covered in the second part. Various innovative initiatives and support services like

Table 3.5: Progress under Microfinance–Savings of SHGs with Banks Region-wise/State-wise/Agency-wise position as on 31 March 2012

(Amount ₹ lakh)

Sr. No	Region/ State	Commercial Banks		Regional Rural Banks		Cooperative Banks		Total	
		No. of SHGs	Loan Disbursed Amount	No. of SHGs	Loan Disbursed Amount	No. of SHGs	Loan Disbursed Amount	No. of SHGs	Loan Disbursed Amount
A.	**Northern Region**								
1	Chandigarh	619	102.10	0.00	0.00	0.00	0.00	619	102.10
2	Haryana	22655	1618.17	18114	1848.28	3415	211.90	44184	3678.35
3	Himachal Pradesh	29621	1362.48	7101	868.17	28919	1057.97	65641	3288.62
4	Jammu & Kashmir	4324	341.00	774	22.34	1251	69.74	6349	433.08
5	New Delhi	3451	299.59	0.00	0.00	85	25.43	3536	325.02
6	Punjab	4662.61	27600	3967.79	4257	286.50	5486	408.32	37343
7	Rajasthan	108277	4168.29	67927	4268.20	75450	4350.61	251654	12787.10
	Total	196547	11859.42	98173	7293.49	114606	6123.97	409326	25276.88
B.	**North Eastern Region**								
1	Assam	102764	5991.53	149291	3039.10	24510	815.35	276565	9845.98
2	Arunachal Pradesh	6983	103.14	959	54.20	421	28.98	8363	186.32
3	Manipur	5955	103.34	5784	106.06	972	9.98	12711	219.38
4	Meghalaya	9057	231.30	2507	143.16	2527	40.28	14091	414.74
5	Mizoram	2104	43.57	2202	507.04	670	22.30	4976	572.91
6	Nagaland	6353	132.93	679	50.99	3679	190.56	10711	374.48
7	Sikkim	4626	178.21	0.00	0.00	654	81.79	5280	260.00
8	Tripura	11636	252.68	16696	2736.28	5689	388.99	34021	3377.95
	Total	149478	7036.69	178118	6636.83	39122	1578.23	366718	15251.75
C.	**EASTERN REGION**								
1	A & N Islands	1699	50.21	0.00	0.00	3822	81.07	5521	131.28
2	Bihar	150445	9741.92	154668	4300.44	0.00	0.00	305113	14042.36
3	Jharkhand	58869	5133.27	30734	1588.48	0.00	0.00	89603	6721.75
4	Odisha	235829	12366.26	226745	17948.26	77455	5821.89	540029	36136.41
5	West Bengal	350641	23145.43	199733	6505.83	135074	8043.15	685448	37694.40
	Total	797483	50437.08	611880	30343.01	216351	13946.11	1625714	94726.20
D.	**CENTRAL REGION**								
1	Chhattisgarh	47850	2649.77	58756	3596.71	23248	1147.98	129854	7394.46
2	Madhya Pr.	85730	8444.15	64452	2337.03	13406	447.87	163588	11229.05
3	Uttar Pradesh	196140	26179.94	265849	10409.82	9195	231.68	471184	36821.44
4	Uttarakhand	24377	4160.55	16019	1397.83	7745	354.89	48141	5913.27
	Total	354097	41434.41	405076	17741.39	53594	2182.43	812767	61358.23
E.	**WESTERN REGION**								
	Goa	5400	491.72	0.00	0.00	3014	376.98	8414	868.70
	Gujarat	136741	9767.96	58713	2982.96	31172	1212.31	226626	13963.23
	Maharashtra	430614	45357.05	94519	3882.05	301914	23122.65	827047	72361.75
	Total	572755	55616.73	153232	6865.01	336100	24711.94	1062087	87193.68
F.	**SOUTHERN REGION**								
	Andhra Pradesh	1062591	114991.38	405904	31827.84	27409	2196.34	1495904	149015.56
	Karnataka	260010	39995.55	176156	23425.98	192477	36791.34	628643	100212.87
	Kerala	494562	31602.93	42879	1264.23	78273	8503.95	615714	41371.11
	Lakshadweep	171	12.48	0.00	0.00	0.00	0.00	171	12.48
	Puducherry	11485	886.21	3242	301.50	3186	495.20	17913	1682.91
	Tamil Nadu	718907	61425.14	52708	4314.65	153777	13299.98	925392	79039.77
	Total	2547726	248913.70	680889	61134.20	455122	61286.81	3683737	371334.70
	G. TOTAL	4618086	415298.04	2127368	130013.93	1214895.45	109829.49	7960349	655141.45

Source: Status of Microfinance in India 2012, NABARD.

capacity building of all stakeholders of microfinance programme etc. is covered in the third part.

SHG-Bank Linkage Programme

The number of saving linked SHGs now stands at 7.96 million with a membership of over 103 million poor households as on 31st March 2012. While bulk of these savings is used for internal lending within the Group (over 70%), the balance is maintained in the savings accounts with the financing banks. Over 79 per cent of SHGs linked to banks are exclusive women groups, which is one of the most distinguishing features of microfinance sector in the country. The balance in the savings accounts of the banks as at the end of March 2012 stood at ₹ 6551.41 crore. Among the major States, Karnataka SHGs maintain the highest Savings Bank balance of over ₹ 16.000 per SHG followed by Punjab of nearly ₹ 12,500 per SHG. Among the regions, southern region is highest at ₹ 10,080 per SHG and northeastern region recorded the lowest balance of ₹ 4159 per SHG. On an average, the SHGs maintain a balance of ₹ 8230. Commercial Banks account for 58 per cent of the savings account maintained by SHGs and RRBs 27 per cent and Cooperative Banks the remaining 15 per cent.

NABARD as Facilitator of Microfinance

Besides, conceiving the SHG-Bank Linkage Programme two decades back, NABARD had assigned to itself the role of a facilitator and a mentor of the initiative. The focus was on bringing in various stakeholders on a common platform, building capacity among the stakeholders to take the movement forward while extending 100 per cent refinance to all banks participating in the programme. A large number of seminars, workshops and training programmes were organized to create awareness about the microfinance programme among all the stakeholders– the bankers, the Government agencies, the NGO partners and more importantly the SHG members. The NGO sector who played the key role of organizing and nurturing the SHGs as the Self-Help Promoting Institutions – later joined by many others including the rural financial institutions, Farmers Clubs, etc. – were encouraged by way of promotional grant assistance by NABARD

Table 3.6: Loans to MFIs by **Banks/Financial Institutions**

Financing Agency	*Period*	*Loans disbursed to MFIs during the year*		*Loan outstanding against MFIs as on 31 March*	
		No. of MFIs	*Amount (₹ in crore)*	*No. of MFIs*	*Amount (₹ crore)*
All Commercial Banks	2008-09	522	3718.93	1762	4977.89
	2009-10	645	8038.61	1407	10095.32
	2010-11	460	7601.02	2153	10646.84
	2011-12	336	4950.98	1684	9810.98
Regional Rural Banks	2008-09	59	13.40	153	31.20
	2009-10	46	24.14	103	52.22
	2010-11	9	4.16	23	42.01
	2011-12	113	13.28	128	37.51
Cooperative Banks	2008-09	NA	NA	NA	NA
	2009-10	0	0	3	0.01
	2010-11	NA	NA	NA	NA
	2011-12	4	1.61	19	4.75
SIDBI	2008-09	NA	NA	NA	NA
	2009-10	88	2665.75	146	3808.20
	2010-11	2	843.78	139	3041.77
	2011-12	12	239.42	129	1597.11
Total by all agencies	2008-09	581	3732.33	1915	5009.09
	2009-10	779	10728.50	1659	13955.75
	2010-11	471	8448.96	2315	13730.62
	2011-12	465	5205.29	1960	11450.35

NA—Not Available
Source: Status of Microfinance in India 2012.

for taking up such work. The phenomenal growth of SHG-Bank linkage programme during the last 20 years owe a great deal to these promotional efforts actively supported by NABARD and participated by the stakeholders. The rapid growth of the SHG linkage programme and its success in taking financial services to the poor, led to its recognition as the most important tool for financial inclusion—the main focus of the Eleventh Five Year Plan. Simultaneously, efforts were also on to experiment innovative initiatives in improving the efficacy and reach of the programme with the involvement of all microfinance practitioner facilitated by NABARD. A glimpse of the facilitator role played by NABARD, the ICT initiatives taken, policy changes etc. in this sector during 2011-12 is narrated in the following paras.

Refinance to Banks

During the initial years of the movement NABARD was extending refinance to the extent of 100 per cent to banks for lending to SHGs since the SHG–Bank Linkage Programme was launched. Initially, this was intended to encourage the banks to actively participate in the programme. As the banks gained confidence in lending to SHGs and realized the business potential in extending financial services through SHGs, they have been increasingly deploying their own resources in a mutually beneficial relationship with the SHGs. SHGs had been instrumental in bringing in more business for the financing banks by way of improving credible client base, also promoting rural and inclusive banking. Banks have also extended other financial services like remittance, housing, insurance, etc, though in a limited way, to this segment. As a result, the banks have started 'owning up' the movement, as a sound business proposition and became less dependent on promotional support from NABARD. The refinance support from NABARD, however, continues to supplement resource mobilization for the programme. During 2011-12, NABARD extended refinance to the extent of ₹ 3072.59 crore as against ₹ 2545.36 crore disbursed during the previous year. Cumulative disbursement of refinance by NABARD for SHG lending now stands at ₹ 18,479.60 crore.

Support for Training and Capacity Building of Microfinance Clients

NABARD has been continuously imparting training to various intermediaries, partners and stakeholders of SHG Bank Linkage Programme such as bankers, NGOs, CSOs, government officials, SHG members, Micro entrepreneurs and trainers. During 2011-12, about 1.87 lakh officials of various agencies participated in NABARD supported training programmes and exposure visits and cumulatively 28.48 lakh officials have been trained and educated knowledge in the area of microfinance. NABARD in association with GIZ has initiated the process of revising the content, coverage of training modules. Training needs of all the stakeholders are being assessed for the purpose.

Grant Support to Partner agencies for Promotion and Nurturing of SHGs

Ever since the SHG-Bank Linkage Programme was launched by NABARD, the Self-Help Promoting Institutions (SHPI) such as NGOs, Banks (RRBs, DCCBs), Farmers Clubs and Individual Rural Volunteers (IRV) are being extended grant support to organize and nurture SHGs of the poor. In fact, the phenomenal growth of SHG-Bank Linkage Programme in the country is the result of the pains taking efforts put in by these agencies in forming and nurturing SHGs especially in areas where the concept never existed.

Table 3.7: Grant Support to Partner Agencies as on 31.3.2012

Agency	*Cumulative Sanction*		*Cumulative Achievement*	
	Amount	*SHG Nos.*	*Amount*	*SHG Nos.*
NGOs	16200.59	499909	4882.31	283007
RRBs	542.19	53145	197.10	56070
Coop. Banks	857.81	71695	289.19	47515
IRVs	733.58	43223	86.02	13105
Farmers Clubs	83.16	7689	73.81	17356
Total	18417.33	675661	5528.43	417053

Source: NABARD

Financing of Joint Liability Groups

Joint Liability Groups (JLG) are informal groups of 4-10 members who are engaged in similar or independent economic activities like crop production, dairy farming or other allied agriculture or non-farm based activities and who are willing to undertake jointly (mutual guarantee) to repay the loans taken by the Group from the Banks. Unlike in the case of SHGs, JLGs are intended basically as credit groups of tenant farmers/small farmers who do not have proper title of their farmland and are unable to provide tangible collateral security for their borrowing from banks and other financial institutions. Regular savings by group members is purely voluntary and intended to bind the members. Credit needs of the group members are to be met through loans form financial institutions and such loans could be individual loans or group loans.

Financing of Joint Liability Groups was introduced as a pilot project in 2004-05 by NABARD in 8 states of the country with the support of 13 RRBs. Apart from extending refinance support to Banks, NABARD also extending financial support for awareness creation and capacity building of all stakeholders of this Programme. NABARD also extends grant-in-aid support for formation and nurturing of JLGs to banks and other JLG promoting agencies. An amount of ₹ 36.68 crore was sanctioned as grant for promotion of 1.95 lakh JLGs across the country as on 31st March 2012. During the year, 1,91,662 new JLGs were promoted (which is 36% growth over the previous year) and fresh loans to the extent of ₹ 1700.39 crore (48% increase over the previous year) was disbursed to JLGs by banks taking the cumulative number of JLGs to 3,32,707 and the cumulative loan disbursed to ₹ 2845.69 crore.

List of Top 20 Microfinance Institutions in India

Table 3.8 shows the top 20 Microfinance Institutions operating in India rated by CRISIL as on 30th September 2008. Out of 20 top MFI in India 17 of them are from southern India. Andhra Pradesh and Tamil Nadu account the highest number of six top MFI each followed by Karnataka with four top MFI. None of the MFI falls in western India and North Eastern India. In case of lending model 14 of MFIs followed the Joint Liability Group Model and 5 of MFIs follows the SHG model in lending microfinance services.

Significance of Microfinance in Indian Planning

Since 1951, Government of India is planning its Five Year Plans regularly. During each and every plan, government is keeping more emphasis on development of women initially and later on microfinance. The following paragraphs will highlight about the significance of microfinance in Indian planning.

Development of women in the First Five Year Plan (1951-56) was clubbed with the welfare of disadvantaged group like destitute, disabled, aged, etc.

The Second to Fifth Five Year Plan (1956-79) continue to reflect the same welfare approach besides giving priority to

Table 3.8: CRISIL List of Top 20 Microfinance Institutions in India

Sl. No	*Name of Microfinance Institution(s)*	*HQ*	*Legal Status*	*Lending Model*	*No of Branch*	*Loan O/S (₹mn)*
1	SKS Microfinance Ltd (SKSMPL)	Secundrabad Andhra Pradesh	Pvt Ltd Co. (NBFC)	JLG	1,413	18,227
2	Spandana Sphoorty Financial Ltd (SSFL)	Hyderabad Andhra Pradesh	Public Ltd Co (NBFC)	JLG Individual	696	11,987
3	Share Microfin Limited (SML)	Hyderabad Andhra Pradesh	Public Ltd Co (NBFC)	JLG Individual	666	8,568
4	Asmitha Microfin Ltd (AML)	Hyderabad Andhra Pradesh	Public Ltd Co (NBFC)	JLG	363	4,944
5	Shri Kshetra Dharmasthala Rural Development Project (SKDRDP)	Dharmasthala Karnataka	Trust	SHG	22	4,060
6	Bhartiya Samruddhi Finance Limited	Hyderabad Andhra Pradesh	Public Ltd Co (NBFC)	Diversified	87	3,882
7	Bandhan Society	Kolkata West Bengal	Society	JLG	385	3,389
8	Cashpor Micro Credit (CMC)	Varanasi Uttar Pradesh	Section 25 Company	JLG	247	1,431
9	Grama Vidiyal Micro Finance Pvt Ltd (GVMFL)	Tiruchirappalli Tamil Nadu	Pvt Ltd Co. (NBFC)	JLG	126	1,316
10	Grameen Financial Services Pvt Ltd (GFS)	Bangalore Karnataka	Pvt Ltd Co. (NBFC)	JLG	62	1,287
11	Madura Micro Finance Ltd (MMFL)	Chennai Tamil Nadu	Public Ltd Co (NBFC)	SHG	46	1,223
12	BSS Microfinance Bangalore Pvt Ltd	Bangalore Karnataka	Pvt Ltd Co. (NBFC)	JLG	51	1,157
13	Bandhan Financial Services Pvt Ltd	Kolkata West Bengal	Pvt Ltd Co. (NBFC)	JLG	171	1,028
14	Equitas Micro Finance India Pvt Ltd (Equitas)	Chennai Tamil Nadu	Pvt Ltd Co. (NBFC)	JLG	36	1,007
15	Sarvodaya Nano Finance Ltd (SNFL)	Chennai Tamil Nadu	Public Ltd Co (NBFC)	SHG	113	949
16	BWDA Finance Limited (BFL)	Villupuram Tamil Nadu	Public Ltd Co (NBFC)	SHG	25	935
17	Ujjivan Financial Services Pvt Ltd	Bangalore Karnataka	Pvt Ltd Co. (NBFC)	JLG Individual	96	837
18	Future Financial Services Chittoor Ltd	Chittoor Andhra Pradesh	Public Ltd Co (NBFC)	SHG	50	811
19	ESAF Microfinance & Investments Pvt. Ltd	Thrissur Kerala	Pvt Ltd Co. (NBFC)	JLG	96	765
20	S.M.I.L.E Microfinance Limited	Chennai Tamil Nadu	Public Ltd Co (NBFC)	JLG	87	757.7

Source: CRISIL

women's education and launching measures to improve maternal and child health services, supplementary feeding for children, and expectant and nursing mother.

Sixth Plan (1980-85) has marked a clear shift in its approach from welfare to development oriented plans towards women. Multi-disciplinary approach with thrust on health, education and employment.

Seventh Five Year Plan (1985-90) aimed at raising women's economic and social status and bringing them into the mainstream of national development. The thrust was on generation of both skilled and unskilled employment through proper education and vocational training.

Eighth Five Year Plan (1992-97) gave more emphasis on the development of women in the country. The Eighth Five Year Plan has given priority to the economic development of scheduled caste families. The scheduled caste and scheduled tribe development corporations have to strengthen their activities to enable proper identification of beneficiaries. In this plan the poverty alleviation programmes like IRDP have been insured and it provides infrastructure support where necessary to enable the group of beneficiaries to take up their group. This programme arranges for inputs such as supply of raw-material, marketing of finished goods etc. and monitors the implementation of the projects.

In the Ninth Five Year Plan (1997-2002), the poverty alleviation programmes have been more effectively integrated with area development programmes and the various sectorial programmes within the umbrella of Panchayati Raj Institutions (PRIs). In addition, the Voluntary Organisations (VOs) will have to play a more dynamic role in empowering the poor through advocacy, awareness generation and formation of SHGs.

NABARD initiated a Pilot project to link Banks with Self-Help Groups (SHGs), with the objective of meeting the credit needs of the poor through formal financial institutions. Evaluation studies show success with increase in loan volume of SHGs, shift to income generating activities, nearly 100 per cent recovery and reduction in transaction costs. 85 per cent of the groups linked with banks were exclusively of women.

Tenth Five Year Plan (2002-2007) continues with the strategy of 'Empowering Women' as an agent of social change and development through social empowerment, economic empowerment and gender justice. The SGSY recognises the need to focus on key activities and the importance of activity clusters. The programme has in-built safeguards for the weaker sections. It insists that 50 per cent of the Self-Help Groups must be formed exclusively by women and that 50 per cent of the benefits should flow to SCs and STs. There is also a provision for disabled beneficiaries.

The Eleventh Five Year Plan aims at inclusive growth and faster reduction of poverty. Microfinance can contribute immensely to the financial inclusion of the poor without which it will be difficult for them to come out of the vicious cycle of poverty. Eleventh Plan strategy for SGSY would have to necessarily take the best out of what has evolved in the Self-Help movement across the country over the last few years and integrate it with the programme. Likewise a few aspects of the SGSY programme that have failed to give the desired results require a fresh look and if necessary, dropped. The current mechanism of fund flow to the SHGs through a graded system requires a comprehensive review. The current scheme allows a Revolving Fund entitlement of up to ₹ 10,000 for the Grade-I SHGs that will also entitle them to draw cash credit from a financial institution. The rate of attrition between the Grade-I and Grade-II indicates that a large number of SHGs fizzle out mid-way after availing the Revolving Funds. Further, the SHGs that have cleared the Grade-II stage seem to wait for long periods before getting an opportunity to avail the subsidy assistance. Close to 3 lakh such SHGs are waiting in the wings for such assistance. Thus, almost all the Five Year Plans of the government have given more emphasis on women development and poverty alleviation which is consider as centric point for microfinance development for inclusive growth of the country.

Government's Role in Microfinance

The initiative of 1992 to make the traditional and formal banks to extend financial services to deprived sections through informal Self-Help Groups (SHGs), has now blossomed into a "monolith" microfinance initiative. It has been recognised as a decentralised, cost effective and fastest growing microfinance initiative in the world, enabling over 103 million poor households' access to a variety of sustainable financial services from the banking system by becoming members of the Groups the facility of not only pooling their thrift/savings and access to credit from the banking system, but also created a platform through which they could launch a number of livelihood initiatives and also facilitate the empowerment process specially to womenfolk.

Major Initiatives Taken by the Government in Microfinance

Government's initiative to reduce poverty by improving access to financial services to poor started since independence. India's overwhelming majority of poor is located in rural areas and this motivated the government to give special attention to rural credit. Following the report of All India Rural Credit Survey in mid-1950's the union government took crucial steps in reviewing cooperative structure including the partnership of state in cooperatives. Also the policy initiative of 'social banking' concept described as "the elevation of the entitlements of previously disadvantaged groups to formal credit even if this may entail a weakening of the conventional banking practices" led to the nationalisation of commercial banks in 1969, adoption of direct lending programmes to rural areas and development of credit institutions such as Regional Rural Banks (RRBs). Government initiatives during the Fourth Plan focused on marginal farmers and agricultural labourers bringing activity was promoted through subsidized lending under Integrated Rural Development Programme (IRDP) and its subsequent variations including the current self-employment programme known as Swaranjayanti Gram Swarozgar Yojana (SGSY).

SEWA Co-operative Bank (1974)

The implementation of formal lending programmes towards the poor suffer from the difficulties such as of exact targeting, screening problems of distinguishing good and bad borrowers and usually lending agencies won't be able to ensure the productive usage of loans. Also, the high transaction costs incurred in lending to the poor made the formal lending agencies leave the poor un-banked.

The Indian cooperative credit structure meant to empower the poor was not very successful as it was captured by a few powerful and because of excessive governmental interference and regulation. The search for an alternative to the formal banking sector and an effective financial system to cater to the needs of the poor, especially the rural poor, continued. The origin of microfinance can be traced to the establishment of the SEWA cooperative bank in 1974, to provide banking services to the poor women employed in the unorganised sector in Ahmedabad in Gujarat.

Shivaraman Committee (1978)

Looking into all aspects of consumption credit for the poor, the Expert Committee on Consumption Credit (Chairman: Shri B. Shivaraman. Member. Planning Commission) recommended for allowing a line of credit to poor households by the formal banking sector. Examining the consumption need of the poor in 1976, the Committee recommended a line of credit equal to ₹ 750 per household. The specific consumption demands identified by the Committee were:

(a) medical expenses (33%),
(b) marriage (33%),
(c) education (13%),
(d) birth, death and religious purposes (10%), and
(e) general consumption (10%).

The co-operative credit structure was to be the main pillar of this drive. The Committee further recommended for legislative reforms in all states and union territories for universal membership in all the Primary Agricultural Cooperative Credit Societies (PACSs) across the country. In regard to the rate of interest, the Committee observed that the rate charged by both cooperative banks and commercial banks on consumption loans should be the same as crop loans. It further observed, 'The cost of servicing the consumption loans will perhaps be even higher than the agricultural loans, therefore, to expect the societies to operate on smaller margins than on the agricultural loans will be unrealistic. On the premise that the risk to the banking sector in the case of consumption loan is higher than the production loan, the committee recommended for a higher percentage (10%) of risk cover by the Government than usually done for other (rural) loans extended by the cooperative and commercial banks. On the estimated demand for consumption loans of ₹ 170 crore (in 1976), it provided for ₹ 17 crore as Risk fund. This fund moreover was required to be shared equally by the central and state governments.

However, despite all its moorings there was not much progress in regard to flow of consumption credit to the poor by the formal banking sector. Legislative reforms *vis-a-vis* universal membership in PACS were introduced, but the co-operative banks themselves became weaker and weaker in the subsequent years. The introduction of bank-SHG linkage programme in the 1990's has in some ways addressed the need of consumption credit of the poor. Under this system, the banks lend to the SHGs who, in turn, are free to disburse loan to their members in their best judgement, whether for production or for consumption purposes.

All India Rural Credit Surveys of Reserve Bank of India

The All India Rural Credit Surveys conducted by the RBI during the various years, show the following transformation in rural credit, *viz.* (i) The share of non-institutional sector in rural credit that was 91 per cent in 1951 went down to 45 per cent in 1991, (ii) The share of institutional sector that stood at 9 per cent in 1951 went up to 53 per cent in 1991, (iii) The share of credit cooperatives in rural credit that was 4.6 per cent in 1951 went up to 29 per cent in 1981, but declined subsequently to 19 per cent in 1991, and (iv) The share of commercial banks in rural credit that was 1.1 per cent in 1951 went up to 29 per cent in 1981 and has remained at the same level in 1991.

The above mentioned percentages are, however, based on aggregate figures and do not throw much light in regard to transformation in rural credit *vis-a-vis* micro-finance. There has not been any rural credit survey at the all-India level since 1991. A survey was nevertheless organised by the World Bank and NCAER in 2003. It utilised a sample of 6,000 households (in Andhra Pradesh and Uttar Pradesh) and throws light on the condition of micro-finance as well. According to this study, around 87 per cent of marginal farmers/landless labourers do not access credit from the formal banking sector. In other words, the same as during 1951most of the benefits of the so called extensive banking infrastructure have gone to the relatively better-off people;

around 66 per cent of large farmers have a deposit account and 44 per cent have access to credit.

Formal/Banking Sector Initiatives

Various programmes were initiated by banks to inculcate savings habit and to provide financial assistance. The initiatives are as follows:

1. *Pigmy Deposit Scheme* – The Pigmy deposit scheme intended to collect tiny deposits from the depositors from their doorsteps. The scheme was implemented by a few banks by engaging local people. The experience of the banks was not encouraging as there were large scale cash leakages, frauds and reconciliation problems.
2. *Mobile Banks* – Some of the banks started mobile banks in rural areas. The location and time of operation are usually synchronized with the market days so that the large number of people could transact its business.
3. *Regional Rural Banks* (RRBs) – were intended to serve the people not covered by co-operatives and commercial banks. But they were not able to serve the purpose as they were more focused on profitability and strong balance-sheets. In spite of this, it was found that the RRBs are better equipped than the commercial and co-operative banks to undertake micro finance operations because of the understanding of the local conditions.
4. *Local Area Banks* (LABs) – aimed to mobilize rural savings by institutions and makes them available for investment locally. They were set up in private sector and regulated by RBI. The working of LABs was not very encouraging. One serious drawback was absence of refinancing facility. Krishna Bhima Samruddi, the local area bank in Andhra Pradesh is only one into the business of micro finance on a large scale.

India to-day has an extensive banking infrastructure comprising over 30,000 rural and semi-urban branches of commercial banks. Over 14,000 branches of Regional Rural Banks (RRBs), around 12,000 branches of District Cooperative Credit

Banks (DCCBs) and 1,12,000 Primary Agricultural Credit Societies (PACSs) at the village level.

Self-Help Groups (SHGs)

Government initiatives during seventies and the Fourth Five Year Plan focused on small and marginal farmers and agricultural labourers. Integrated sustainable income generation activity was promoted under Integrated Rural Development Programme. Inadequacies inherent in running programmes focused on individual households called for shift to a group based approach. The first step towards setting up Self-Help Groups (SHGs) was taken by MYRADA and it built upon rural chit funds and informal lending networks to evolve a credit management group.

National Bank for Agriculture and Rural Development (NABARD)

In 1991-92, NABARD launched the SHG-Bank Linkage Programme on a pilot basis to finance SHGs across the country through the formal banking system. High repayment rates by the SHGs encouraged the banks to finance SHGs. The NABARD SHG-Bank linkage programme, has proved to be a decentralised cost-effective and the fastest growing microfinance initiative in the world. As on 31 March 2011, there were 74.62 lakh savings-linked Self-Help Groups (SHGs) and 47.87 lakh credit-linked SHGs covering 9.7 crore poor households under the micro-finance programme.

Rashtriya Mahila Kosh (RMK), 1993

The success of the concept of micro-credit through Self-Help Groups (SHGs) has encouraged the Government of India to establish a National level Micro-Credit organization/Rashtriya Mahila Kosh (RMK) (National Credit Fund for Women) under the Ministry of Women and Child Development in 1993, with an initial corpus of ₹ 31 crore. During the year 2010-11, credit amounting of ₹ 12.78 crore were sanctioned, benefiting 13,362 women beneficiaries. The cumulative sanctions and disbursements at the end of the year were ₹ 30,752 lakhs and ₹ 25,182 lakhs respectively benefiting 6,87,512 poor women beneficiaries. The objective was to help women organise income generating activities to improve their social economics status.

Small Industries Development Bank of India (SIDBI), 1994

In 1994, Small Industries Development Bank of India (SIDBI) launched a pilot scheme to provide financial assistance by way of loans to NGO's for providing credit to the poor households, especially women. A small amount of grant also accompanied the loans so as to build capacity of the intermediates and end-users. The programme did not achieve the desire objective. SIDBI reoriented its Micro Finance Programme in 1999 by addressing the weakness of the pilot scheme, with an objective to create a national network of large and viable Micro Finance Institutions from the formal and informal sector. The programme provides need based assistance by way of term loans to partner institutions for meeting their on lending fund requirements.

The cumulative assistance (including loans, grants, equity and quasi-equity) sanctioned under SIDBI's microfinance initiatives up to March 31, 2012 aggregated ₹ 8,164.41 crore, while cumulative disbursements aggregated ₹ 7,069.37 crore. The outstanding micro credit portfolio of the Bank stood at ₹ 2,153.96 crore, including investments as on March 31, 2012. The number of MFIs assisted by SIDBI and having loaned outstanding with the Bank as on March 31, 2012 stood at 130. The assistance through SIDBI has benefited about 317 lakh disadvantaged people, most ofthem being women.

SHG-Bank Linkage Programme 1996

In 1996, Reserve Bank of India included financing of SHGs as a mainstream activity of banks under the priority sector lending programmes. The SHG Bank linkage programme covered over 79.60 lakhs number of SHGs with a corpus fund of ₹ 6551.41 crore as on 31st March 2012, of which 62.99 per cent are women's Self-Help Groups.

Microfinance Development and Equity Fund (MD & EF), 2001

The Microfinance Development and Equity Fund is being utilized for promotion of various microfinance activities such as formation and linkage of SHGs through SHPIs, training and capacity building of stake holders, livelihood propagation, studies, documentation, etc. During 2011-12, ₹ 33.31 crore was released of which ₹ 28.68 crore was grant support for promotional activities and ₹ 4.63 crore for capital support and lending resources to MFIs. As against a total corpus of ₹ 200 crore contributed by RBI, NABARD and commercial banks, the actual (cumulative) utilization of the fund stood at ₹ 278.31 crore as on 31 March 2012. NABARD has been augmenting this fund from its own resources and has also been crediting interest on the unutilized portion of this fund. There have been no further receipts forthcoming from other contributor of this fund.

During 2011-12, ₹ 33.31 crore was released under Micro-Finance Development and Equity Fund (MFDEF); of which, ₹ 28.68 crore was grant support for promotional activities and ₹ 4.63 crore for CS/RFA to MFIs, as against ₹ 29.95 crore and ₹ 17.43 crore, respectively, in the previous year.

Micro Finance Programme (MFC) 2004

In March 2004, the Ministry of Small Scale Industry introduced the Microfinance Programme along with the SIDBI. The Government Provides funds for Micro Finance Programme to SIDBI called "Portfolio Risk Fund (PRF)". This fund is used for security deposit required of the MFIs/NGOs to get loan. At present SIDBI takes fixed deposit equal to 10 per cent of the loan amount. The share of MFIs/NGOs is 2.5 per cent of the loan amount (i.e. 25% of security deposit) and balance 7.5 per cent (i.e. 75% of security deposit) is adjusted from the funds provided by the Government of India. The MFIs/NGOs avail of loan from SIDBI for further on lending on the support of the deposit. Up to December 2006, a total of 39 MFIs have been disbursed loan to the tune of ₹ 102 crore, thereby utilizing an amount of ₹ 7.64 crore from the PRF. This has benefited approximately 3.20 lakh beneficiaries, mainly women.

During 2011, loans amounting to ₹ 14,547.73 crore were disbursed to 11,96,134 SHGs. As on 31 March 2011, there were more than 74.62 lakh savings linked Self-Help Groups (SHG) and more than 47.87 lakh credit-linked SHGs covering 9.7 crore poor households under the micro-finance programme.

Eligibility for Priority Sector Lending

The Reserve Bank of India (RBI) encouraged banks to participate in microfinance by reckoning lending to the sector as part of their priority sector lending, which needs to account for 40 per cent and 32 per cent of net bank credit in the case of domestic and foreign banks respectively.

Micro Finance Bill (2006)

The Micro Financial Sector (Development and Regulation) Bill was introduced in the Parliament. The few important silent features of the draft Micro Finance Bill (2006) are:

(a) Enactment of the bill will give the NABARD explicit powers to regulate the micro finance and so ensure greater transparency, effective management and better governance. These will facilitates the flow of Micro Finance Services in a more efficient way to the un-banked population.

(b) The Bill defines the Micro Finance services as provision of financial assistance to the eligible clients either directly or through group mechanism for small and tiny enterprise, agriculture, allied activities including consumption up to an amount not exceeding ₹ 50,000 in aggregate and up to ₹ 1,50,000 for housing purpose or such other amounts for the above purpose or such other purposes as specified by the NABARD from time to time.

(c) Micro Finance Organization is defined as an Organization carrying on the business of extending Micro Finance Services and includes Society registered under the Societies Registration Act, 1860 or a Trust created under the Indian Trust Act, 1880 or Public Trust registered under any State enactment or a Cooperative Society engaged in Micro Finance service excluding a Cooperative Bank as defined under the Banking Regulation Act, 1949.

Microfinance (Development and Regulation) Bill 2007

In March, 2007, the draft Microfinance Sector (Regulation and Development) Bill, 2007 was introduced in the Indian Parliament to provide for promotion, development and orderly growth of the microfinance sector in rural and urban areas for providing and enabling environment for ensuring universal access to integrated financial services, specially to women and certain disadvantage section of the people and thereby securing prosperity of such areas and regulation of the microfinance organizations not being regulated by any law. The definition of MFOs specifically included societies, trusts and cooperatives. The Bill designates NABARD as the regulator for the sector. Microfinance services are defined to include credit, life insurance, general insurance and pension services. While micro-credit has been defined as loans not exceeding ₹ 50,000 (₹ 1,50,000 in case of housing), the other services have not been defined further. The draft Bill was subsequently referred to a Parliamentary standing committee, though no recommendations have been given by it and the Bill has lapsed.

Capital Adequacy Requirements of NBFC-MFIs

In 2008 RBI increased the capital adequacy ratio of MFIs registered as NBFCs and having an asset size of ₹ 1 billion. As against 10 per cent, their minimum capital to risk assets ratio was required to be 12 per cent by March 31, 2009 and 15 per cent by March 31, 2010.

Committee on Financial Inclusion

The Rangarajan Committee on Financial Inclusion (2008) provided a systematic overview of the issues and suggested that RBI may consider bringing all regulatory aspect of microfinance under a single mechanism. The committee has also recommended the setting up of a Financial Inclusion Technology Fund to support the costs of technology adoption for financial inclusion purposes. It also suggested that NBFCs focused on microfinance (MF NBFCs) could be permitted to offer thrift, credit, and micro-insurance and remittance products up to specified amounts.

Raghuram Rajan Committee Report 2008

The Planning Commission of India had in 2007 set up a High Level Committee for looking into reforms to be made in the national microfinance sector. The committee was chaired by Raghuram G. Rajan who was a professor in Graduate School of Business of the University of Chicago. The committee had provided its report during September 2008.

In its report the committee had stated that the microfinance sector of India was a successful one but several factors were limiting its progress. A major issue was the capability of the microfinance institutions (MFI) to generate substantial capital. The approximate demand for micro-credit in India is a significant one and so the MFIs needed to have several sources for generating their finances, in addition to loans from banks that may be regarded as a traditional source of finance.

Yet another major problem in this regard was the regulatory scenario that was in a far from desirable condition. The management information system in India at that time was also not developed well enough, thus adding to the problems. The supply of management staff, which is properly trained, was a major hindrance as well. The report stated that if this problem could be addressed properly then the microfinance companies could think of increasing their operations substantially.

Micro Finance (Development and Regulation) Bill 2010

The proposed bill was presented to provide for promotion, development and regulation of the microfinance organisation in rural and urban areas and thereby for securing easy access to credit, thrift and other financial facilities to women and certain disadvantaged section of the people.

Malegam Committee Report 2011

Reserve Bank of India had set up a sub-committee under the chairmanship of Shri Y.H. Malegam, to address the several issues concerning the Microfinance Sector and RBI released the report of recommendations by the sub-committee on 19th January, 2011. The sub-committee was to review the scope and objectives of regulations governing MFIs with regard to interest rates, lending and recovery practices, applicability of existing money lending legislations, need for grievance redressal machinery and other issues concerning the sector.

Microfinance industry had recently come under the scanner when the Andhra Pradesh government passed an Ordinance calling the borrowers to stop paying their loans, making it illegal for the micro lenders to ask for weekly repayments and also required them to get a no objection from the local authorities before providing for a second loan to a borrower, bringing a jolting halt to the ₹ 20,000 crore industry in India and exposing the inherent problems in the sector. Sub-committee recommended creation of a separate category of NBFCs, NBFC-MFIs, providing short-term, and unsecured loans to the low income borrowers for income generating activities.

Some of the Qualifications for NBFC-MFIs are:

1. The NBFC-MFI to hold not less than 90 per cent of its total assets (other than cash and bank balances and money market instruments) in the form of qualifying assets. The sub-committee also mentions that a non-NBFC-MFI cannot have loans to the microfinance sector exceeding 10 per cent of its total assets.
2. Individual ceilings to loans to a single borrower of ₹ 25,000 is applicable.
3. Not less than 75 per cent of the loans given by the MFI should be for income-generating purposes.
4. There is a restriction on the other services to be provided by the MFI which has to be in accordance with the type of service and the maximum percentage of total income as may be prescribed.
5. The report recommends all NBFC-MFIs to have a minimum net worth of ₹ 15 cores.

Recommendations of the Committee

Following are the few important recommendations of Malegam Committee report submitted to the Government:

1. A borrower can be a member of only one Self-Help Group

(SHG) or a Joint Liability Group (JLG). Not more than two MFIs can lend to a single borrower. Tenure of the loan to vary with amount.

2. There should be a minimum period of moratorium between the disbursement of loan and the commencement of recovery.
3. Problem of Ghost Borrowers is addressed by sanctioning and disbursement of loans from a central location.
4. A Credit Information Bureau has to be established to avoid multiple lending and over borrowing.
5. The primary responsibility for avoidance of coercive methods of recovery must lie with the MFI and its management. Regulators to monitor, MFIs have a proper code of conduct for field staff for prevention of coercive methods of recovery.
6. The Reserve Bank must prepare a draft Customer Protection Code to be adopted by all MFIs. All MFIs must observe a specified Code of Corporate Governance.
7. There must be grievance redressal procedures and establishment of ombudsmen may be recommended by RBI to lead banks.
8. For loans not exceeding ₹ 15,000, the tenure of the loan should not be less than 12 months and for other loans the tenure should not be less than 24 months, however there would be no prepayment penalty.
9. MFIs can charge insurance premium, interest charges and loan processing fees which should not exceed 1 per cent of the gross loan amount. Also only the actual cost of insurance should only be recovered.
10. To improve transparency in providing loan and MFIs should make borrowers aware of the effective interest rate charged, this would enable comparability.
11. Provisioning of loans should not be maintained for individual loans but an aggregate provision for loan losses should be maintained by the MFIs.
12. Disclosures to be made in the financial statements of MFIs with regard to the outstanding loan pools securitized.
13. Bank lending to MFIs would continue to be entitled to priority sector status. A cap of 24 per cent is provided

for interest on individual loans and an average margin cap of 10 per cent for MFIs having loan portfolio of ₹ 100 crores and above and cap of 12 per cent for smaller MFIs.

14. Sub-committee also recommended that entities governed by the proposed Act, (Micro Finance Development and Regulation) Bill 2010 should not be allowed to do business of providing thrift services.

The report also recommends that all the recommendations must be accepted and implemented by 1st April, 2011. The thought behind microfinance is to assist the poor to work their way out of poverty as the traditional sources of funding is not available to them. Microfinance provides easy and cheap access to loans, without the need for collateral. The constraints of catering to this sector are high transaction costs, no understanding of banking amongst the borrowers and need for the lenders to handhold the borrowers for generating income, savings and repayments. The intent of the report is to ensure that right balance between the pursuit of social objective and interest of shareholder is maintained through responsible financing. MFIs cater to the vulnerable section of the society and are pivotal for achieving financial inclusion. The recommendations of the committee work towards achieving the purpose of financial inclusion in a proper business environment. The pertinent question here is will these recommendations resolve the grappling issued facing the industry today and achieve its purpose of financial inclusion yet being sustainable?

Micro Finance (Development and Regulation) Bill 2011

The Microfinance Institutions (Development and Regulation) Bill 2011 was put up in the Parliament. The bill provide access to financial services for the rural and urban poor and certain disadvantaged sections of the people by promoting the growth and development of microfinance institutions as extended arms of the banks and financial institutions and for the regulation of microfinance institutions for matter connected therewith and incidental thereto.

The Microfinance Institutions Bill 2012 (Bill No. 62 of 2012)

The Microfinance Institutions (Development and Regulation) Bill 2012 introduced in the Parliament on the 22nd of May comes with modifications to the earlier Bill introduced in 2007. The industry, too, has broadly welcomed the Bill as a much better version of the 2007 Bill, which lapsed on account of the dissolution of the Lok Sabha (the lower house of India's Parliament).

The introduction of this Bill brings a much needed strengthening of the regulatory framework and consumer protection norms of the microfinance industry in India. Regulation of financial services is necessary to protect current and future clients, but it must also be undertaken with care in order to maintain access to those services. A controversial law passed in the wake of the Andhra Pradesh crisis, for example, saw the asset base of the microfinance industry shrink and led to a drastic increase in bad debts due to restrictions on collection practices. Such stress on MFIs has the potential to decrease their ability to offer loans and other financial services to those who need them.

This new Bill both seek to protect consumers and recognize the need to maintain access, stating clearly that its purpose is "facilitating access to credit, thrift and other microfinance services to the rural and urban poor and certain disadvantaged sections of the people and promoting financial inclusion." If approved in its entirety, the Bill will take MFIs outside the purview of state-level legislation, such as the Andhra Pradesh law mentioned above, and provide a clear regulatory framework that applies to the entire country. The Bill has to be passed by both houses of Parliament before it becomes law.

The Broad Features of the Bill include–

1. Defining microfinance broadly and beyond just lending, to include savings, insurance, money transfers, etc.
2. Inclusion of Non-Banking Financial Company (NBFC) MFIs in its purview, in addition to NGO-MFIs.
3. Recognition of the Reserve Bank of India. (RBI) as the sole regulator of NBFC MFIs and exclusion of MFIs from

the purview of the Money-Lender Act. The Bill seeks to empower the RBI to specify sector related benchmarks and performance standards pertaining to methods of operation, fair and reasonable methods of recovery of loans advanced by MFIs.

4. Strengthening of client protection norms-including the establishment of advisory councils at the central, state and district levels and restrictions on pricing and profitability. The Bill provides for the constitution of the microfinance development council to advise the Central Government on formulation of policies, schemes and other measures required to be taken in the interest of orderly growth and development of Microfinance institutions. It also provides for the establishment of State Micro Finance Councils in each state or for two or more states, considering the extent of microfinance activities in such states. This council would have to report to the Central Government on the implementation of the measures undertaken for the promotion and development of microfinance institutions.
5. Establishment of a Microfinance Development Fund to enable lending, equity investment, capacity building and research. Under the proposal, the RBI will be empowered to set up this fund, which can be applied for providing loans, grants or seed capital as well as for training of personnel engaged in microfinance institution services.

This Bill has the potential to herald the next stage of microfinance growth in India. After witnessing a decade and a half of rapid expansion and subsequent overheating and politicization.

Challenges of Microfinance Regulation in India

Regulation of the microfinance sector poses different challenges. They are worth enumerating as there appears to be inadequate appreciation of these challenges in India. The CGAP (Consultative Group to Assist the Poor), an international consortium of public and private development agencies evolved a set of "Microfinance regulation consensus guidelines" which have been adopted by its donor agencies. These guidelines are general in nature and each country is expected to evolve its own regulatory framework based on considerations of likely effectiveness and cost of supervision. The lending models used in microfinance have peculiarities and hence regulation of microfinance poses certain unique challenges which are different from banking regulation.

First, MFIs may not pose systemic challenges in the sense that it is unlikely that even the largest MFIs are *"too big to fail"*. For example, the asset size of one of the largest MFIs in the country, SKS Microfinance Private Limited in March 2009 was ₹ 24.6 billion while that of the largest private sector bank in the country, ICICI Bank, was around ₹ 3,793 billion, approximately 154 times as large (www.icicibank.com and www.sksindia.com). MFIs however deal with low income groups least likely to bear downside risks, in a democratic country, politically the MFIs may be "too sensitive to fail". The implicit contingent liabilities are on the state, making their effective regulation in the interest of the Government.

Second, in case of banking regulation, banks are often required to make full provisions for loans without collateral. In case of MFIs, most loans are collateral free and hence no such measures are possible. On-time repayments on microfinance loans however tend to be high, though experience shows that once a loan is overdue, the ultimate collection of the loan is less likely, than in the case of loans that are backed by collateral (Rosenberg, 2008). As a result, provisioning already delinquent loans needs to be more aggressive for micro-credit loans as compared to other loans.

Third, while bank failures may be contagious in the sense that the failure of one bank is likely to impact solvency of others due to the interdependent nature of the payments system, the interdependencies between group members in microfinance can lead at times to a different kind of contagion effect. Widespread defaults can occur either if some members start consistently defaulting or if there are rumours of MFI failures. An important incentive for repayment of collateral free MFI loans is the ability to obtain larger loans in the future. Any event which makes the possibility of future loans reduce considerably, has the potential to trigger widespread defaults. A regulator of MFIs has therefore, to be highly sensitive to these realities.

Fourth, MFI customers are often first time users of financial services and usually have low education. The responsibility on the MFI to offer the right products which suit their members' needs as well as provide adequate financial education and training to them is considerable. Regulating needs to necessarily oversee this important element of MFI operations.

Fifth, merely formulating regulation regarding codes of conduct for MFIs and providing channels for dispute resolution regarding MFI practices is not sufficient. MFI customers need to be made aware of them by using appropriate communication. Moreover, the channels need to be easily accessible.

Sixth, the cost that MFIs would incur in complying with regulation needs to be considered, as it may have an impact on their lending rates. As in the case of regulation of any financial institution, two basic issues arise in regulating MFIs, prudential and non-prudential. The first relates to issues regarding solvency of the institution which is important to maintain confidence in the financial system and protect depositors. The second, non-prudential regulation includes all other matters such as guidelines on interest rate, truth-in-lending laws and anti-money laundering rules.

The CGAP guidelines on microfinance regulation favour a clear distinction between the supervisor of depository (deposit accepting) and non-depository MFIs, as the former require closer monitoring. Housing the supervision of non-depository MFIs separately would help to avoid confusion and more importantly so as to prevent the public from being misled into believing that the authority is vouching for the financial health of these MFIs when it is not (and should not be) closely monitoring their financial health. The guidelines provide that for deposit taking MFIs, the supervisory body most appropriate would be the authority which supervises commercial banks. This leverages existing supervisory skills and reduces incentive for regulatory arbitrage. The supervisory staff needs however to be trained in the particular portfolio characteristics of MFIs. Another alternative suggested for supervisor of MFIs is "delegated supervision" which refers to an arrangement where the Government delegates direct supervision to an outside body while monitoring and controlling the body's work.

In conclusion, it is time to address regulatory issues to enable the microfinance sector to contribute more effectively to the goal of financial inclusion, and to provide an environment in which all stakeholders can participate with confidence.

Summary

Microfinance has been considered as a powerful instruments for alleviation of poverty by the government. Over the last few decades, government has been undertaking various schemes and packages for effective implementation of microfinance so that it can reach to the ultimate beneficiaries. Various Five Years Plans has gave emphasis for microfinance by the government. NABARD has been given special attention for the promotion and development of microfinance. Since 1974 various initiative has been undertaken by the Government of India for development of women in particular and microfinance in general through various committee recommendations, microfinance bills, etc. To pass a bill on microfinance is still in process and it will be remain futile all efforts of government until and unless Microfinance Act is passed in the parliament.

FOUR

Microfinance in North East India

"One of the most distressing consequences of globalization is the increase in the wealth of a few while hundreds of millions of people still live in poverty. However, microfinance is a powerful tool to begin to change that."

— *Marilou van Golstein Brouwers*

Introduction

The eight states of Northeast India together have a population of 38.7 million (Census 2001) which is around 3.8 per cent of the country's total population. The region however, has 8 per cent of the country's land mass and hence the population density of the region is lower than the national average. It ranges from a low of 13 persons per square km in Arunachal to a high of 340 persons per square km in Assam. Assam is the biggest state having almost 69 per cent of the total Northeast population. The region is mostly hilly and home to over 160 scheduled tribes and over 400 other tribal and sub-tribal communities. The literacy rate in Northeast is 65.9 per cent which is marginally higher than the national average of 65.4 per cent. However, of greater significance is the fact that the Northeast is predominantly rural with 84 per cent of the population living in villages. Therefore, compared to the national average of rural literacy of 59.4 per cent, the literacy rate of 65.9 per cent of Northeast is considerably higher to the rest of rural India.

Microfinance Scenario in North East India

Literature on Microfinance found that there is late entrance of Microfinance in the region. Except Assam and Manipur, other states of the region have started Microfinance activities with a slow pace of development. Following paragraphs have highlighted microfinance activities in eight sister states of the region.

Microfinance in Arunachal Pradesh

Under Microfinance Vision-2011 special care would be given for formation and nurturing of Women Self-Help Groups (SHGs). This endeavour will gradually raise the income levels of households and improve their standards. The main objective of the Microfinance movement is to form Self-Help Groups (SHGs) of women entrepreneurs having similar social and economic background voluntarily coming together to save small amounts regularly and agree to contribute to a common fund to meet their emergency needs on mutual help basis. It also provides access to financial services of saving and credits to women especially the poor women who are not in a position to gain access due to limited outreach of banking system in the State. This will also inculcate saving habit and repayment culture and thus gradual shift from subsidy driven programmes to market driven programmes.

During the year 2009-10, Department of Social Welfare, Women and Child Development in collaboration with National Bank for Agriculture and Rural Development (NABARD) conducted Training programme of Master Trainers comprising of Deputy Director, Integrated Child Development Services (ICDS) and Child Development Project Officers (CDPOs) during the month of 9th May and 9th June and there after Department identified 8 (Eight) Districts in the 1st phase viz. Tawang, West Kameng, Lower Subansiri, Papum Pare, Upper Subansiri, West Siang, East Siang and Tirap to implement the scheme. Training programme of Anganwadi workers/helpers is going on in the above said Districts and for which ₹ 20.00 lakh is supposed to be spent during the year 2010-11.

It is also proposed to provide interest subsidy to encourage SHG from SBI, RBI and Commercial Banks other than Arunachal Pradesh State Co-operative Apex Bank Limited would be eligible for interest subsidy of 3 per cent has been commenced from 1st January, 2010. The principal amount of interest subsidy with a corpus fund of ₹ 1.00 crore will be maintained with SBI, Itanagar Branch.

It is also proposed to provide Guarantee Fund of ₹ 100 crore to the Arunachal Pradesh State Co-operative Apex Bank Ltd. to encourage SHGs to undertake commercial activities with bank loan. The credit facility to SHG from Arunachal Pradesh State Co-operative Apex Bank Ltd. would be eligible for interest free loan up to 20 per cent of the total loan amount as guaranteed by the State Government. The Guarantee Fund of ₹ 1.00 crore allotted to Arunachal Pradesh State Co-operative Apex Bank Ltd. will be interest free for further investment by the Bank.

Microfinance in Assam

Assam state is the first state in the region started with the activities of microfinance in 1980s. Major microfinance NGOs and MFIs in Assam have been presented as follows:

ASOMI: Asomi is a leading microfinance institution, currently operating in the state of Assam. With over 53 branches and 235 employees Asomi has just within a space of 9 years, established itself as one of Assam's leading NGO engaged in social transformation. Supported by leading governmental and private finance institutions, such as NABARD, Central Bank of India, Assam Gramin Vikash Bank, IDBI, State Bank of India (SBI) etc., Asomi is a professionally managed organization that has been accredited by leading rating agencies like CRISIL, MiCRIL etc.

Rashtiya Gramin Vikas Niddhi (RGVN): RGVN was founded as an autonomous non-profit organization in April, 1990 and is registered under the Societies Registration Act XXI of 1860 in the State of Assam, with Head-Quarters at Guwahati. It is also registered with the Foreign Contribution Regulation Act. RGVN has obtained exemptions under Section 80G of the Income Tax Act, 1961, providing tax concessions to donors Founded as organizational innovation in support of social action. It operates in 14 states of the country; RGVN chose to focus on north eastern India including Sikkim initially as this region lacked NGOs as well as donors. It is head-quartered at Guwahati to ensure special focus on the Northeast and eastern India. Programme activities were gradually extended to the "poverty pockets" of eastern India-eastern Uttar Pradesh, Bihar, Jharkhand, Orissa, North-eastern, Andhra Pradesh and the eastern region of Chhattisgarh.

Suraj Mukhi Banijyik Kendra (SMBK), North Lakhimpur: Established in the year 1995, SMBK started with microfinance activities in an around Lakhimpur district. However, it is also promoting livelihood activities like Poultry, Goatary, Duckery and sale of Handloom and Sanitary products in their area of operation.

Mahila Shakti Kendra (MASK), Sonitpur: With a strong community presence in Balipara Block of Sonitpur district, MASK is a federation of 100 SHGs established in the year 2002. Recently, it has taken the shape of an NGO. It is mainly involved in doing Microfinance. Also, SHG members associated with the organization are proactive in pursuing livelihood activities like Piggery, Poultry, Weaving, Pickle Making, etc.

People Action for Development (PAD), Dhemaji: PAD was established in the year 2001 with an objective to ensure the rights of the tea tribes. It has been successful in forming 66 SHGs with Piggery and Fishery as major activities besides experimenting Microfinance in Revenue villages and Tea Gardens. Currently, PAD is running 3 schools, one outside the tea garden and 2 in the tea gardens.

Social Economic Development Organization (SEDO), Dhemaji: Established in the year 2002, SEDO started with SHG promotion and bank linkages which resulted in successful formation of 98 SHGs. Currently, the organization is mainly involved in supervising Anganwadis under ICDS in 45 villages in 9 blocks of the district under a project granted by ANT, Bongaigaon. It is also working in the field of Reproductive Child Health under NRHM.

Grameen Silk Producer's Company Ltd (GSPCL), Kamrup Rural: GSPCL has been recently established as a Producer's Company in March 2012 under the Companies Act of 1956. The entity is especially working in the field of 'Silk' like Eri and Tassar. In collaboration with Central Silk Board, Small Industries Development Bank of India, NABARD it is proving spinning machines to the beneficiaries in subsidy, skill building training on Eri spinning through CSTRI (spinning) Machines and also capacity building support on design development. Their area of operation is Chaygaon situated in the Kamrup district.

Lok Seva Samity (LSS), Baksa: LSS was established in the year 1999. It is currently promoting SRI under SDTT and Mushroom Cultivation under JRDTT in Baksa district. Previously LSS has successfully implemented livelihood project on Bee keeping under CML in their area of operation.

Microfinance in Manipur

Some of the leading microfinance NGOs/MFIs in Manipur has been discussed as follows:

Loyalam Bank Project (LBP): Under the umbrella of Rural Development Organization (RDO), Manipur, Loyalam Bank Project was set up as pilot project for bottom poor in Imphal West on 2nd October, 1992 with the support from the Grameen Trust, Bangladesh, National Bank for Agriculture and Rural Development (NABARD) and Rashtriya Mahila Kosh (RMK). The RDO is the first organization which starts microfinance in the state with the objective of to introduce and institutionalize a non-traditional banking system in rural areas which would provide credit facilities under special terms and conditions. It has been covering only rural areas, far-flung and inaccessible or hilly areas in Manipur. So far LBP has covered the four districts of Manipur. The goal of the project is to contribute in the alleviation of poverty through Micro credit by expanding the outreach to 10,000 poor families by the year 2015 in Manipur.

Youth Volunteer's Union (YVU): YVU, Thoubal–Manipur, enter in the field of microfinance with the establishment of Women Credit and Thrift Project (WCTP) in Manipur on 2nd October, 1996 under the leadership of Akoijam Tikendrajit Singh, with a capital of ₹ 35,000 and small grant assistance from Evangelische Zentralstelle (EZE), Germany. Now YVU is no longer dependency to donor agency for its own survival. It is operating in three states i.e., Assam, Delhi and Manipur. YVU microfinance is working as NBFC under the banner of *YVU Financial Service Ltd* and it is register under the company act 1956.

Machaleima Microfin: Machaleima Microfin has been started on 1st November 1997 as a microfinance programme for women through SHG under the organization called Manipuri Chanura Leishem Marup (MACHA LEIMA), Palace Compound - Imphal. The organization is run only by the women from top to bottom.

It is one of the unique features of this orgnization. The main objective of this project is to give comprehensive livelihood support to poor but able-bodied women and a collective obligation towards a better society.

Chanura Microfin: CMM has been working relentlessly to reduce poverty and introducing positive changes in the lives of the poor since its inception in April, 2007. Its main target is to reduce poverty from the society gradually. During the first year (2007-08), pilot testing of SHG and JLG model had been conducted by observing client friendliness, cost effectiveness and loan security. During this reporting period of 2 years of microfinance programme, CMM has decided to follow only the JLG methodology.

Microfinance in Meghalaya

Followings are some of the MFIs/NGOs in Meghalaya.

Grace Foundation, Ri-Bhoi: Formed in the year 2003 with its office at Ri-Bhoi district, Grace Foundation is one of the oldest NGOs working for the development of a few villages in the Ri-Bhoi district. The major activities which the organization has taken up since its inception are running of a school up to tenth standard for the underprivileged children, proving capacity building support to the CBOs and a project on ginger cultivation supported by RGVN.

Association for Rural Development (ARD), West Khasi Hills: With its office in Mawkrywat in the West Khasi Hills district, ARD has been working in the handicraft sector with their beneficiaries in the remotest corners of Mawkrywat. They have been able to link their beneficiaries to the market through participation in different trade fairs and exhibitions.

Rilum Foundation, East Khasi Hills: Based at Smit in East Khasi Hills district, Rilum foundation had been working on rights based approach since 1999 to 2009. Post 2009, the organization undertook the work of social audit in 2 blocks to facilitate its work on livelihood. Thematic areas for intervention in the coming years are goatary and bird keeping formed.

Baite Tribal Social Welfare Association (BTSWA), Jaintia Hills: Based at Jowai, BTSWA was formed in the year 1982 with the mandate of working for the upliftment of the Baite tribe. The target community is located at Saipung block which is 70 kms away from Jowai. Since its inception, BTSWA has taken up several activities like providing solar lamps to around 250 villages in the Saipung block, construction of foot bridges, distributing looms and lanterns to around 630 artisans and doing several cane and bamboo work.

Microfinance in Mizoram

The National Bank for Agriculture and Rural Development (NABARD) today expressed concern over insufficient Self-Help Group—SHG-Bank linkage programme—in Mizoram. Talking to UNI, NABARD's Assistant General Manager Pillai Santhanam said "it has been felt that the SHG has not been percolated well among the bankers at branch level and also among the various NGOs in the state" "At time the SHG-bank linkage programme has been understood as SGSY programme of the government, which is a conceptual abbreviation", he added. He also pointed out as 2006 declared as the year of "microfinance" by the United Nations, NABARD had convened a meeting with the chief executives of all the commercial banks including SBI, Vijaya Bank, UCO bank, Mizoram rural bank and Mizoram co-operative Apex Bank to discuss the modalities to improve the SHGs in the state. The meeting emphasised the need to create a credit linkage with SHGs in the region, he added. The CEOs of these banks also volunteered to help for the formation of SHGs and opening of bank accounts to 1020 new SHGs during next fiscal, he said and stressed the need to create a core group of mobile trainers to create awareness about micro finance. Mr Pillai said they would organise more SHG sensitization programmes across the region for women and various NGOs. "Till now the entire organised programme throughout the state was well received by the bankers as well as NGOs, who took active part in these meetings".

Shri R.K. Das, GM, NABARD, informed the house that a target of 1500 SHGs has been given for the current year. He also informed that various NGOs have been involved in this process and requested all the banks to come forward and help in formation and credit linkage of SHGs.

Microfinance in Nagaland

Following are the few selected MFIs/NGOs working in the field of microfinance in Nagaland.

Microfinance in Nagaland is of recent origin. Unlike other parts of the country and general practice followed worldwide, the Microfinance programme in Nagaland is unique. Though, the programme is under the Department of Rural Development yet the approach is two-fold viz. Microfinance through Self-Help Groups (SHGs) and Microfinance through Village Development Board (VDB).

Realising the growing importance of SHG bank linkage programme and as per the recommendations of the NABARD Working Group, the RBI decided to extend SHG-bank linkage programme beyond the pilot phase and advised the banks to make it a part of their mainstream banking function. As an effect, microfinance through SHGs has gradually emerged in Nagaland. The State Governments and NABARD are playing a more proactive role in this area by identifying various NGOs/MFIs, organizing training programme for capacity building, etc.

Nagaland has been the pioneer in the concept of Decentralized Planning through active participation of the village community. The Village Development Boards are empowered in the entire process of implementation of all its rural developmental activities including Microfinance. This innovative approach to involve the VDBs in the process of credit related Micro-Financial Intermediaries Activity is now firmly rooted in Nagaland. Almost all the VDBs are now involved as Micro-Financial Intermediaries. In order to promote micro finance activities in Nagaland, initially, 25 VDBs were selected as Financial Intermediaries as Pilot projects. A Corpus Fund of ₹ 1.00 lakh was created through the contribution of VDBs, State Government, Central Government and NABARD at the rate of 40:20:20:20 respectively. With the successful implementation of the Pilot Projects, the State Government has decided to cover all VDBs under this umbrella phase-wise.

It is observed that out of 6,057 SHGs, 4,744 SHGs were registered with public sector commercial banks, 308 SHGs were registered with Regional Rural Banks and 1,005 SHGs were registered with Central Cooperative Bank. The total number of SHGs members registered with the Public Sector Banks stood at

30,435. The total savings of the SHGs was 157.65 lakhs as on 31st March 2009. Out of the total savings, Public Sector Banks accounts for the largest share of 111.22 lakhs representing 70.55 per cent. RRB accounts for 11.51 lakhs representing 7.3 per cent, while Central Cooperative Banks accounts for 34.92 lakhs representing 22.15 per cent. It is, therefore, concluded that Public Sector Banks with large network in the State is responsible for assuming great responsibility for the SHG growth in Nagland.

Community Development Foundation (CDF), Dimapur: Based in Dimapur, CDF started its intervention in 2003 by providing MF services in the different villages of Dimapur. CDF is currently involved in a project on Microfinance in Dimapur. Previously it was involved in a Piggery project in 4 villages of Kohima supported by SDTT, Mumbai.

Sisterhood Network (SN), Dimapur: Sisterhood Network is a woman based NGO based in Dimapur established in 2001 with the sole objective of empowering Naga women. SN provides basic vocational training in tailoring, craft-making etc. to the girls and also helps them in getting placed in some units.

Rongmei Baptist Association (RBA), Peren: Located at Jalukie in Peren district, RBA started its development activities in 1992 in collaboration with the World Vision to support school education among children of Peren district. Later on, it also received support from NICORD, Shillong and EED, Germany for the same project. Currently, RBA is involved in horticulture, skills training and microfinance.

Exotic Echo, Dimapur: Located in Deziephe village in the outskirts of Dimapur, Exotic Echo started with the promotion of SHGs since there were already formed SHG groups in the village before the existence of the organization. Their second line of activity is providing trainings on weaving and making.

Chakhesang Women Welfare Society (CWWS), Phek: Based in Pfutsero in Phek district of Nagaland, CWWS was set up with the basic idea of uplifting Chakhesang women. CWWS is currently involved in promoting SHGs, horticulture, vocational training and food processing.

Microfinance in Sikkim

Speaking on the status of microfinance in Sikkim in a session

B.K. Dey, General Manager/Officer In-charge, NABARD, Sikkim said that SHG movement shows a very poor progress in Sikkim because of absence of credible NGOs, poor connectivity particularly during rainy and winter seasons, banks being not pro-active, absence of RRBs and above all, groups formed being taken away for SGSY financing by DRDA. Dey said that bank personnel were not very interested to promote SHG activities in Sikkim despite that there is a potential for forming 10,000 more SHGs.

One of the participants raises the question that women empowerment rate was high in Sikkim and SHG could do better there. Another said that SHG group may work on eco-tourism and green state formation activities. In Sikkim most of the contribution flowed from Government as subsidy and hence, the people of Sikkim were not willing to take any loan from formal financial organizations. Sikkim can do with it because of generous budgetary support from centre but how many states have a population of nearly 7 lakh and a budget of nearly 1400 crore?

Microfinance in Tripura

NABARD continued to provide technical support to the State support project on SHGs being implemented by the Government of Tripura for credit linkage of 11,500 existing SHGs, forming and credit linking 35,000 new SHGs and promoting livelihood activities among the 3 lakh members up to 2012.

Demand and Supply of Microfinance in the North East India

Microfinance demand arises from the financial requirements of low income households. To date, the Northeastern region has been underserved and neglected from a financial inclusion standpoint. In this section we try to estimate the demand for microfinance in the region and compare it with the data available on supply of microfinance through institutional sources.

(i) Micro-credit Demand of the Region

The total annual micro-credit demand for the region is estimated between ₹ 22.9 billion and ₹ 38.0 billion. It is commonly acknowledged that dwelling units reflect the economic status of households. The Census of India provides useful data on the socio-economic profile of the population and this includes information on dwelling units 10 we have used this data to determine the demand for micro-credit the Northeast. The Census classifies dwelling units on the basis of the material used for roof construction. We have selected households that used Grass, Thatch, Bamboo, Wood, Mud, Plastic, Polythene, Tiles, or Slate as those which were economically weak and had a demand for microfinance.

There were over 2.54 million such households in Assam according to the Census of 2001. If one assumes that the micro-credit demand in 2001 for a rural household was ₹ 3,000 and for an urban household was ₹ 5,000, one gets an annual microfinance demand of ₹ 7.8 billion. If the demand from a rural household was ₹ 5,000 and an urban household was ₹ 8,000, the annual demand comes to ₹ 13.0 billion. However, this range reflects the demand range for microfinance in the year 2001. A 10 per cent Compounded Annual Growth Rate (CAGR) yields a demand range of' 16.8 billion to ₹ 27.9 billion in 2009.

The demand for the other states has been calculated in a similar manner and this is distributed across the eight states in the following way:

Table 4.1: State-wise Distribution of Microcredit Demand

States	*Lower limit (₹ bn)*	*Upper limit (₹ bn)*	*% of total*
Arunachal Pradesh	0.87	1.45	3.8
Assam	16.79	27.91	73.4
Manipur	1.03	1.71	4.5
Meghalaya	1.12	1.87	4.9
Mizoram	0.28	0.45	1.2
Nagaland	0.74	1.23	3.2
Sikkim	0.12	0.20	0.5
Tripura	1.93	3.21	8.4
Total	22.88	38.03	100.0

Source: NABARD.

This analysis reveals that over 70 per cent of the demand emanates from Assam while Sikkim contributes less than 1 per cent to it.

(ii) Microcredit Supply Channels

The important channels of microfinance supply in the Northeastern region are the commercial banks, regional rural banks, cooperative banks, SHGs linked to banks and direct lending by MFIs. There are also some indigenous mechanisms organized as ROSCAs and ASCAs, which help in rotating internally pooled savings. Namghars, Marups, Sanchay Samitis, are some unique examples of such mechanisms. They have been discussed below:

(a) *Lending by Commercial Banks*: Scheduled Commercial Banks, Regional Rural Banks and Cooperative Bank operating in each states provide direct credit for a range of activities such as microenterprises and other economic oriented activities and personal consumption. Banks also provide remittance and saving services.

(b) *Lending by banks to SHGs under SHG-Bank linkage Model*: SHG-Bank linkage is another important channel. Due to absence of MFIs in the region, SHPIs gain a lot of significance in nurturing SHGs and linking them to banks.

(c) *Lending by Microfinance Institution*: Direct microfinance can be a crucial delivery channel, as MFIs have a revenue model to sustain themselves and to scale up fast. However, in Northeast the MFIs have still not flourished. There are only around ten MFIs, of which only four to five MFIs have attained significant size. Most of these MFIs are operating in Assam while other Northeastern have no MFI presence at all.

(d) *Lending by IFAD*: IFAD project for rural and backward development in the region is spread into three states of Assam, Meghalaya and Manipur. IFAD is providing financial assistance through its microfinance wings to SHGs forming under the project.

(e) *Indigenous Institutions*: There are several indigenous lending institutions operating in the region. These institutions have been in existence for many years and play significant roles in providing financial security as well as social security to their members. These are community managed institutions which have evolved in the absence of formal financial importance, but are part of the culture of many communities. These indigenous institutions are primarily Rotating Saving and Credit Associations (RoSCAs) e.g. Marups in Manipur and Accumulating Saving and Credit Associations (ASCAs) e.g. Sonchay, Somobay, Got in Assam. Other institutions such as Namghars, Pujaghars, Shinglups, and Mahari mainly provide social security in emergency situations such as death and the funds are also utilized in the common welfare of the community (Appendix-VI)

(iii) Credit Supply Estimation

The supply of credit has been estimated based on the two major channels of credit i.e. the SHG-Bank linkage and direct microfinance. While there are also indigenous institutions providing credit facilities locally, due to lack of data it is difficult to ascertain its size. However, considering the total demand, its share is still insignificant.

Agencies-wise Progress of Microfinance–Savings of SHGs with Bank in North Eastern Region

SHGs have been linked to commercial banks, RRBs as well as cooperative banks. The total supply of microcredit for the North East through SHGs bank linkages was at ₹ 15,251.75 lakh arson 31st March 2012. Assam state account the highest number of SHGs among the eight sister states as on 31st March 2012. Among the three components, Regional Rural Banks accounts the highest contribution to the total number of SHGs followed by Commercial Banks and cooperative banks respectively. The distribution of this supply across states and the nature of bank are given in Table 4.2.

State-wise Progress of Microfinance–Savings of SHGs with Banks in Northeast India

Below given Table 4.3 represents the state-wise progress of microfinance in northeastern states from 2009-10 to 2011-12 respectively. Assam state being a big brother contribute 74.72 per cent and 75.42 per cent of SHGs and 60.49 per cent and 64.55

Table 4.2: Agencies-wise Progress of Microfinance–Savings of SHGs with Bank in North Eastern Region as on 31st March 2012

(₹ in Lakhs)

States	Commercial Banks		RRBs		Coop Banks		Total	
	No. of SHGs	Amount (₹Bn)	No. of SHGs	Amount (₹Bn)	No. of SHGs	Amount (₹Bn)	No. of SHGs	Amount (₹Bn)
Arunachal	6983	103.14	959	54.20	421	28.98	8363	186.32
Assam	102764	5991.53	149291	3039.10	24510	815.35	276565	9845.98
Manipur	5955	103.34	5784	106.06	972	9.98	12711	219.38
Meghalaya	9057	231.30	2507	143.16	2527	40.28	14091	414.74
Mizoram	2104	43.57	2202	507.04	670	22.30	4976	572.91
Nagaland	6353	132.93	679	50.99	3679	190.56	10711	374.48
Sikkim	4626	178.21	0	0.00	654	81.79	5280	260.00
Tripura	11636	252.68	16696	2736.28	5689	388.99	34021	3377.95
Total	149478	7036.69	178118	6636.83	39122	1578.23	366718	15251.75

Source: NABARD, 2012.

per cent of SHG credit during 2009-10 and 2011-12 respectively. Next to Assam, Tripura and Meghalaya contribute 2nd and 3rd position respectively.

Table 4.3: State-wise Progress of Microfinance–Savings of SHGs with Banks in Northeast India as on 31 March 2012

(Amount ₹ in lakh)

Sl. No	State	2009-10		2010-11		2011-12	
		No. of SHGs	Savings Amount	No. of SHGs	Savings Amount	No. of SHGs	Savings Amount
1.	Arunachal	6418	164.89	7079	186.31	8363	186.32
2.	Assam	218352	7359.94	245120	8196.6	276565	9845.98
3.	Manipur	10831	218.56	10306	240.23	12711	219.38
4.	Meghalaya	11787	360.25	10653	376.12	14091	414.74
5.	Mizoram	5097	251.04	4592	178.11	4976	572.91
6.	Nagaland	5926	334.37	9866	362.99	10711	374.48
7.	Sikkim	2428	141.98	2811	168.94	5280	260.00
8.	Tripura	31349	3335.07	34312	3395.03	34021	3377.95
	Total	292188	12167.09	324739	13104.06	366718	15251.75

Source: Status of Microfinance in India 2012.

Microcredit through MFIs in Northeast India

Table 4.4 highlight the extent of microcredit through different MFIs operating in the region. Both in terms of number of clients covered and also the amount of loan outstanding as on March 2009, RGVN-CSP of Assam emerge as number one MFI in the region followed by ASOMI in the region.

Table 4.4: Micro-credit through MFIs in North East India as on March 2009

MFI	*State(s)*	*Clients*	*Loans Outstanding (₹ bn)*
ASOMI	Assam	19,253	0.21
IIRM	Assam	8,140	0.041
RGVN – CSP	Assam	65,052	0.36
Prochesta	Assam	8,610	0.007
Grameen Sahara	Assam	4,200	0.002
Others*	Assam	NA	0.15
Youth Volunteer's Union (YVU)	Manipur	4,111	0.05
Volunteers for Village Development (VVD)	Manipur	779	0.003
WSDS	Manipur	2,226	0.001
Others*	Manipur	NA	0.25
Others in other states	Various states	NA	0.08
Total		112,371	1.15

* Other include MFIs such as Bandhan, UNACO, NEREFS and small NGO- MFIs.

Source: NABARD.

Micro-insurance

Microfinance institutions typically provide life insurance to their clients and their spouses by acting as agents for mainstream insurance companies. In some cases, they also provide health insurance. Data indicates that MFIs are able to provide insurance coverage at an annual premium of ₹ 10 per ₹ 1,000 sum insured. Assuming that an aggregate insurance cover of the total microfinance demand is required, the insurance premium potential for the Northeast region is ₹ 230–380 million of which an insignificant portion has been trapped to date.

Key Stakeholders for Microfinance Development in Northeast India

In order to achieve financial inclusion in the region, various stakeholders have come together, leverage their work to date, and differentiate their roles in the development of a Northeast microfinance sector. Few of them are:

(i) Centre for Microfinance and Livelihood (CML)

Microfinance and Livelihood (CML) is a recently formed umbrella organization for capacity building, research, collaborative interventions and policy advocacy in the social sector. CML was established in 2008, under the active support of Tata Social Welfare Trust, (TSWT) an affiliate of Sir Dorabji Tata Trust, Mumbai. CML is centrally located in Guwahati, Assam. CML has been formed to provide a platform for resource and capacity building support to social sector in Northeast. CML along with RGVN conducted the first microfinance and livelihood conference for northeast in February 2010. CML can take up the role of a resource and advocacy platform for microfinance in northeast.

(ii) Rashtriya Gramin Vikas Nidhi (RGVN)

RGVN is a non-profit organization founded in April, 1990 and is registered under Societies Registration Act and its Head Quarters at Guwahati. RGVN operates in 14 states of the country but its focus is on northeastern India. RGVN is a very reputed NGO in northeast and has high outreach in different states of northeastern region. Apart from other social activities, in microfinance RGVN has supported several smaller organizations through its NGO-Support Programme (NGO-SP) and NGO Microfinance Programme (NGO-MF). NGO Support Programme aims at reinforcing livelihood systems of poor people who have little or no access to mainstream assistance. NGO SP aims to promote, nurture, and develop NGOs.

RGVN takes the credit risk to work with these NGOs with borrowed fund and grooms them into sustainable MFIs. RGVN also has a separate microfinance programme of its own called RGVN-Credit and Savings Programme (RGVN-CSP). Table 3.5

Table 4.5: RGVN NE-State-wise Commitment and Disbursement of NGO-MF During Financial Year 2009-10

(₹ in lakh)

State	*Proposal*	*Commitment*			*Disbursement*		
		RG	*NRG*	*Total*	*RG*	*NRG*	*Total*
Arunachal	9	18.72	0	18.72	13.12	0	13.12
Assam	88	368.90	0	368.90	396.86	0	396.86
Manipur	6	77.525	0	77.525	27.95	0	27.95
Meghalaya	0	0	0	0	0	0	0
Mizoram	1	1.65	0	1.65	6.50	0	6.50
Nagaland	4	47.00	0	47.00	27.00	0	27.00
Sikkim	0	0	0	0	0	0	0
Tripura	13	77.4	0	77.4	128.00	0	128.00
Total	121	591.195	0	591.195	599.43	0	599.43

Source: RGVN Annual Report 2009-10.

shows the state-wise commitment and disbursement of NGO-MF under RGVN in North East India.

(iii) Rastriya Mahila Kosh (RMK)

RMK has formulated a concessional package for the voluntary organisations of the North-Eastern region for easy access of credit from RMK to meet the credit needs of the poor women of the region in order to remove the uneven presence of micro-credit in the country which is witnessed mostly in North-Eastern region due to poor presence of banking network, lack of infrastructure and awareness, the concessions are:

- The organization having completed one year of its registration (previously 3 years) can apply for the loan.
- Margin on loan reduced from 10 per cent to 5 per cent.
- The grace period on repayment of loan enhanced from 6 months to 12 months.
- The repayment period of loan enhanced to five years invariably for all schemes.
- The NGOs to be supported with 10 per cent of the loan sanctioned as capacity-building assistance.
- To provide second class sleeper rail fare and where there

is no rail link, cheaper class to and from Air fare to the members of NGOs (up to 2 numbers) for coming to Delhi for execution of documents.

Table 4.6: State-wise Details of Sanctions and Disbursements under the Main Loan Scheme and Composite Loan Scheme of RMK during the Years 2009-10 and 2010-11

(₹ in lakhs)

	2008-09		2009-10		2010-11	
	No.	Amount Disbursed	No.	Amount Disbursed	No.	Amount Disbursed
Assam			—	9	—	451
Manipur			1	22		
Nagaland					1	5

Source: Annual Report, RMK 2010-11.

(iv) Apex institutions

NABARD: NABARD is the Apex Development Bank with a mandate for facilitating credit flow for promotion and development of agriculture, small-scale industries, cottage and village industries, handicrafts and other rural crafts. It also has the mandate to support all other allied economic activities in rural areas, promote integrated and sustainable rural development and secure prosperity of rural areas. NABARD being an apex development financial institution with mandate for microfinance and the originator of SHG-Bank Linkage Programme in the country is a key stakeholder for provision of microfinance in northeast. NABARD has its Regional Offices in each of the eight states in northeast.

SIDBI: SIDBI has one of its five Zonal/Regional offices in Guwahati for the northeast region. Apart from the Zonal office SIDBI has branch offices in each of the eight northeastern states; these are located in Agartala, Aizawl, Dimapur, Gangtok, Guwahati, Imphal, Itanagar and Shillong. SIDBI being an apex financial institution with significant presence in the northeast and being an agency which spurred the growth of microfinance at national level becomes a natural stakeholder for catalysing growth of microfinance in northeast.

Table 4.7: Progress under Microfinance-Bank Loan disbursed during the year 2011-12 for North East States

States	*Commercial Bank*		*RRB*		*Cooperative Bank*		*Total*	
	SHGs	*Rs.*	*SHGs*	*Rs.*	*SHGs*	*Rs.*	*SHGs*	*Rs.*
Assam	10072	8228.09	16279	8691.61	1661	1827.28	28012	18746.98
Arunachal	48	94.12	15	24.50	67	39.34	130	157.96
Manipur	828	554.37	433	185.65	47	117.50	1308	857.52
Meghalaya	168	138.87	391	220.21	132	130.14	691	489.22
Mizoram	7	11.48	542	640.18	26	38.54	575	690.20
Nagaland	466	475.86	44	112.31	352	33.12	862	621.29
Sikkim	356	324.08	00	0.00	40	99.62	396	423.70
Tripura	1104	1729.29	16301	19469.51	1624	1943.07	19029	23141.87
Total	13049	11556.16	34005	29343.97	3949	4228.61	51003	45128.74

Source: NABARD, Status of Microfinance in India 2011-12.

The Banks accord special and focused attention for the development of North Eastern Region (NER) in terms of micro-finance, rural industrialization, handicraft, entrepreneurship development, marketing support, etc. During the year, total assistance of ` 33.20 lakh was extended under various programmes in NER, which are briefly given below:

- Under the Bank's Flagship P&D Programme, viz. MEPP, 22 districts in the region have so far been covered, out of which, 10 are currently under implementation. These MEPPs have cumulatively resulted in promotion of about 2,500 units including 223 units during FY 2011-12. The Bank has supported 39 Cluster Development Programmes (CDPs) in different states of NE covering activities like bamboo mat weaving, carpet weaving, handicrafts, handloom weaving, etc. These cluster development initiatives would benefit about 6,000 artisans. Out of the above, skill and entrepreneurship training programmes are presently being conducted in 9 different clusters of northeastern region.
- A Micro Enterprise Business Information Counsellors (MEBICs) Centre has been set up by SIDBI at Guwahati for fostering entrepreneurship by providing counselling, initial handholding and development of micro-enterprises in northeastern region. Rashtriya Gramin Vikas Nidhi

(RGVN) has been supported for operating this Centre. Till March 31, 2012, the Centre has rendered service to more than 1,400 existing and prospective micro entrepreneurs.

- A Memorandum of Understanding was executed with NEDFI in March 2012 for providing various financial and developmental services including MSME finance, Micro Finance and also for undertaking various P&D activities in NER. Under this arrangement, Credit Counselling Centres were also opened. There are five such centres in operation in NER, which includes Shillong (Meghalaya), Silchar (Assam), Aizawl (Mizoram), Gangtok (Sikkim) and Agartala (Tripura).

NEDFI: North Eastern Development Finance Corporation Ltd. (NEDFI) was incorporated under the Companies Act, 1956, on August 9, 1995 with its registered office at Guwahati, Assam, for the development of industries, infrastructure, animal husbandry, agri-horticulture plantation, medicinal plantation, sericulture plantation, aquaculture, poultry and dairy in the North Eastern states of India.

NEDFI has been jointly promoted by several financial institutions including IDBI, ICICI, SBI, IFCI, SIDBI, UTI, LIC and GIC. After the creation of DONER, NEDFI has come under the administrative control of this Ministry. NEDFI is the premier financial and development institution of the North East of India. NEDFI with its products and services aims to be a dynamic and responsive organization catalysing the economic development of the Northeast region of India.

NEDFI has been playing a proactive role by financing MFIs and also organizing capacity building programmes for them. NEDFI aims to continue its support to microfinance, which makes it one of the stakeholders.

The microfinance scheme, an effective instrument for financial inclusion, was launched to meet the needs of smaller entrepreneurs in the remote areas of the region. During the financial year, loans sanctioned under the scheme aggregated to ₹ 33.35 crore covering 21 projects and 51,304 beneficiries. Till the FY 2010-11 cumulative sanctions and disbursements were ₹ 101.19 crore and ₹ 95.45 crore respectively to 422 NGOs/MFIs/CBOs from 8 North

Eastern states to reach out to 1,59,983 beneficieries, of which 83 per cent are women.

Table 4.8: Financial Assistance supported by NEDFI for Microfinance in Northeast India

(₹ in Crore)

Micro Finance	*2009-10*	*2010-11*
Sanctions	17.12	33.35
Disbursements	16.96	39.85
No. of Projects	28	21
No. of SHGs/JLGs Groups assisted	3,904	9,838
No. of beneficiaries	24,802	51304
No. of women beneficiaries	22,370	50,293

Source: Annual Report 2011-12, NEDFI.

FWWB: Friends of Women's World Banking-India (FWWB-I), was promoted in 1982 by SEWA Bank, as an affiliate of Women's World Banking, a global network created to focus on the need for women's direct access to financial services. FWWB-I's mission is to provide financial and capacity building services to organizations promoting livelihoods and self-reliance of poor women.

FWWB provides the following services such as institution building, capacity building, monitoring and assessment services for Microfinance institutions, community based organizations and Enterprises. Supporting partner organizations that use innovative ways of poverty alleviation, focusing on enhancing and introducing sustainable livelihood activities for women.

Table 4.9: FWWB financial support to NE Region in 2008-09

State	*Functional Domain*	*Grant (₹)*	*Soft Loan (₹)*
Arunachal Pradesh	Horticulture intervention with tribals and Budhists in rain shadow region	Nil	500,000
Assam	Scale up and linkage of weavers of Boro and Karbi tribes in highly decentralized and remote communities of Assam	Nil	13,00,000

Source: Annual Report 2009, FWWB.

Table 4.10: Progress under Microfinance-Bank Loan disbursed by Commercial Bank in North Eastern Region

(₹ *in lakh*)

States	*2008-09*		*2009-10*		*2010-11*		*2011-12*	
	SHGs	₹	*SHGs*	₹	*SHGs*	₹	*SHGs*	₹
Arunachal	387	228.38	911	312.13	937	441.00	48	94.12
Assam	11775	8300.78	11760	9075.23	8042	9631.52	10072	8228.09
Manipur	574	388.54	233	174.23	203	140.74	828	554.37
Meghalaya	396	293.39	1425	672.32	765	480.71	168	138.87
Mizoram	347	154.29	39	98.52	45	49.15	7	11.48
Nagaland	94	200.51	603	637.83	243	194.39	466	475.86
Sikkim	924	1189.81	389	198.32	267	108.31	356	324.08
Tripura	1791	591.41	1292	1368.67	1300	871.65	1104	1729.29
Total	16288	11347.11	16652	12537.25	11802	11917.47	13049	11556.16

Source: NABARD, Status of Micro Finance in India.

North East has been a special area of focus for FWWB-I and FWWB have been providing financial and capacity building support to MFIs. This included: exposure visits, MIS support, trainings, workshops on governance, etc.

(v) Commercial Banks

There are several public sector banks operating in northeast India. State Bank of India is the biggest bank in outreach in the region. Private sector banks are also now expanding in northeast. Apart from these banks, regional rural banks and cooperative societies are also key stakeholders. The importance of these financial institutions is in providing loans to SHGs as well as MFIs. They are chief sources of fund for MFIs and SHGs and hence are indispensable stakeholders.

(vi) Consultants

Consultants based in Northeast or outside Northeast will have to play a key role in providing technical support in building the sector. Microfinance consultants will have to provide mentoring support, help MFIs in developing products, systems and processes and help in their overall growth. The consultants can also carry out research, studies and assessments which are necessary for maintaining standards and transparency in the sector. There are several microfinance consulting companies such as M2i Consulting, Intellecap, and Microsave, etc. which can play a role in Northeast. Access Development Services itself can also play a role in capacity building of MFIs, policy advocacy and to address various other sector issues. Apart from microfinance consultants, IT and technology consultants will also have a role in making available affordable technology solutions for the northeastern MFIs.

(vii) Academic Institutions

As microfinance expands in the Northeast, it will need trained and educated human resources. The quality of human resource will ultimately define the quality of microfinance programmes. Various institutes in the Northeast can cater to this vital demand for high-quality human resources and can feed into the multi-level. The academic institutions will also be needed for and publications, further adding to their important role as a key stakeholder.

(viii) SHPIs and MFIs

SHPIs and MFIs are the channels to provide the financial services. SHPIs groom SHGs which ultimately deliver financial services. The quality of SHGs being nurtured depends on the SHPIs and their own capacity. SHGs are an important financial services delivery channel and hence SHPIs gain a lot of importance. These SHPIs are several NGOs operating in all the states of northeast and are key stakeholders in one of the streams of Microfinance. MFIs provide financial services directly to the clients and hence are the main stakeholders. Some of the major MFIs operating in northeast including RGVN-CSP, ASOMI, IIRM, Bandhan, Prochesta, Youth Volunteers' Union (YVU), Volunteers for Village Development (VVD), NEREFS and UNACCO.

(ix) Donors

As the microfinance industry is in its infancy in Northeast (in some states it has not even started), support will be imperative during this early phase. Since, there is a massive need for capacity building and creating infrastructure for the MFIs, donors can play an important role in providing that initial support. Also the fact that MFIs typically take two to three years to break even, (in case of Northeast it may take even longer), some support will be needed by these MFIs during the initial loss phase. Donors therefore, become stakeholders in supporting MFIs on one hand and also in investing in creating an enabling environment in the region for microfinance to flourish over the long-term.

(x) Government

Both the state and Central Government will play a critical role in designing a conducive framework. The national and statutory authorities can really help create a favourable system that welcomes donor funding, minimizes interference, and creates a facilitating regulatory environment.

The study on Microfinance in the Northeastern region points out that many diverse traditional systems and even geographical conditions of the region make it almost impossible to transplant the model of SHGs adopted elsewhere in India into this region. The micro-finance movement started late in the region and is confounded by many regional complexities that must be understood, appreciated and incorporated into policy if the plans to make affordable loans to low income groups in the region are to bear any fruit. The state of the SHG movement varies from state to state, and within states from one district to another. The SHG movement is yet to take off in any major way in Arunachal Pradesh. In Manipur, too, it is not significant despite, or perhaps because, many traditional systems of organising savings and lending still hold away.

Summary

Unlike other parts of the country, Microfinance is late entry in northeastern region of India. Assam and Manipur are the two states started microfinance activities in early 1980s. Remaining states, though late, started microfinance activities for the promotion of micro-enterprise activities as of today. On the other hand, only few prominent microfinance institutions have started their campaign for microfinance in the region like RGVN, RMK, FWWB, IFAD and Bandhan. Besides few microfinance promotion NGO-MFI of the region also plays a key role in the development of microfinance in the region. But due to present law and order problems and other sociological, geographical and economical problems, the microfinance movement in the region is progressing at a very slow rate. A concerted effort of the government, NGO-MFI, SHGs, JLGs and Micro enterprenuers are the need of the hour for microfinance development as well as micro-enterprise development of the region.

Five
Research Design

> "This is not charity. This is business: business with a social objective, which is to help people get out of poverty."
>
> —*Muhammad Yunus*

Introduction

Today, Microfinance is widely practicing all over the globe spreading into five continents and different countries. Among the different continents, Asia is the top microfinance continents and emerging markets in the world. India and Bangladesh are the two most important countries when we talk about the microfinance industry. India is one of the most potential for microfinance industry and it has been considering as one of the effective tool to mitigate several social and economic problems of rural mass. Despite of concerted efforts undertaken by the government of India over the last few decades, still there is a huge gap to bridge between the targeted objectives and its reality. Thus, there is need to study how microfinance institutions are functioning in the country in general and more particularly the state and region towards eradication of poverty.

Statement of the Problem

Microfinance is one of the most effective tools for alleviating poverty in the world. It is the largest scheme undertaken by the government for mitigation of rural poverty through engaging socio-economic oriented activities. Knowing the significance and importance of this sector, Government of India has been trying to pass the Microfinance Bill in the Parliament in 2006 and also in 2012. But it fails to materialise in the form of Act. The microfinance scheme have direct impact on the alleviation of rural poverty by giving small financial assistance, microcredit, micro-insurance and other facilities for upliftment of rural poor. The scheme have also gave direct relieve from local money-lender towards the micro-entrepreneurs. The socio-economic conditions of rural population have helped to great extent through this scheme by improving their earnings, living standards and also minimising idle period of works. Despite of having all these benefits, the microfinance have also serious issues due to high rate of interest charge by the lenders and also rigorous methods of collection which result in suicide in Andhra Pradesh and other parts of the country few years back.

Having seen the problems facing the industry, this study was attempted for several reasons. It was felt that ample scope for self-employment as well as employment generation existed in this sector, if appropriate measures could be taken. This would be a blessing to a country where unemployment levels are very high and the population is growing at an explosive rate.

Since microfinance is mostly implemented in the rural, backward far-flung areas in general, improvements affected in these sectors will have its beneficial effects in such areas of the country. And finally, the urban and semi-urban centres in the country are experiencing rush from the rural and semi-urban areas for better living standards, jobs, thrills of big city life, etc. If the lot of micro-entrepreneurs could be improved in the backward areas this flow can be checked to some extent. Thus, attaining better growth of these backward areas and stoppage of flow of rural population to already crowded and poorly maintained towns and cities, more teeth should be given for promotion and development of microfinance industry. And, it is also believed that these findings will be helpful to policy-makers for better decisions.

Significance of the Study

In the developing world, micro-enterprises employ a significant share of the workforce, particularly of the female workforce, and generate a significant share of household income, particularly in low-income households. Several studies of the microfinance field provide a closer look at the impacts to service recipients and the significance of their micro-enterprise. In rural areas, self-employment provided by micro-enterprise through microfinance has become a means to alleviate the poverty in one side and unemployment in other side. And in urban areas where corporate and government downsizing on employment have affected to communities, micro-enterprise programmes are often able to reach potential entrepreneurs with increased efficiency and breadth of services.

Participation in different activities in Microfinance is positively associated with woman's empowerment such as physical mobility, economic security, ability to make various purchases on her own, freedom from domination and violence within the family, political and legal awareness, and participation in public protests and political campaigning.

Micro-enterprises play a critical role in the economic development of any economy, but particularly so in those economies which are undergoing a transition from the traditional subsistence to a modern industrial economy. It has been playing a prominent role in the socio-economic development of the country for the past two decades. The country accorded high priority to this sector on account of its employment generation potential, low requirement of capital, short gestation period, promotion of balance regional development, utilization of local resources of both human and raw materials, production of exportable products, the micro-enterprise sector will continue to play a significant role in eradicating poverty and promoting higher levels of gainful employment to reduce the problems of unemployment.

Micro-enterprise credit has become an increasingly popular development tool for addressing issues of poverty and unemployment. Since its birth in Asia in the early 1980's, it has spread to every corner of the globe (Ghate, 1992). In Bangladesh the "programmatic" success of the micro-credit scheme of Grameen Bank among poor women in Bangladesh became a demonstration of a successful development strategy (Rahman, 1998). It has proven very effective in providing support to street vendors, market vendors, and small-scale home-based businesses. Micro-enterprise credit is based on the premise that small loans made to individuals with little or no collateral can help sustain and develop self-employed initiatives (Berger *et al.*, 1989). A micro-enterprise is a business activity run by individuals or families with less than five workers (Lubell, 1991 and PREALC, 1978). The goods for sale are usually home-produced or purchased and sold in small quantities.

Micro-enterprises are considered as growth engine that triggers developmental process. They had emerged as a real boon to the poor those who are living below poverty line in one side and at the mercy of local money-lenders on the other side. Besides, solving the problems of unemployment and poverty, it helps to generate additional income for families. It trains them to acquire entrepreneurial ability to the younger generation and at the same time, obtain economic independence. Micro-enterprises sector is being accepted as key to sustainable economic growth.

In India, the micro and small industries sector has a long historical tradition and since independence has contributed significantly to the overall economic development of the country. During the last few years, Non-Governmental Organizations (NGOs) especially MFI and SHPI have begun to play a significant role in facilitating the poor to increase their income levels through micro-enterprises. MFIs prefer to give loans to women groups to ensure that repayment is prompt. Self-employment through micro-enterprises can play a considerable role in poverty alleviation for the millions of poor in the country. Women in India are having more integrity in financial matters. They are more responsible, hardworking. Dignity and honour are their credentials.

Hence, the present study has significant impact on the socio-economic development of the people of the state those who are living below poverty line. Establishment of micro-enterprises through microfinance scheme and financial linkage by banks and MFI, SHPI in the state shall enable to mitigate the alarming growth of unemployment problems of the state in particular and region and country in general.

Review of Literature

Throughout the world, poor people are excluded from formal financial systems. Exclusion ranges from partial exclusion in developed countries to full or nearly full exclusion in less developed counties. Absent access to formal financial services, the poor have developed a wide variety of informal; community based financial arrangements to meet their financial needs. In addition, over the last two decades, an increasing number of formal sector organizations have been created for the purpose of meeting those same needs. Microfinance is the term that has come to refer generally to such informal and formal arrangements offering financial services to the poor.

Scholarly interest in microfinance has lagged behind industry development, but it too is now growing rapidly. Before 1997, academic journals published only an occasional article on microfinance, but since that time, academic journals have published hundreds of peer reviewed articles on the topic. Nonetheless, microfinance has yet to break into finance journals. This despite the term finance in microfinance and the fact that the basic products offered by Microfinance Institutions (MFIs)—namely investing (savings), lending (credit services), and insurance (risk management)—are all well-established topics of mainstream finance research.

A literature is account of what has been published on a topic accredited scholars and researchers. The purpose of writing the literature review is to convey to the readers matters what knowledge and ideas have been established on a topic and what their strength and weaknesses are as. It is very difficult to review all the relevant studies since proper documentation of such studies is still to be ensured. Therefore, available relevant studies, particularly case studies, workshops, seminars and symposia, have been critically reviewed in the following few paragraphs.

Yarn (1994) underlined that the microfinance institutions remain most successful ones in terms of outreach and performance in delivering credit services to the poorest of the poor women, and small artisans in the rural and urban areas, reduction in adverse selection of borrowers, development of collateral substitutions, offering cost effective approaches to formal institutions.

Hal Kane (1996) many little things done in many little places by many little people will change the face of the world. Micro-enterprise offers an alternative to the conventional strategy for bringing development to poor nation making large loans to government for massive power or infrastructure projects. More investment in smaller local industries would bring economic and social benefits at far less cost.

Abdul Hayes et al. (1998) analysed the relationship between poor women's participation in micro credit programmes and their empowerment by taking both SHGs and non-SHGs members in rural Bangladesh.

Yunus (1999) revealed that when a destitute mother starts earning her dreams of success invariably centres on her children. When a destitute father earns extra income he focuses more attention on himself. Thus, money entering a household through a woman brings more benefits to the family as a whole.

Ahmad (1999) through a case study on Thrift Groups in Assam highlighted that women are coming to the administration directly for their just rights and to address their grievances boldly. It proved that Self-Help Groups are successful in North East India even in the midst of insurgency.

Nagayya (2000) maintains that an informal arrangement for credit supply to the poor through SHG's is fast emerging as a promising tool for promoting income generating enterprises. He has reviewed the initiatives taken at the national level with a view of institutional arrangements to support this programme for alleviation of poverty among the poor, with focus on women. He maintained that NABARD and SIDBI are playing a prominent role at various stages of implementation of this programme. There are other national level bodies also supporting NGOs/VOs, viz. Rastriya Mahila Kosh (RMK), Rashtriya Gramin Vikas Nidhi (RGVN) etc. He called for an imperative need to enlarge the coverage of SHGs in advance portfolio of banks as part of their corporate strategy, to recognize perceived benefits of SHGs financing in terms of reduced default risk and transaction costs.

Gurumoorthy (2000) maintained that SHG is a viable alternative to achieve the objectives of rural development and to get community participation in all rural development programmes. SHG is a viable organizational setup to disburse micro credit to the rural women for the purpose of making them entrepreneur and encouraging them to enter into entrepreneurial activities. Credit needs of the rural women can be fulfilled wholesomely through the SHG's. The women led SHG's have successfully demonstrated how to mobilize and manage thrift, appraise credit needs, maintain linkages with the banks and enforce financial self-discipline. SHG's enhance the equality of status of women as participants, decision-makers and beneficiaries in the democratic, economic and social and cultural spheres of life. They encourage women to take active part in the socio-economic progress of the society.

Malhotra (2000) in his study of 174 women beneficiaries, in Rae Bareilly of the State of Uttar Pradesh, drawn and covered randomly from four formal agencies of credit i.e. CB's, RRB's, PACS, and ARDB's revealed that less than half per cent of female population against 3.5 per cent of male population in the study area were clients of the banks. Furthermore, only 7.64 per cent of the total number of cases financed and only 6.96 per cent of the total quantum of credit extended by RFI's have gone to women. It was observed that 83 per cent of loan cases availed by women; male members were primarily responsible for the end use of credit.

Dasgupta (2000) in his paper on informal journey through Self-Help Groups observed that micro-financing through informal group approach has effected quite a few benefits viz,: (i) savings mobilized by the poor; (ii) access to the required amount of appropriate credit by the poor; (iii) matching the demand and supply of credit structure and opening new market for FI's; (iv) reduction in transaction cost for both lenders and borrowers; (v) tremendous improvement in recovery; (vi) heralding a new realization of subsidy less and corruption less credit, and (vii) remarkable empowerment of poor women. He stressed that SHGs should be considered as one of the best means to counter social and financial citizenship not as an end in itself.

Puhazhendhi *et al.* (2000) assessed the living conditions of SHG members after they were linked to banks. The study covered 560 member households of 223 SHGs from 11 states of the country. These states spanned the central, southern, northern, western and eastern regions of the country. The findings showed that the social impact of the post-SHG period was such that there was an increase in self-worth, in communication, an increased awareness of social evils (this was tested by asking questions about the abuse of women in films) and a small decrease in family violence.

Datta and Singh (2001) evaluated the impact of SHG on the income of the members taking BPL households without bank loan and BPL and APL households with bank loan in Punjab. It was observed that SHGs belong to the BPL households generated 70 per cent of the saving and the remaining by APL households.

Kallur (2001) analysed the impact of SHG supported by NGO namely MYRADA on women empowerment in Karnataka. It was found that the loans were taken for productive purposes, interest charged were high to cover the expenses of the group, the recovery rate was higher compared to formal credit and income generation is small.

Ragavendra (2001) studied three SHGs run by forward, SC/ ST and backward communities in Karnataka to assess the performance. He found member no longer borrow from moneylenders. It was suggested that with vision, participation and motivation, forward community SHGs could sustain in changing farm based activities into market basedactivities.

Rao (2001) in a comparative study on SHGs in Karnataka and Andhra Pradesh underlined that SHGs are sustainable, have replicating, stimulate saving and in the process-helped poor to come out of vicious circle of poverty. Claiming that more than 2 million poor families have been brought within the fold of formal banking sources, he held that SHGs concentration in Southern region.

Baonkar (2001) studied the impact of SHGs on women in Goa and observed that individual loans were mostly for productive purposes with cent per cent recovery. Monthly interest rate charged is high with 24 to 36 per cent but it goes to group fund. SHGs made a lasting impact on the lives of the poor and the quality of life is improved on the family in terms of increase in income, savings, consumption expenditure, gaining self-confidence, productive use of free time, getting opportunity to improve hidden talents. It has contributed to address poverty and unemployment and able to bring social transformation through economic development and social change.

Awasthi *et al.* (2001) in their study in Madhya Pradesh on the impact of SHGs on economic status of women observed that the SHG women were engaged in mahua, mushroom cultivation, amachur, papad making, nursery, etc. With the group loan at 2 to 4 per cent interest per month, they realized an increase in income and employment. SHGs have made a positive impact on creating leadership, improving literacy, consciousness about health and hygiene and skill formation among the group member. However, they suffered from lack of motivation, infrastructure, forward and backward linkages, insufficient loan, inadequate provision of marketing and inputs, lack of systematic monitoring and follow up etc.

Sale *et al.* (2001) in a case study of SHG in Maharashtra found that the SHG group loan was lent to income earning activities such as sheep and goat rearing, poultry, meeting medical and educational expenses. The revolving fund assistance improved their scale of operations and the repayment of 100 per cent. SHGs have inculcated a habit of thrift and fulfilled the needs on priority basis. Expansion of such of such operations would improve a lot of rural poor households.

Sethi (2001) in their study in Orissa found that the average group size was 14 and 82 per cent of the SHGs were formed by women. There has been an uneven growth of SHGs in all the regions. The per capita loan was very low at ₹ 177 per years. Only 28 per cent of the women were able to receive credit support from banks and quantum of credit support was in the ratio of ₹ 650 for ₹ 177 saving. It is suggested that more number of groups should be linked with the banks so that their credit support would be strengthened. Besides, intensive training and skill development may be offered to make the members independent and self-reliant.

Srinivasan *et al.* (2001) in their study on financial performance of rural and urban SHGs in Coimbatore district of Tamil Nadu with 50 SHGs in terms of recovery index, (ratio of total recovery to total lending) thrift credit ratio (ratio of total saving to total lending) and outstanding credit ratio (ratio of outstanding to total lending) revealed that the average membership was 17, the average savings were ₹ 16,333 and the average total lending was ₹ 17,537 and the average of defaults (₹ 956) were found to be higher in rural SHGs than in urban SHGs. Due to higher defaults, the rural SHGs showed lower recovery index (80%) and higher average outstanding credit ratio (0.14%) than the urban SHGs (87% and 0.09% respectively). The average thrift credit ratio of urban SHGs (0.91) was lower than the rural SHGs (0.93), implying that the overall financial performance of the urban SHGs was better than that of the rural SHGs.

Pawar *et al.* (2001) on the review of RRBs as SHPIs evaluated the performance of RRBs and found that the recovery rate was only around 40 per cent. In order to widen the outreach to the poor, an experiment to test the feasibility of an RRB working as SHPI was launched in 1994 in which the officers were entrusted with the additional responsibilities of promoting, nurturing and financing SHGs. The results were encouraging the recovery performance improved more than 60 per cent and hence RRBs linking with SHGs has been suggested as a right strategy to expand to other branches to improve the performance of RRBs.

Mishra and Hossain (2001) in their study to assess the impact of Mahila Mandals a rural SHGs in Orissa in terms of empowerment of rural women through participation and employment generation in the pre and post SHG periods, arrived at the fact that there is a considerable increase in the revolving fund, loan extended, grant availed, savings done etc. The loans were given both for consumption and social obligations. There is a considerable improvement in the socio-economic status in terms of literacy, housing conditions, food security to manage the lean season, nutritious level of food etc. in the post SHGs situation compared to pre-SHG period.

Dadhich (2001) in his study on micro finance a panacea for poverty alleviation analysed the performance of SHGs formed by Oriental Bank of Micro lending and underlined that the project has established beyond an idea of doubt that properly designed and effectively implemented microfinance can be a means not only to alleviate poverty and empower women but also be a viable economic and financial proportion.

Satish (2001) in his paper raise certain issues related to the functioning of SHG's. Adequate care should be taken to ensure homogeneity of socio-economic status of the members, while forming SHG's. The process of SHG formation has to be systematic whether a Bank or an NGO forms it. He emphasized that SHG's experiment has to be spread throughout rural India rather than being concentrated in a few pockets of the country. NGO's are more suited for forming and nurturing of the SHG's, and, therefore, it is essential to strengthen them and their resources so that they should increasingly undertake this work.

Borbora and Mahanta (2001) analysed the impact of micro-financing through SHGs taking the case of Rashtriya Gramin Vikas Nidhi in Assam and found that 80 per cent of the SHG members were from poor families, in the age group of 8 to 50 years. Their socio-economic status has increased after starting SHGs economic oriented activities.

Manimekalai and Rajeswari (2001) studied the impact of SHG

in creating women entrepreneurship in rural areas of Tamil Nadu by taking 150 SHG members. They found that the SHGs have helped to initiate micro-enterprises including farm and non-farm activate, trading and service units.

Harper (2001) in his study on Promotion of Self-Help Groups under SHG Bank Linkage Programme in India has examined and compared the different ways in which self-help promotion institutions promote Self-Help Groups. The study suggested that incentive schemes for NGOs and individual should be redesigned and tested in order to cover the full cost of SHPI. The management of the schemes to encourage SHG promotion should be experimentally delegated to banks in order to avoid the problems caused by NABARD's thin representation and to take full advantage of the banks greater field coverage.

Sharma (2001) maintained that through SHG's women empowerment is taking place. Their participation in the economic activities and decision-making at the household and society level is increasing and making the process of rural development participatory, democratic, sustainable and independent of subsidy, thus, macrofinancing through SHG's is contributing to the development of rural people in a meaningful manner.

Rao (2002) maintain that a review of the genesis and development of SHG's in India reveals that the existing formal financial institutions have failed to provide finances to landless, marginalized and disadvantaged groups. The origin of SHG's could be treated to mutual aid in Indian village community. SHG's are sustainable to have applicability, simulate savings, and in the process help borrower to come out of vicious circle of poverty.

NABARD (2002) in 11 states of India elucidated that there has been a positive result in enhancing the standard of living of SHG members in case of asset ownership. Savings and borrowing capacity, income generating activity and income levels have increased after joining SHGs and its economic oriented activities. The average value of asset including livestock and consumer durable has increased considerably. The housing condition of the people is improved, from the mud-walls to thatched roofs to brick walls and tiled roofs. Almost all members developed saving habit in the post SHG.

Dwarakanath (2002) analysed the characteristics and growth of Self-Help Groups in Andhra Pradesh and found that the SHGs using the loan facilities from the Cooperative Credit Banks, Commercial Banks, Mahila Bank and Maheswaran Banks, have produce more than 50 varieties of products.

Jothy and Sundar (2002) in their study of evaluation the programme of Tamil Nadu Mahalir Thittam found that SHG women are currently involved in economic activities such as production and marketing of agarbathis, candle and soap, readymade garments, pickles, appalam, vathal, fur toys, bags, palm leaf products dhotis, herbal products, fancy sea shell, ornaments, eatables, coir mats and other coir products, mattress, chapels, leather good etc.

Rajesekar (2003) analysed the impact of the economic programmes of SHARE, a NGO in Tamil Nadu on poverty reduction with the help of data collected from the households of 84 women members. The economic programmes have contributed to saving and income increase for the women. However, the member group was not found to be significantly different from the comparison group in terms of control over income and decision-making.

Chitanjaeevulu, (2003) the study entitle "Empowering women through Self-Help Groups, Experiences and Experiment" with an objective to found that women have developed abundant and self-esteem through SHG movement. Not only economic poverty but also social and gender issues can be tackled effectively through this process. Government and Non-Government agencies can play a proactive role in mobilizing, organizing and sustaining SHGs, necessary managerial, technical and marketing skills can be implemented to groups to enhance their livelihood opportunities.

Dutta and Neelakanta (2004) in their paper on Governance in Microfinance have discussed a case of BASIX. They are of the view that the governance is a pervasive entity eight strong intuitive appeal that yet somehow defies precise definition, whose essence, while clear, is somehow impossible to crystallize. Microfinance in deed any credit based activity faces certain unusual pre and post contractual problems such as adverse selection and moral hazard, which arise due to informational asymmetries and incompleteness, as well as imperfect commitment on the part of contracting parties. These problems are a sub-set of the general problem of any organization namely coordination and motivation, and necessitate the incurring of cost, called transaction cost, to solve these problems.

Basu (2005) in her paper on Scaling of Micro Finance for India's Rural Poor has reviewed the current level and pattern of access to finance for India's rural poor and has examined some of the key microfinance approaches in India, taking close look at the most dominant among these, the self-help group, bank linkage initiative. Her paper is based on a household survey supported by World Bank. The survey findings show that India's rural poor currently have a very little access to finance from formal sources. Microfinance approaches have tried to fill the gap. Among these, the growth of SHG Bank linkage has been particularly remarkable, but outreach remains modest in terms of the proportion of poor household served.

Burra, *et al.* (2005) in her edited volume on Micro Credit, Poverty and Empowerment have highlighted the SHG based microfinance and their impact on women empowerment in India. They presented analysis of case studies and modules of microfinance in India. They are of the view that collective strategies beyond micro credit to increase the endowments of poor women enhance their exchange outcomes *viz-a-viz* the family, state, markets and community, and expand socio-cultural and political spaces are required for poverty reduction and women's empowerment.

Kabir (2005) in her study on Microfinance has assessed the impact of microfinance on women's empowerment. The findings suggest that there is need for caution in talking about the impact of microfinance in general. Microfinance offers an important and effective means to achieving change on a number of different fronts, economic, social and political. The success of microfinance organizations in build up the organizational capacity of poor women provides the basis for their social mobilization that may other development interventions have not been able to achieve.

Ravat and Sumathi (2006) conducted a study to analyse the working of SHGs in Trichy district of Andhra Pradesh. They found women empowerment through the SHGs has increased their annual savings and enabled them to play an active role in getting loans and handling cash effectively.

Singh and Pandey (2007) in their study on Empowerment of Scheduled Caste Women have highlighted the impact of microfinance on socio-economic empowerment of Scheduled Caste women in Uttar Pradesh and Uttaranchal. They are of the view that SHG based microfinance is an instrument for overall economic empowerment of rural poor women.

Chander and Vanguri (2007) highlighted the impact of microfinance programmes on women's empowerment in India. They compared Swashakti, Swayamsiddha, Swaranjayanti Gramin Rojgar Yojana and Rashtriya Mahila Kosh microfinance programmes for facilitating rural poor women in their access to micro credit.

Shiralashetti and Hugar (2008), they strongly recommended that the developing countries which have poor people like India need microfinance for alleviating poverty. Because the institutional sources of finance generally finance on the basis of collateral security. But for this group of people they have no collateral security for getting finance from such institutions.

George (2008) opined that still moneylenders are dominated in the rural credit sector. So there is a need to shift the focus from the quantity of credit to the quality of credit by the MFIs. He also suggest that in order to achieve this, emphasis should be given to creation of adequate infrastructure, efficient extension services, processing and marketing facilities etc. It is also suggested that group lending should be encourage than individual lending.

Prabhu (2008), mention that MFIs will always have a comparative advantage over banks in being able to originate, monitor and collect microloans. Gunaranja Sai (2008), in his paper comment about the micro-insurance that a major roadblock for rolling out insurance products for the poor has been the gap between expectations of insurance companies about completing a certain kind of paper work for issuing insurance contracts and what the poor can actually provide.

Rambabu and Venkateshwarlu (2008), from their study in three region of Andhra Pradesh found that 23 per cent of members have brand names for their products whereas, the rest do not have. They have the brand name to the products like, candles, Napkins, papads etc. they also face the competition from the brands of national and MNC companies.

Gupta (2008), mention that the facilities provided by SHG-Bank linkage programme to the poor increases the socio-economic empowerment of rural women. There this programme has proved its efficacy as a mainstream programme for banking and emerged as one of the need-base policies and programmes to cater the neglected groups of society such as women, poor and deprived sections of rural areas.

Pandey (2008) has comment that due to the failure of formal banking system in meeting the credit needs of millions of rural and urban people increases the need of microfinance in India. He also mentions that microfinance is a programme for the poor and by the poor to mobilize the savings and use then to meet their financing needs.

Pangannavar (2008), Self-Help Groups programme is the right approach to create self-employment opportunities so as to supplement the income and assets of the rural poor. The SHG programme provides the rural poor women the access to micro-credit. It encourages rural women entrepreneurship and rural women empowerment.

Rao (2008), in his paper try to show the relationship between the financial inclusion and microfinance and he has mention that building an inclusive financial sector has gained growing global recognition bringing to the fore the need for development strategies that touch all lives, instead of a select few.

Shylendra (2008), there is a massive mobilization of women taking place as a result of the SHG movement. The growth of SHGs incidentally has occurred during the economic reforms period. The SHG movement has a good potential to serve both as a human face of the economic reforms as well as contribute towards women's emancipation.

Sriram (2008), comments that for the Grameen type of microfinance institutions, the subsidies on group formation of the SHGs are hidden because they are usually absorbed by the institution that promotes these groups and these institutions could be grant funded. Therefore the high interest rates have been justified.

Tangirala (2008), comments that the cooperatives are playing a tremendous role in the economic development of its members and in alleviation of poverty in the country. In the advent of the SHGs, the cooperatives have got another tool in its toolbox to quicken the process of developing the members financially.

Agrawal (2009), there has many challenges of micro-insurance in India and one of the major challenges is the acceptance of micro-insurance among the rural poor who not only have low levels of awareness about possible risks to their lives but also lake trust in most financial schemes structured for the long term with no immediate benefits. She also mention that non-availability of authentic admissible documentation during enrollment and claims processing and a lack of facilities for premium remittance further adds to the complexity in insurance administration in the remote and far flung pockets of India.

Ahirrao (2009) opined that small loans can make good business sense among the women. Microfinance gives women an independent means of generating wealth and becoming self-reliant in a society that does not offer them much scope for entrepreneurship.

Ranjan (2009), in their paper comment that Indian microfinance sector in recent years has been the establishment of networks of micro finance practitioners. These networks not only help in creating awareness but also help in formation, experience sharing, etc. These could also develop into a Self-Regulatory Organization of microfinance institutions.

Hema (2009) in their paper shows that rural poor are actually efficient managers of credit and finance. Therefore, availability of timely and adequate credit is essential for them to undertake any economic activity rather than credit subsidy.

Giresh (2009), comment that the SHG form of microfinance help in improving the socio economic status as well as the status of awareness and self-dependency of rural women.

Jennifer (2009) state that India was in danger of declaring microfinance a huge success while tens of millions of poor families continued to lack access to the most basic of financial services. She also comments that no doubt India is one of the most dynamic microfinance markets in the world. A combination of visionary social entrepreneurs, huge demand for microfinance services and the availability of local commercial debt capital has fuelled rapid and enviable growth in the sector. It is estimated that almost 55 million households are currently being reached by specialized microfinance institutions and through the NABARD-supported SHG approach.

Reddy (2009), in his article mention that more than 51 per cent of SHGs in Andhra Pradesh were financed by banks under SHG Bank Linkage programme and this programme increased the saving habit of SHG members.

Sharma (2009), microfinance is one of the ways for achieving financial inclusion and such a financial inclusion of the poor can be more fruitful if the credit disbursed can help them become entrepreneurs than meeting only their consumptions needs.

Gurmeet (2009) tries to show the importance of microfinance institutions in rural development and poverty eradication in his paper, "microfinance—an innovation in rural credit system". He also tries to show MFI is the most suitable credit institutions for the rural poor.

Srivastava (2009) opined that despite micro-credit being given priority in the institutional credit structure for several decades, its accessibility by the poor has not been fully achieved.

Das (2010), comment that microfinance has the capability of improving the standard of living by providing more means to raise money and it also increase the awareness among the women about the hygiene, importance of education, child care, sanitation etc. and Human Development Index (HDI). It is also mention that microfinance is not only associated with the giving loans but also associated with the rural economy.

Chakraborty (2010), comment that even though there has the government involvement in SHGs-based microfinance, still there are several drawbacks that need to be corrected. It is also mention that the biggest challenge in microfinance is to ensure whether the benefits of microfinance reach its true beneficiaries.

Rao (2011) identified that the rural women have now transformed their lives into full time and active entrepreneurs with lot to hope and are able to lead a life with self-esteem. And also mention that SHGs has become a powerful tool in bringing women together, in the remote rural areas and thus helped to emancipate the once mute sufferers in silence, to march forward towards collective community progress on a substantial basis.

Singh and Singh (2011) undertake a research work on Microfinance and Women empowerment-with special reference to Manipur. In their study it is found that Microfinance plays the important role in empowering specially women in the state. Despite of all the benefits derive from microfinance, the higher rate of interest has made beneficiaries a lame duck.

Singh (2012) in his research work on Microfinance in India: Boon or Bane has highlighted the opportunities emerging through microfinance as well as threat emerging out of microfinance. Charging higher rate of interest, harassment while collecting instalment from the microfinance clients, lack of proper control from the government side are few mention boon of microfinance in the discussion.

The review of studies pertaining to microfinance and women empowerment simply demonstrates that there has been significant contribution of self-help group based microfinance in the social change and empowerment of the poor. Moreover, microfinance activities promoted by either non-governmental organizations or government agencies have no doubt created opportunities for promotion of income generating activities and enhance income to the poor. However, most of the studies focus on specific issues and geographical regions. There is paucity of literature and empirical data, which provide basis for analysis of the impact of microfinance activities on women empowerment the national perspective. Thus, the present study attempts to assess the impact of self-help group based microfinance activities on women's empowerment in the national perspective.

From the above literature survey, it is found that when a women enters into the business activities, she has to face lot of problems like finance, marketing, management and maintenance. Women really contribute more time in income formation activities in comparison with men, but still their socio-economic conditions are deplorable. In the recent period SHG plays a vital role in the development of women entrepreneurs (micro enterprise). So, the present study analyses the problems and also SHGs really motivate the women entrepreneurs or not.

Objectives of the Study

The present study has covered the following important objectives:

- To make a macro level analysis of the performance of micro-finance sector in India and its prospects, given the current policy environment, from an international perspective.
- To find out the functioning of various Micro Finance Institutions and their role in linkage of finance with SHGs and banks in the state.
- To identify the successful rate of SHGs *vis-a-vis* individual entrepreneurs who have established their own/group's Micro-enterprise and its impact on poverty reduction, empowerment to women and employment generation.

- To evaluate the role of government for the development of micro-enterprise through microfinance in the state, and
- To know the different problems faced by the micro-enterprise units established under microfinance scheme and also find out the ways and means to short out the problems.

Hypotheses

The following hypotheses has been empirically tested:

1. NGO/MFI has taken important role to set up new micro-enterprises in the state.
2. After getting microfinance loan the income level of the micro-entrepreneurs have been increasing.
3. Microfinance beneficiaries have been reduced their poverty after getting microfinance loan.

Period of Study

The present study has covered a period of ten years starting from 2001-02 to 2011-12.

Research Methodology

Present study is mainly empirical in nature and based on primary data. Besides, collection and analysis of primary data, secondary data and pertinent literature has been compiled, analysed and reviewed accordingly. The main sources of secondary data and pertinent literature include published and documented sources including website. The microfinance institutes, Self-Help Group promotion institute, Non-Governmental Organisations and Microfinance promotion institutes have been consulted for collection of secondary data and literature. To make enable to study efficiently, following sub-heading have been divided, such as:

Universe of the Study

The present study has covered the entire state of Manipur. Hence, the universe of the present study is Manipur state covering all the nine districts such as Imphal East, Imphal west, Thoubal, Bishenpur, Ukhrul, Chandel, Senapati, Tamenglong, and Churachandpur.

Sample of the Study

It will be herculean task if we cover all the intermediaries who are directly and indirectly involve in the promotion of microfinance in the state of Manipur. Hence, the present study has covered 20 Self-Help Group Promotion Institutions (SHPI)/Micro Finance Institutions (MFI)/Non-Governmental Organizations (NGOs) operating in the state. Again from these 20 SHPI/MFI/NGOs, 104 Self-Help Groups have been selected for the study. Further, it is also covered another 200 micro-enterprise units (individual entrepreneurs) who are directly benefited from microfinance scheme.

Collection of Data

Primary data regarding functions and role of Microfinance for the development of micro-enterprise were collected directly through *In-depth Interview Schedule* used to interview the SHG leaders, NGO leaders and bank officials (collectively termed as decision-maker interviews) and *Structured Interview Schedule* from 200 beneficiaries who have started their own micro-enterprise unit. Besides, officials of the government agencies dealing with finance department in the state has also cover for the present study.

Secondary data has collected from the publications of various government agencies, both central and state and also of other organisations involved in promoting microfinance sector in the state. Further, it has also been collected data from books, annual reports, journals and website where found suitable data and information available. During the course of study, the researcher has visited national library at Kolkata, NEC Library Shillong, and other institutions and organisations deals with microfinance in the country.

Framework of Analysis

The collected data has carefully classified, tabulated, analysed, interpreted and presented in the form of report. In the process of analysis various statistical tools and techniques such as correlation analysis, regression analysis, per centage analysis, ranking analysis, F-test, and T-test analysis have been used for presentation where found necessary.

Analysis of Data

The filled in interview schedules were thoroughly checked, edited and processed in computer for the analysis. Inferences, results and conclusion have been drawn out from the analysis of data. The data in tabular form has been analysed, interpreted and discussed in the respective chapters. The policy recommendations are based on critical appreciation of pertinent literature and analysis of research findings. A few case studies of microenterprise have also been given in order to understand and achievement of the projects in the state.

Chapter Scheme

To reflect the different areas of Microfinance for Micro-enterprise development of the state, the present report is broadly divided into nine chapters, they are:

Chapter 1 is delves with the Microfinance highlighting the Historical Background of Microfinance; What Is Microfinance? Significance of Microfinance; top 20 microfinance institutions in the world; Contemporary of Microfinance such as Global Microfinance, Microfinance in Asia and Microfinance Resources.

Development of Microfinance is the title of the Chapter 2. This chapter covers the various emerging areas of microfinance such as gensis of SHGs; SHGs linkage; impact of SHGs on women empowerment; Microfinance Institutions; Microfinance Models at international as well as in Indian context; Microfinance and Micro-credit; Microfinance and Financial Inclusion; Microfinance and Micro-insurance; Microfinance and Micro-enterprise; Microfinance and primary agricultural credit societies

(PACS); Microfinance and Technology; Islamic Microfinance; and microfinance and shopkeepers.

The third chapter is deals on Microfinance in India highlighting on apex microfinance wholesalers; present status of microfinance; SHGs bank linkage programme; NABARD as facilators of microfinance; top 20 microfinance institution in India; significance of microfinance in Indian planning; government role in microfinance and challeges of microfinance regulation.

Microfinance in North East India is the title of fourth chapter covering microfinance scenario in north east India spreading to all the eight states of the region; demand and supply of microfinance in north east India; agencies-wise and state-wise progress of microfinance in north east India; and also the key stakeholders for microfinance development in North East India.

Chapter fifth is presented on Research Design covering various methods deals with the present research work. It covers Statement of Problem; Significance of the study; Review of literature; Objectives of the Study; Hypotheses; Period of study; Universe of the Study; Sample size; Chapter Scheme and Limitation of the Study.

Microfinance in Manipur is the title of Chapter six highlighting the main areas such as Historical Background of Microfinance in the state of Manipur; Microfinance and Local Moneylender; Microfinance and indigenous saving; District-wise allocation of Microfinance and its Development initiatives; District-wise Microfinance Promotion Institute like RGVN, RMK, and FWWBs etc.

Chapter seven devoted on the title Development of Micro-enterprise Manipur spreading into Micro-enterprise through government agencies and Micro-enterprise through Microfinance.

Data Analysis and interpretation is the title of the Chapter eight. The present data represent the analysis and interpretation ofMFIs/SHGs, Beneficiaries Micro-enterprise and finally hypothesis testing of the study.

Chapter nine give emphasis on Findings of the study, Recommendation and Conclusion.

Limitation of the Study

For any study based on primary data collection has encountered

few limitations. The present study is also no exception. In records, more than 70 MFIs are operating in the state but while visiting by the team of researchers most of them have already closed down and only few have found actively functioning in the state at present. Most of the SHGs as well as Micro-enterprises were not maintaining proper record and accounts, hence it has been considered as main challenges for the researchers to get the data required for the study at fullest extent possible.

Summary

The present chapter covered the design of the study spreading into objectives of the study, hypotheses, sample size, literature review, chapter scheme and also the limitation of the study.

Six
Microfinance in Manipur

> "The key to ending extreme poverty is to enable the poorest of the poor to get their foot on the ladder of development. The ladder of development hovers overhead, and the poorest of the poor are stuck beneath it. They lack the minimum amount of capital necessary to get a foothold, and therefore, need a boost up to the first rung."
>
> — *Jeffrey Sachs*

Introduction

Manipur is one of the industrially and economically backward states of North East India bordering with Myanmar in the east, Nagaland in the north, Mizoram in the south and Assam in the west. The economy of the state is mainly agrobase economy. More than 75 per cent of the total economy is contributed from the agriculture. Despite of rigorous effort made by the government to rise the economy from industrial sector, except small scale and micro-enterprises, other industrial sector has failed to contribute in the economy of the state. Among the micro and small enterprises, food processing and agro-processing base industries play the significant role in the contribution from the industrial sector to the economy of the state. In addition, handloom and handicrafts industries have also equally play the important role in the socio-economic development of poor people of those who are living below poverty line. The state is suitable for micro and small enterprises where low capital investment is required in one side and availability of large human resources in other side. Hence, development of such micro and small enterprises at large scale have a significant impact on the solution of unemployment problems of the state in particular and region and country in general.

The evolution of microfinance movement in the state had started since 1990s when the Rural Development Organization (RDO) started the setting up of SHGs and linkage with financial assistance through Revolving Fund Assistance under NABARD with a corpus fund of ₹ 50 lakh. Since then, many NGOs have come forward and taking initiation for setting up of SHGs and linkage with different model of Microfinance in the state. In the recent past, with the instruction of central government, many commercial banks, regional rural banks and cooperative banks in the state have been taking major role in the development of Microenterprise though Microfinance scheme.

There are approximately 20,000 SHGs, 76 NGOs-MFIs-SHPIs out of 541 NGOs are directly and indirectly working for the promotion and development of microfinance in the state. In Manipur microfinance activities are mainly contributed from the Model-II where SHGs are formed by formal agencies other than banks such as Non-Governmental Organizations (NGOs) and Community Based Organizations (CBOs), but is financed by banks. Whereas in other part of North Eastern states Model-I is popularly implemented where SHGs are formed and financed by banks. The contribution of Model–II is 51.77 per cent followed by Model-I with 19.56 per cent and Model-III with 0.52 per cent respectively in the state.

However, most of these SHGs and their members were utilized microfinance loan mainly for their consumption purpose such as to meet their day to day financial needs, children education, medical purpose and repayment of debt to local money lenders. Only a few of them have come out as micro entrepreneurs engaging in different economic oriented activities and also enable to escape from the grips of poverty. The prevailing successful rate of microenterprises through microfinance in southern state of the country has shown a significant impact on the alleviation of poverty. Poor people as well as government have more confident on it as important tool for poverty alleviation. Keeping in this view, the present area of study have been undertaken by the researcher as main problems of study.

Demographic Profile of Manipur

Manipur is one of the eight sisters state of North Eastern Region of India. It is an isolated hill-girt state stretching between 92°58'E to 94°45'E longitudes and 23°50'N to 25°42'N latitudes. The state has 352 kms long international border with Myanmar to the south-east and 502 kms long border with the adjacent states of Nagaland on the north, Cachar District of Assam on the west and Chin Hills (Myanmar) and Mizoram on the south and the south-west and Surma Tract and upper Chindwin of Myanmar on the East. Manipur has a geographical area of 22,327 sq.kms which constitutes 0.7 per cent of the total land surface of India. Ninety per cent of the total geographical area of the state i.e., 20,089 sq.kms is covered by hills; the remaining area is a small valley covering only 2,238 sq.kms and accounting for only one-tenth of the total area of the state. The state of Manipur splits up naturally into two tracts viz, the hills and the dales. The hill comprises of five districts namely, Chandel, Churachandpur, Senapati, Tamenglong, and Ukhrul while the valley consists of four districts viz., Bishnupur, Imphal East, Imphal West, and Thoubal.

According to 2001 census the population of Manipur was 22.9 lakh and the sex ratio was 974 female per 1000 male. For the recent census of 2011 it has been increased to 27.2 lakh of population with the sex ratio of 987 female per 1000 male. The population density of the state according to 2011 census is 122 persons per sq.km as against 103 persons per sq.km in 2001. The progress of urbanisation of the state is found to be very slow. The number of towns and cities has grown at a low rate. It has risen from 1 town in 1951 to 33 towns in 2001. But Manipur ranks second among the North Eastern State of India in respect of urbanisation. The urban population has increased from 5.06 lakh in 1991 to 5.76 lakh in 2001.

Banking Profile of Manipur

A well-developed banking system is the prerequisite for all other development activities of a state, region or a country. Manipur is no exception from this well-developed banking systems before undertaking any development activities both in rural as well as in urban areas. The profile of banking in the state is not encouraging in comparison with other states of the region. By the end of March, 2012 there were altogether 119 scheduled commercial banks branch offices in the state (SLBC report). The average population per bank offices of the state was about 22 thousand against about 38 thousands Average Population Per Bank Office (APPBO) in the year 2007.

Comparative Statement of Banking Key Indicators in Manipur

Below Table 6.1 highlighted the comparative statement of banking key indicators in Manipur since June 2009. There is steady growth of bank branches in the state from 97 in 2009 to 100 in 2010, 106 in 2011 and 122 in 2012.

Table 6.1: Comparative Statement of Banking Key Indicators in Manipur (As on June 30th)

Sl. No.	*Particulars*	*2009*	*2010*	*2011*	*2012*
1.	Total no. of branches	97	100	106	122
	• Rural	51	51	53	64
	• Semi-Urban	20	22	23	28
	• Urban	26	27	28	30
2.	Deposits (₹ in crore)	2837.92	3512.76	4164.79	
3.	Net Bank Credit	1358.78	1409.16	1720.81	
4.	C.D. Ratio (60%)	48	40	41	
5.	Priority Sector Advance	861.86	964.64	1080.51	
6.	% to P.S. Advance to NBC (40%)	63	68	63	

Source: 31st SLBC Meeting, Manipur.

District-wise Banking Status

According to 30th State Level Bankers' Committee Report, Manipur, there are 127 bank branches in the state. The distribution of bank branches in all 9 different districts of the state has been shown in the above Table 6.2. From the Table 6.2 it is understood that maximum numbers of bank branches are located in Imphal East and Imphal West district. The two districts covered the 45 per cent of the total bank branches in the state. Even though there has the highest number of bank branches in these two districts of the state, the maximum number of lack of customer access

Table 6.2: District-wise distribution of bank branches in the state as on 30th September 2012

Sl. No	District	Rural	Semi-urban	Urban	Total	CBs	RRBs	Co-op. banks	Total
1.	Bishnupur	8	1	0	9	3	3	3	9
2.	Chandel	5	1	0	6	4	2	0	6
3.	Churachandpur	6	6	0	12	10	1	1	12
4.	Imphal East	5	11	4	20	12	4	4	20
5.	Imphal West	7	4	28	39	27	5	7	39
6.	Senapati	14	0	0	14	9	4	1	14
7.	Tamenglong	7	0	0	7	3	3	1	7
8.	Thoubal	7	6	0	13	7	4	2	13
9.	Ukhrul	7	0	0	7	4	2	1	7
	TOTAL	66	29	32	127	79	28	20	127

Source: 31st SLBC Meeting, Manipur.

banking facilities from these two districts. Due to the high population per bank branches in the state many customers are queuing every day in the bank particularly in Imphal East and Imphal West districts. Another important reason for rushing to the bank branches of Imphal East and Imphal West districts are, maximum government offices and establishment are in these two districts, in addition to this these two districts are the most populated in the state. Still a large number of people who are in the villages and far from the district headquarter cannot access the normal banking facilities in this globalized world. Therefore, government should take more initiation for opening up of new bank offices in the state particularly where there are no bank branch offices.

Historical Background of Microfinance in Manipur

The banking profile of the state shows an insignificance growth in comparison with other neighbouring states of the region. The non-availability of banking facilities and other financial services were the root causes of growth of microfinance activities in the state.

Since time immemorial microfinance activities has been practicing in the state in different forms. It is very helpful to those poor people who could not bought small amount of capital for setting up of their business and other domestic purposes. Looking at the stages of evolution microfinance activities operating in the state, it can be broadly classified into (a) Traditional Microfinance and (b) Modern Microfinance.

Traditional Microfinance

Before 1992, small form of financing activities was practicing in the state in the form of cash, goods and kinds through 'Marup' literally known as 'friendship'. Under this system of traditional microfinance, either cash or goods are collected with equated instalment on daily, weekly and monthly basis from the members. The collected amount has been given to the needy person or through lottery basis so that receiver can start his or her small micro-enterprise units and repay back on instalment basis to the organiser of Marup on daily, weekly and monthly basis.

Modern Microfinance

In Manipur modern form of microfinance was started since 1992 by Loyalam Bank Project under Rural Development Organization (RDO), replica of the Grameen Bank Model with the support from Grameen Trust, Bangladesh; Revolving Fund Assistance (RFA) of National Bank for Agriculture and Rural Development (NABARD) and Rashtriya Mahila Kosh (RMK). Later NABARD started microfinance in the state since 1997 and now many NGOs and financial institutions like RMK, RGVN, FWWB, SIDBI, Commercial Banks, Cooperative Banks, and Regional Rural Bank (RRB), etc. are playing an integral role in promotion and development of microfinance. In addition to this, there are many private financial institutions and NGOs which provide microfinance services in the state.

The early and mid-1990s can be call the era of microfinance in the state because in this period the prominent and leading NGOs of the state have started their microfinance activities. Some of the prominent NGOs are Loyalam Bank Project (under RDO), The Youth Volunteers' Union (YVU), and Machaleima Microfinance, etc.

According to NGO partnership system, Planning Commission, Government of India (August 2012; *http://*

ngo.india.gov.in/ngo_state schemes_ngo.php) there were 44,361 VOs/NGOs signed up on the NGO-PS in India out of this 1,017 VOs/NGOs were in Manipur. Manipur stood the second largest number of NGOs in North-East India next to Assam. More than 50 per cent of them have started with the activities including microfinance in the state. But the sorry figure is that most of them were not undertaking microfinance activities in the state. Hence, the figure between registered VOs/NGOs microfinance and current VOs/NGOs microfinance has shown quite different from the original. Due to unorganized nature of microfinance functioning in the state, it is very difficult to find out the exact number of MFIs or NGOs deals with microfinance in the state. For the present study the researcher has try to find out by collecting all information from the reliable sources like., ICM, NGO Forum Manipur, NEDFi, RMK, RGVN, NABARD, SIDBI, SLBC's reports and information from related NGOs etc.

Progress Under SHG-Bank Linkage

Table 6.3 given below explains the district-wise progress of microfinance under SHG-Bank linkage model in Manipur during 2011 and 2012 with target, deposit linkage and achievement

Table 6.3: District-wise Progress of Microfinance Under SHG Bank Linkage in Manipur

District	*As on 30-09-2011*			*As on 30-09-2012*		
	Target	*Deposit linkage*	*% Achieve-ment*	*Target*	*Deposit linkage*	*% Achieve-ment*
Bishnupur	120	29	24	170	25	15
Chandel	85	112	132	130	59	45
Churachandpur	85	112	132	150	33	22
Imphal East	190	112	59	395	109	28
Imphal West	399	328	82	860	233	27
Senapati	500	209	42	430	63	15
Tamenglong	35	21	60	140	50	36
Thoubal	150	150	100	280	51	18
Ukhrul	72	33	46	150	109	73
TOTAL	1636	1106	68	2705	732	27

Source: State Level Bankers' Committee Meeting Manipur (28th & 32nd).

parameters. There was a poor performance in 2012 as compared with 2011 performance of the state. Among the districts Churachandpur and Chandel districts have performed better with 132 per cent achievement each in the year 2011. However, during 2012, the performance of both the districts have come down to 22 per cent and 45 per cent respectively. Ukhrul district emerge the first in rank with 73 per cent. Among the valley districts, Thoubal district with 100 per cent achievement in 2011 and Imphal east district with 28 per cent achievement in 2012.

District-wise Position of Self-Help Groups in Manipur

District-wise position of Self-Help Groups in Manipur have been presented in Table 6.4. As on 30th September 2012 there were 22,183 SHGs formed in Manipur of which 20,913 had taken up economic oriented activities and 19,626 SHGs were purely formed by the women groups.

Table 6.4: District-wise Position of Self-Help Groups in Manipur as on 30.09.2012

Sl No	District	No of SHGs formed		No of women SHGs		No of SHGs taken up economic activities	
		No.	%	No.	%	No.	%
1	Bishnupur	2281	10.28	2051	10.45	2154	10.30
2	Chandel	948	04.27	866	04.41	906	04.33
3	Churachandpur	1533	06.91	1256	06.41	1492	07.13
4	Imphal East	2431	10.96	2097	10.68	2192	10.48
5	Imphal West	5438	24.51	4344	22.13	4935	23.60
6	Senapati	3507	15.81	3362	17.13	3433	16.42
7	Tamenglong	662	02.98	593	03.02	631	03.01
8	Thoubal	4083	18.41	3889	19.82	3911	18.71
9	Ukhrul	1300	05.86	1168	05.95	1259	06.02
	TOTAL	22183	100	19626	100	20913	100

Source: 32nd SLBC Report, Manipur.

Among the districts, Imphal west district has formed the largest SHGs with 5,438 followed by Thoubal district with 4,083 SHGs, 3,507 SHGs in Senapati district and Imphal east district with 2,431 SHGs respectively. Tamenglong district has only 662 SHGs of the total SHGs formed in Manipur.

Microfinance and Local Moneylender

Moneylender lends the small and micro amount of money to the borrowers But they are different from microfinance because there is no rule and regulation of moneylender and they have charged the interest whatever they want looking at the advantage of needy clients. There is no other facility from them except money borrowing facility. Even though moneylender has provided the micro-credit they are quite different from microfinance because microfinance has provided different services for the beneficiaries unlike moneylenders do.

Microfinance and Indigenous Saving

As we know microfinance includes the services provided by a normal commercial bank but in the small quantity such as financing, saving, insurance, credit, etc. Even all these have not exist in the Manipuri society in the early time, the people of the state have the habit of small saving and lending of money after collection of small amount of contribution from a group of people which are made themselves. The saving and lending models in traditional ways have been discussed separately as under.

Traditional Saving: There is a habit of saving among the people of Manipur since time immemorial particularly among the women folk. Saving can be broadly classified into two i.e., *money saving* and *property saving* base on its nature. In Manipuri society women have been taking the main role in family management. In comparison with men they have a good family management skill. They carefully manage money and materials which are used in day-to-day life particularly in family management.

- *Money (coin) Saving:* For the saving of money in the ancient time, they used some traditional model such as saving at bamboo hole, making a hole nearby fireplace of house (type of piggy bank) and piggy bank etc. In the early time most of the houses were built up by bamboo. So people use to make a hole to one of the bamboo pillars of the house and some coins every day or whenever, they have. They withdraw the whole coins and invest it to their new property or business when the opportunity prevails. This type of saving is commonly used in the early time and still it is practicing in rural areas which are far from the city and where no banking facilities are availed.

Another form of money saving which have been commonly used in the early time is saving to the fire place in the house. This type of saving is bound by the religion and tradition of Manipuri society especially in Meitei community. Traditionally in every household of the Meitei society they have a tradition to maintain a *Phunga* (traditional fire place in the house) where people believe the *Emoinu* (Goddess of wealth) exist. Just nearby this *Phunga* they make a place for worship with a piggy bank where the coin drops at the time of worship every day. When the piggy bank is full or occasionally they use that money for the purchase of new item and other purpose of the family too.

- *Property Saving*: Not only saving money, but also people of Manipur had the habit of saving their day-to-day consumable food items too. As a tradition and believe while preparing the food for both meal of a day they retain one or three handful of rice from the share of the day. They have believed that if they do like this there will have no insufficient food throughout the year and they will live with enough food. Though it is traditional believe it is true because if there is retain of one or three handful of rice every meal than after some days with that small quantity of rice accumulated will become a share of a meal and so. Therefore, it is the methods of saving property in the traditional way.

Microfinance Promotion Institutions in Manipur

In the previous paragraphs, we have discussed about the growth and evolution of microfinance in the state. Despite of its late entrance, the pace of microfinance development in the state is very impressive in comparison with other neighbouring state of the region. Various government agencies, INGOs, VOs, NGOs, commercial banks and other private financial institutions plays the important role in promotion and development of microfinance in the state. Following paragraphs explain the role of various microfinance promotion institutions in the state.

NABARD

National Bank for Agricultural and Rural Development (NABARD) is an apex body and playing a key role for the promotion and development of microfinance in the state since 1992 when the first microfinance institutions Rural Development Organisation started functioning microfinance activities in the state. NABARD has been taking a significance role in microfinance development through schedule commercial banks in the state. Table 6.5 shows the performance of commercial banks, Manipur Rural Banks and Cooperative banks in the state.

SIDBI

Small Industries Development Bank of India is another Microfinance promotion institutions keenly operating in the state for the promotion and development of microfinance. Table 6.6 shows the sanction and disbursement of funds allocated for microfinance along with grants in aid from 1995 to 2012 with a total disbursement of ₹ 7.54 crore against the sanction of ₹ 8.54 crore.

Rashtriya Mahila Kosh (RMK)

Instituted under the National Credit Fund, Rashtriya Mahila Kosh, the first and the only scheme for the welfare of the women in India was implemented by the Union Ministry of Women and Child Development in 1993. The benefit of the Rashtriya Mahila Kosh (RMK) scheme has been already extended to around 2700 women in Manipur, nodal officer of Rashtriya Mahila Kosh has appealed to all the people for co-operation in ensuring that the implementation of the scheme may be expanded to cover more beneficiaries.

Organisations like NGOs, VOs, WDCs, COSs, Indira Mahila Block Samitis, agencies of the State Government, Urban Co-operative Banks and VAs which have a track record of working for the welfare of the women in society and registered under the Rashtriya Mahila Kosh for a minimum of three years are entitled to get the loan. At present, 31 organisations in Manipur have been given the permission for granting the loan under the Rashtriya Mahila Kosh.

Table 6.5: Progress under Microfinance – Savings of SHGs with Banks Agency-wise position of Manipur as on 31 March 2012 under NABARD

(Amount ₹ lakh)

Sr. No.	Year	Commercial Banks		Manipur Rural Banks		Cooperative Banks		Total	
		No. of SHGs	Loan Disbursed Amount	No. of SHGs	Loan Disbursed Amount	No. of SHGs	Loan Disbursed Amount	No. of SHGs	Loan Disbursed Amount
1	2007-08	3449	213.17	4496	154.78	–	–	7945	367.95
2	2008-09	4803	121.71	4671	70.07	–	–	9474	191.78
3	2009-10	4973	118.44	4723	80.00	1135	20.12	10831	218.56
4	2010-11	5027	145.18	5279	95.05	0	0.00	10306	240.23
5	2011-12	5955	103.34	5784	106.06	972	9.98	12711	219.38

Source: Annual Report NABARD, 2012.

Table 6.6: Financial Assistance under Microfinance by SIDBI in Manipur From 1995-2012

(₹ in '000)

Date of sanction	*Name of NGO/MFI*	*Sanction*		*Disbursement*	
		Loan	*Grant*	*Loan*	*Grant*
11.02.93	Youth Volunteers Union (MFN)	750	350	750	350
09.01.95	All Manipur Women's Social Reformation & Development Society	100	—	100	—
05.09.95	National Association of Fisherman	384	25	384	25
27.02.96	Youth Volunteers Union-SFMC I, Thoubal, Manipur	450	50	450	50
31.12.96	Sugnu Kendra Ex-Serviceman Multipurpose Development Assn	114	25	114	25
31.12.96	The Top Makha Leikai Embroidery and Tailoring	125	25	125	25
31.03.00	Youth Volunteers Union-SFMC II, Thoubal, Manipur	2000	250	2000	250
28.10.02	Youth Volunteers Union-CB, Thoubal, Manipur	—	550	—	550
08.02.05	Youth Volunteers Union-SFMC III, Thoubal, Manipur	1500	600	1500	600
02.05.06	Youth Volunteers Union-FCB, Thoubal, Manipur	—	325	—	325
24.01.07	Youth Volunteers Union-SFMC IV, Thoubal, Manipur	10,000	1600	10,000	1600
29.08.08	Youth Volunteers Union-SFMC V, Thoubal, Manipur	20,000	1450	20,000	1450
27.03.09	WSDS Initiate	2500	—	2500	—
14.03.11	Youth Volunteers Union-SFMC VI, Thoubal, Manipur	20,000	—	10,000	—
23.03.10	Chanura Microfin Manipur	2500	—	2500	—
17.09.12	Youth Volunteers Union-SFMC II, Thoubal, Manipur	20,000	—	20,000	—
30.10.12	Chanura Microfin, Manipur	5000	—	5000	—
	Total	85,423	5250	75,423	5250

Source: SIDBI, Imphal Branch.

Rastriya Grameen Vikash Nidhi (RGVN) (Northeast) Microfinance Ltd

Rastriya Grameen Vikash Nidhi (RGVN) is a pioneer Microfinance Institution operating in Northeast and other parts of the country. It provides financial assistance and technical support to all the states of the region for the promotion of microfinance. Table 6.7 depicts the commitment and disbursement of finance under NGO microfinance in Manipur during 2008-09 and 2009-10. It was ₹ 31.80 lakhs and ₹ 27.95 lakhs disbursed during the year 2008-9 and 2008-10 for the promotion of microfinance in the state.

Table 6.7: RGVN Commitment and Disbursement of Finance under NGO-MF in Manipur

(₹ in lakh)

Year	Proposal	Cmmitment			Disbursement		
		RG	NRG	Total	RG	NRG	Total
2008-09	12	51.73	0.00	51.73	31.80	0.00	31.80
2009-10	6	77.525	0	77.525	27.95	0	27.95

Source: Annual Reports, 2009-10, RGVN.

Friends of Womens World Banking (FWWB)

Understanding the Clients of Microfinance a Household Level Studies has been conducted in Manipur (March 2009). The centrality of clients' lives and livelihoods to microfinance is one of FWWB's major research themes currently. We began our research efforts in this area with a series of studies among the clients of our partners in the north-eastern region. This study had conducted in three microfinance organisations in Manipur– Weaker Sections Development Society (Initiate), Chanura Microfin, and Organisation for Rural Improvement (ORI).

Weaker Sections Development Society (WSDS) initiate operates in more than 80 villages spread across the hilly district of Senapati. It became a partner of FWWB India in 2007 when the later extended its activities in the North East as part of a new initiative that focuses on underserved regions. WSDS has a mandate to attend to the special economic issues that face the hills of Manipur through diverse activities related to NRM, microfinance and micro-enterprise development, community health and social security. Unlike WSDS, Chanura and ORI work in the valley region comprising of the districts of Imphal East and West, Bishnupur and Thoubal. REEP is the MF programme of the Organisation for Rural Improvement and has been in operation since 2003-04 replicating the Grameen methodology. Chanura is a newer organisation having commenced its microfinance operations in April 2007. This too is the MF programme of an NGO, Rural Agricultural and Industrial Development (RAID) Centre, and works mainly in the Imphal East and West districts. Chanura works in both rural and semi-urban areas, whereas REEP has an exclusive rural focus. Both the organizations share a common vision of enhancing the economic status of the poorer households in Manipur by working through the women.

International Fund for Agricultural Development (IFAD)

International Fund for Agricultural Development (IFAD) is an organisation taking important role in undertaking different activities for the promotion and development of rural in backwards and hilly region of the country. The scheme has been starting in selected states and districts of the country. In Manipur, Ukhrul district and Senapati district have been introducing this schemes few years (1999) back funded by IFAD head office Rome. Along with other different rural development activities, microfinance is also provided to SHGs directly and through ACCORD in Senapati project and UDWIM in Ukhrul projects. Table 6.8 is the financial assistance sanction for the promotion and development of microfinance in these two districts of Manipur.

Year-wise financial assistance under International Fund for Agricultural Development in two districts of Manipur is shown in Table 6.8. UDWIM and UDCRMS has been given financial assistance since 2005-06 till 2012-13 except two years i.e., 2008-09 and 2009-10. On the other hand ACCORD, SEDCORMS has been started its microfinance funding since 2009-10 till 2012-13.

Table 6.8: Financial Assistance by IFAD for Microfinance in Manipur

Year	UDWIM, Ukhrul		ACCORD Senapati	
	No. of SHGs	Amount in ₹	No. of SHGs	Amount in ₹
2005-06	260	26,00,000	NA	NA
2006-07	240	30,20,000	NA	NA
2007-08	477	1,21,37,000	NA	NA
2008-09	—	—	NA	NA
2009-10	—	—	127	65,70,000
2010-11	201	1,00,63,350	167	78,50,000
2011-12	221	78,05,350	184	1,22,45,000
2012-13	276	91,67,500	140	1,37,90,000

Source: UDCRMS and SEDCORMS, IFAD Project Manipur.

Financing of SHGs in Manipur through Commercial Banks

All commercial banks such as SBI, UBI, CBI and BOI including MRB and cooperative banks play the important role in financing microfinance in the state over the last few years. Table 6.9 highlights the financing of SHGs by the commercial banks operating in the state in cumulative figure from 2009 to 2012. The number of SHGs covered by commercial banks has increased from 7,229 in 2009 to 10,555 in 2012. Further, it has been seen that the amount of financing also increased from ₹ 3216.38 lakhs in 2009 to ₹ 5,387.26 in 2012.

Table 6.9: Financing of SHGs in Manipur by all Commercial Banks in cumulative as on 30th June

(*₹ in Lakh*)

2012		2011		2010		2009	
No.	Amount	No.	Amount	No.	Amount	No.	Amount
10555	5387.26	9044	4246.84	8111	3746.88	7229	3216.38

Source: 27th and 31st SLBC Report, Manipur.

Commercial Banks Financing under SHGs in Manipur

Bank-wise performance of financing under SHG in Manipur as on 30th September 2012 is shown in Table 6.10. United Bank of

India and State Bank of India were the two lead banks in the state and occupied the major contribution for the promotion of microfinance in the state. SBI and UBI have a deposit linkage with the SHGs during the year with 9,305 SHGs and 3,493 SHGs respectively. Further, the credit linkage to SHGs by the two commercial banks was ₹ 2,987.86 and ₹ 3,540.78 respectively. Out of the total 5,805 SHGs linkage with credit, 2,076 and 3,729 SHGs were linkage under SGSY and direct SHGs respectively.

Manipur Rural Banks

Manipur Rural Banks has also play the important role in financing microfinance in the state. As on 30th September, the rural bank of Manipur provide the direct credit linkage to 4,735 SHGs with an amount of ₹ 1,451.74 lakhs whereas only 11 SHGs with an amount of ₹ 11.75 lakhs SHGs linkage under SGSY in the state.

Table 6.10: Financing under SHGs in Manipur by Commercial Banks as on 30th September 2012

(Amount ₹ in Lakhs)

Bank	*Deposit Linkages*		*Credit Linkages*					
			Under SGSY		*Direct SHGs*		*Total*	
	No.	*Amount*	*No.*	*Amount*	*No.*	*Amount*	*No.*	*Amount*
ALB	63	2.00	0	0.00	5	1.23	5	1.23
AXIS	0	0.00	0	0.00	0	0.00	0	0.00
BOB	550	110.98	111	82.00	171	43.00	282	12.500
BOI	0	0.00	0	0.00	0	0.00	0	0.00
CBI	359	9.11	72	108.93	50	75.25	122	184.18
HDFC	0	0.00	0	0.00	0	0.00	0	0.00
ICICI	0	0.00	0	0.00	0	0.00	0	0.00
IOB	25	0.24	15	18.60	10	6.55	25	25.15
PNB	219	23.05	37	5.97	19	2.11	56	8.08
PSB	29	0.55	11	1.98	0	0.00	11	1.98
SBI	9305	572.35	736	670.81	3376	2317.05	4112	2987.86
UBI	3493	1116.08	989	344.43	23	10.35	1012	3540.78
UCO	266	9.91	103	71.50	25	59.24	128	130.74
VJB	62	26.31	2	2.50	50	50.00	52	52.50
ACSB Total	14371	1870.58	2076	1306.72	3729	2564.78	5805	3871.50

Source: 32nd SLBC meeting Manipur.

Table 6.11: Financing under SHGs in Manipur by Manipur Rural Banks as on 30th September 2012

(Amount ₹ in Lakhs)

Deposit Linkages		*Credit Linkages*					
		Under SGSY		*Direct SHGs*		*Total*	
No.	*Amount*	*No.*	*Amount*	*No.*	*Amount*	*No.*	*Amount*
6173	108.50	11	11.75	4724	1439.99	4735	1451.74

Source: 32nd SLBC meeting Manipur.

State Co-operative Banks

There are four branches of cooperative banks operating in the state such as Imphal Urban Cooperative Banks, Manipur State Cooperative Bank, Moirang Primary Cooperative Banks and Manipur Women Cooperative Bank. All the cooperative banks were actively financing microfinance to the beneficiaries in the state. Table 6.12 highlight the financing under SHGs in Manipur by Cooperative banks as on 30th September 2012.

Table 6.12: Financing under SHGs in Manipur by Co-operative Banks as on 30th September 2012

(Amount ₹ in Lakhs)

Co-op Banks	*Deposit Linkages*		*Credit Linkages*					
			Under SGSY		*Direct SHGs*		*Total*	
	No.	*Amount*	*No.*	*Amount*	*No.*	*Amount*	*No.*	*Amount*
IUCB	413	5.03	0	0.00	131	23.03	131	23.03
MSCB	1621	22.39	47	117.50	5	1.15	52	118.65
MPCB	62	0.25	62	54.75	8	4.00	70	58.75
MWCB	5	0.05	0	0.00	5	0.50	5	0.50
Co-op Total	2101	27.72	109	172.25	149	28.68	258	200.93

Source: 32nd SLBC meeting Manipur.

Development Initiatives

Microfinance is an important tool for alleviation of poverty. Keeping this in view, Central Government and Government of Manipur have been taking various development initiative for the promotion and development of microfinance in the state. To implement the various microfinance promotion schemes, NABARD, SIDBI, Commercial Banks, Manipur Rural Banks and Cooperative Banks have taken lead role. Besides, RMK, RGVN, FWWB, and other microfinance promotion institutions also took initiative for microfinance development in the state. However, the expected level of development have not achieved in the state.

Summary

Microfinance in Manipur is started with the initiation of Rural Development Organisation during 1990s under NABARD and Grameen Bank Bangladesh. Loyalam Bank Project is the replica of Grameen Bank Model of Bangladesh of Rural Development Organisation, Manipur. Since then, the movement of microfinance in Manipur has started. Today, various microfinance promotion institutes/agencies such as NABARD, SIDBI, RMK, RGVN, FWWB and commercial banks are taking keen interest for the promotion and development of microfinance along with NGO-MFIs in the state.

Seven

Development of Micro-Enterprise in Manipur

> "Small loans can transform lives, especially the lives of women and children. The poor can become empowered instead of disenfranchised. Homes can be built, jobs can be created, businesses can be launched, and individuals can feel a sense of worth again."
>
> —*Natalie Portman*

Introduction

India is the second largest populated country in the world next to China. Poverty is predominantly rural in character and is more pronounced among vulnerable groups like schedule castes, schedule tribes and other backward women in the country. These social groups belong to landless and small farming classes, experience unemployment and are dependent on wage employment. Mostly they are engaged in low production activities of agriculture and other allied activities. Therefore, the poverty alleviation needs increase in agricultural productivity and transfer of substantial proportion of labour-force from farm-sector to non-farm sector including other more productive employment areas. The most commonly adopted poverty alleviation approaches have been state-driven, donor-funded and top-down approach. However, many cultural, economic and political barriers effectively prevent the poor from having any real stake in development activities. Therefore, reaching the poor requires working with them to learn about their needs, understanding how development decisions are made in their communities and identifying institutions and mechanisms that can get opportunities and resources into their own hands.

In India, over 260 million populations are falls under the category of poverty. The poor are victims and sufferers of high level of unemployment, low level of income, and significant debt. Many of them are trapped in this financial position. They rarely can offer collateral against their loans and therefore are continually denied access to formal credit institution. Even when loans are awarded, high interest rate and unrealistic repayment schedules leave families unable to escape the poverty cycle.

In this context, micro-enterprises have been recognized for their significant role in poverty alleviation by creating self-employment opportunities, supplementing agricultural income, linking agricultural households to local markets through the sale and exchange of products and providing a source of employment for household members where wage employment is scarce.

Micro Enterprises Development through Microfinance

Micro-enterprises are consider as an integral part of any developing economy. World over, micro or small enterprises are an important source of livelihoods for majority of the people. This section is devoted to understanding the role of micro enterprise in development and specifically the relationship between microfinance and micro-enterprise development strategy. We also review some studies that have looked at the impact of micro-enterprise development on poverty and livelihood promotion. The objective is to gain more insight and understand factors that determine how microfinance programmes help in establishing and sustaining enterprises.

The Micro, Small and Medium Enterprises (MSME) sector is an important pillar of the Indian economy by way of creating employment of about 70 million through 30 million units, manufacturing more than 6,000 products, contributing about 45 per cent to manufacturing output and about 40 per cent of exports, directly and indirectly for earning foreign exchange for positive balance of payment.

Understanding Micro Enterprises

Micro-enterprises are referred to as home based work or self-employment taken up on a small scale. Researchers have identified these enterprises as businesses operated by poor or group of poor people with support of sponsoring organizations and operated either by individuals or individuals along with their family members (Midgley, 2008). As micro enterprises are overwhelmingly operated by poor, it is one of the significant livelihood promotion strategies adopted across the world.

According to ADB Report 1997, the major objectives of micro-enterprise development projects are, "poverty alleviation, women empowerment, employment generation and enterprise development"

Micro-enterprises can be developed under two different frameworks such as (i) livelihood promotion, and (ii) growth oriented enterprise development. Livelihood promotion programmes have main objective of poverty reduction and in the process the programmes help to increase the productivity of the enterprises. Growth oriented micro-enterprise programmes, on the other hand, have main objective of enterprise development. These programmes attempt to have micro-enterprises to achieve the high level of sustainability and long-term growth by providing services like training, technical assistances, credit and business skill. Given the nature of these two approaches, it is seen that the livelihood programmes make a short-term impact on poverty by creating self-employment whereas growth oriented micro-enterprise development programmes make long-term impact on poverty. However, the problem with long term growth oriented programme strategy is that it reaches only a smaller number of enterprises. Livelihood promotion programmes on the other hand can reach much higher number of poor people (ADB Report 1997, pp. 9).

Definition of Micro, Small and Medium Enterprises

In accordance with the provision of Micro, Small and Medium Enterprises Development (MSMED) Act, 2006 the Micro, Small and Medium Enterprises (MSME) are classified in two classes:

(a) *Manufacturing Enterprises*: The enterprises engaged in the manufacture or production of goods pertaining to any industry specified in the first schedule to the industries (Development and Regulation) Act, 1951. The Manufacturing Enterprise is defined in terms of investment in Plant and Machinery.

(b) *Service Enterprises:* The enterprises engaged in providing or rendering of services and are defined in terms of Investment in equipment.

The limit for investment in plant and machinery/equipment for manufacturing/service enterprises, as notified vide S.O. 1642(E) dated 29-09-2006 are as under:

Manufacturing Sector	
Enterprises	*Investment in plant and machinery*
Micro-Enterprises	Does not exceed twenty five lakh rupees
Small Enterprises	More than twenty five lakh rupees but does not exceed five crore rupees
Medium Enterprises	More than five crore rupees but does not exceeds ten crore rupees
Service Sector	
Enterprises	*Investment in equipment*
Micro-Enterprises	Does not exceed ten lakh rupees
Small Enterprises	More than ten lakh rupees but does not exceed two crore rupees
Medium Enterprises	More than two crore rupees but does not exceed five crore rupees.

Fig. 7.1: Category of Enterprise and Investment

Micro, Small and Medium Enterprises (MSME)

The Micro, Small and Medium Enterprises (MSME) sector has been recognised as engine of growth all over the world. Many countries of the world established a SME Development Agency as the development of this sector. In the case of India, also Medium establishment has for the first time been defined in terms of separate Act, governing promotion and development of Micro, Small and Medium Enterprises (MSME), i.e. Micro Small and

Medium Enterprises (MSME) development Act, 2006 (which has come into force from 2nd October, 2006) the Office of Development Commissioner (Micro, Small and Medium Enterprises) functions as the nodal Development Agency under the Ministry of Micro, Small and Medium Enterprises (MSME).

Office of Development Commissioner (SSI) was established in 1954 on the basis of the recommendations of the Ford Foundation. Over the years, it has seen its role evolve into an agency for advocacy, hang holding and facilitation for the small industries sector. It has over 70 offices and 21 autonomous bodies under its management. These autonomous bodies include Tool Rooms, Training Institutions and Project-cum-Process Development Centres. Office of the Development Commissioner (MSME) provides a wide spectrum of services to the Micro, Small and Medium Industrial sector. These include facilities for testing, tormenting, training for entrepreneurship development, preparation of project and product and energy audits etc. Office of the Development Commissioner (MSME) provides economic information services and advises Government in Policy formulation for the promotion and development of SSIs. The field offices also work as effective links between the Central and the State Governments.

Consequent to the increased globalization of the Indian economy, MSMEs are required to face new challenges. Office of the Development Commissioner (MSME) has recognised the changed environment and is currently focusing on providing support in the fields of credit, marketing, technology and infrastructure to MSMEs.

Table 7.1: Working MSMEs with their Employment, Fixed Investment and Production of Manipur as on 2011-12

Year	*No. of Enterprise*	*Employment (person)*	*Fixed Investment (₹ in crore)*	*Production (₹ in crore)*
2006-07	4492	19960	96.76	199.80
2007-08	4530	20129	97.58	201.49
2008-09	4670	20751	100.59	207.72
2010-11	4759	21146	102.51	211.68
2011-12	4881*	21689	105.14	217.10

Source: Annual Report 2011-12, MSME, Government of India.

Commercial Banks for Promotion of Micro-enterprise

Like other microfinance promotion institutions, Commercial Banks have been taking a major role in providing financial support for development of microenteprise in Manipur. The SHGs members beneficiaries have undertaken various economic oriented activities in the form of establishing their own microenterprise units with the financial support from the commercial banks.

Table 7.2: Bank-wise summary of finance to Micro-Enterprise in Manipur as on 30th June 2012

(₹ in lakh)

Banks	*Disbursal during the Qtr.*		*Outstanding at end of Qtr.*	
	No.	*Amount*	*No.*	*Amount*
ALB	0	0.00	239	531.40
AXIS	0	0.00	14	303.29
BOB	2	10.00	914	2277.00
BOI	0	0.00	9	49.20
CBI	45	323.36	727	2568.00
HDFC	0	0.00	1	5.50
ICICI	0	0.00	0	0.00
IOB	6	8.30	318	630.06
PNB	30	127	349	1091.00
PSB	10	85.00	591	709.41
SBI	910	1491.98	22363	31350.72
UBI	603	1781.52	6398	15163.36
UCO	5	5.20	963	1874.51
VJB	17	25.00	372	714.00
SCB TOTAL	1628	3857.36	33248	57267.44
MRB	158	179.92	3213	2604.18
CO-OP BANK	175	428.96	12387	14890.11
G TOTAL	1961	4466.24	48848	74761.73

Source: 31st SLBC Report, Manipur.

NEIIPP-2007 and Micro-enterprise

The cabinet committee on Economic affairs gave its approval to the North East Industrial and Investment Promotion Policy (NEIIPP), 2007. Its main features are:

(i) Under NEIIPP, 2007, all new units as well as existing units which go in for substantial expansion, unless otherwise specified and which commence commercial production within the 10 year period from date of notification of NEIIPP, 2007 will be eligible for incentives for a period of 10 years from the date of commencement of production.

(ii) The incentives under the NEIIPP, 2007 shall be available to all industrial units, new as well as existing units on their substantial expansion, located anywhere in the North Eastern Region.

(iii) Under NEIIPP, 2007 incentives on substantial expansion will be given to units affecting 'an increase by not less than 25 per cent in the value of fixed capital investment in plant and machinery for the purpose of expansion of capacity modernization and diversification as against an increase by 33.5 per cent prescribed at present.

(iv) Under NEIIPP, 2007, 100 per cent excise duty exemption will be continued as at present on finished products made in the North Eastern Region. However, in cases, where the CENVAT paid on the raw materials and intermediate products going into the production of finished products (other than the products which are otherwise exempt or subject to nil rate of duty) is higher than the excise duties payable on the finished products, ways and means to refund such overflow of CENVAT credit will be separately notified by the Ministry of Finance.

(v) 100 per cent income tax exemption will continue under NEIIPP, 2007 as at present.

(vi) Capital investment subsidy will be enhance from 15 per cent of the investment in plant and machinery to 30 per cent and the limit for automatic approval of subsidy at this rate will be ₹ 1.5 crore per unit as against ₹ 30 lakh at present. Such subsidy will be applicable to units in the private sector, joint sector, cooperative sector as well as the units set up by the State Governments of the North Eastern Region. For grant of capital investment subsidy higher than ₹ 1.5 crore but up to a maximum of ₹ 30 crore, there will be an Empowered Committee.

(vii) Interest subsidy will be made an available @ 3 per cent on working capital loan in the NEIIPP, 2007 as at present.

(viii) Under NEIIPP, 2007 new industrial units as well as the existing units on their substantial expansion will be eligible for reimbursement of 100 per cent insurance premium under the comprehensive Insurance Scheme.

(ix) To include tobacco and tobacco products, pan masala, plastics carry bags and goods produced by refineries, in a host of industries which would not be eligible for incentives under NEIIPP, 2007.

(x) To provide incentives to service sector, bio-technology and power generating industries.

(xi) To continue North Eastern Development Finance Corporation Ltd. (NEDFi) as the nodal agency for disbursal of subsidies under NEIIPP, 2007.

The provisions of the NEIIPP, 2007 would provide the requisite incentives as well as an enabling environment to speed up the industrialization of the North Eastern Region which is otherwise less than 4 per cent per annum against a national average of 8 per cent.

The Industrial and Investment Policy of Manipur, 2011

The draft Industrial and Investment Policy of Manipur 2011 is proposed to extend the following incentives and services for the promotion of micro-enterprise in particular and other small, medium and large scale industries in general.

1. *Allotment of land*: The State Government will endeavour to provide: (a) developed land with all infrastructural facilities at major infrastructural Centres, and (b) undeveloped land, to manufacturing and Service Sector Enterprises/industrial units.

- The developed land will be allotted on lease basis for a period of 30 (thirty) years, renewable before the expiry of lease.
- The State Government will subsidise the cost of land development at the rate given below:
  - (i) Micro, Small Enterprise, 25 per cent
  - (ii) Micro, Small Enterprise for EOU, and Micro, Small Enterprise units owned and managed by Weaker sections, 30 per cent
  - (iii) Medium and Large scale Industries/Enterprises. 15 per cent
- The Government will constitute a Committee/Agency

by notification for allotment of land for industrial purposes, and Rules for allotment of land shall be framed and notified by the State Government.

2. *Allotment of sheds to Micro, and Small enterprises*: The Government will endeavour to provide built up factory sheds to Micro, Small enterprises on monthly rental basis at industrial estates, industrial park, growth enters, and at built-up industrial locations.

3. *Special scheme for the development of Handicraft*

- *Land and building*: The State Government will endeavour to provide developed land with built-up buildings in cluster with common facilities centre, to develop handicraft villages for the Handicraft artisans on hire purchase basis with suitable terms of instalments, as a special scheme, at suitable location in all districts. The State Government will provide adequate forward and backward linkages, to enhance their activities and earnings.
- *Special Subsidy for Handicraft unit in the rural areas, construction of work-shed/store-room*: The State Government will provide subsidy to the Handicraft Unit in the fold of Micro Enterprise, located in the rural areas for the construction of work-shed/store room, to the extent of 50 per cent.
- *Special Subsidy for Handicraft unit in the Rural, Urban and Semi Urban areas*: The Government will endeavour to provide subsidy to the Handicraft unit in the fold of Micro Enterprise, located in the Rural, Urban and Semi Urban areas for hiring of building used:
  (i) as the work-shed,
  (ii) as the store-room,
  (iii) as the show-room,

The subsidy will be entitled to the Handicraft unit/Enterprise, against the number of artisan employed producing items for sale:

(i) Employing 20 to 50 artisans, 50 per cent concession on floor space rentals or to the extent of ₹ 50,000 whichever, is less per year, for a duration of five years.

(ii) Employing above 50 artisans, 50 per cent concession on floor space rentals or to the extent of ₹ 1,00,000 per year, for a duration of 5 years.

(iii) Employing above 100 artisans, 50 per cent concession on floor space rentals or to the extent of ₹ 20,00,000 per year, for a duration of 5 years.

The State Government will constitute a Committee, by notification, with the Secretary in charge, of Commerce and Industries as the Chairman of the Committee to oversee these schemes. The Committee will decide the number of unit to be benefited during a Financial Year, examining at least the following criteria:

(i) concentration of artisans,
(ii) availability of raw material at source or by transport,
(iii) capacity of production,
(iv) market trend/demand,
(v) market linkages.

4. *Manpower Development*: Industrial Units which depute their workers for technical training in Central Government, State government Training Centres, Central Government undertakings, ITI, Government recognized Centre will be eligible for subsidy/reimbursement of the admission fee incurred to the extent of 50 per cent. The enterprise has to submit an undertaking to the State Government that such trained person will be employed by the industrial unit on successful completion of training, and in case of mis-representation of the facts under the scheme the sponsoring enterprise has to refund the subsidy/incentives in full within a period prescribed by the State Government. The ITI passed-out candidate and candidate passed from the Polytechnic/Engineering college, and from the other Training centres/Institutes, recognised by the State Government will be eligible for reimbursement of the admission fee, as well as course fee to the extent of 50 per cent, for in plant training, or Tool-room training at State Government recognised centres inside, and outside the State.

5. *Incentives to the Innovator/Inventor*: The State Government will encourage innovator/inventor by providing financial assistance up to 90 per cent of the cost involved in R&D. The incentive will be granted on production of documentary proof. The innovator/inventor to avail the benefit under the scheme is to get registered/enlisted with the District Industries Centres, before starting the innovation/invention work.

6. *Subsidy for Feasibility Study and Project report Preparation*: A subsidy to the extent of 50 per cent will be admissible for the

enterprise in the fold of Micro, Small and Medium to meet the cost of feasibility study and project report preparation in each case. The study/report should be prepared by an approved consultant registered either with the Government of Manipur or the Government of India. The Manipur Handloom and Handicrafts Development Corporation will also be eligible for the subsidy. An enhanced subsidy to the extent of 60 per cent will be admissible in case of Weaker sections and EOUs.

7. *Subsidy for Technical Know-How*: A subsidy to the extent of 50 per cent will be admissible for the enterprise in the fold of Micro, Small and Medium to meet the cost of technical know-how obtained from organisations approved by Government of Manipur. The subsidy will be released only on commencement of commercial production. The subsidy will be 55 per cent for EOUs, units using raw materials produce from organic farm and Weaker Section. The enterprise is to obtain prior permission of the State Government to qualify under the scheme

8. *Exemption of Earnest Money and Security Deposit*: Micro and Small enterprise, established in this State, are exempted from payment of earnest money, and security deposits, for the item/items for which they filled Part-II of the "Entrepreneurs Memorandum" (EM) under the provision of the Micro, Small and Medium Enterprise Act, 2006, with the District Industries Centre, on purchase of "Tender" floated by the State Government Department/Office/State Government undertakings/Public Sector Undertakings/State Government Company/Corporation/Autonomous Board/Local Self-Government Office/Semi-Government Organisation/Grant-aid-Institutions/Non-Governmental Organisation getting assistance from the State Government, etc.

9. *State Capital Investment Subsidy*: The State Government will provide Capital Investment Subsidy to all eligible new as well as existing units, including Service Sector Enterprise/unit, in the fold of Micro, Small enterprises and in the case of service sector up to Medium scale, at the rate of 20 per cent on the total capital investment on plant and machinery/machinery or equipment for Service sectors per unit. For EOUs, units using raw materials produced from organic farm and Weaker Section the rate of subsidy shall be 25 per cent per unit.

10. *Interest Subsidy*: Micro, Small and in the case of service

sector up to Medium scale Enterprises, both in the fold of Manufacturing and Service sectors, will be provided an interest subsidy up to 4 per cent per annum on term loan and 3 per cent on working capital loan taken from Bank and Financial Institution. This subsidy will be available for the first five years from the date of commercial production or from the date of release of loan, extendable for another five years on expansion/ modernization/diversification, on the consideration of the State Government on case to case basis.

11. *Power Subsidy:*

- Power subsidy will be provided to eligible units on power tariff paid by the unit on actual units consumed for a period of 5 years at the rates fixed by the Government from time to time from the date of commercial production subject to ceiling given below: Connected load/Rate of subsidy Ceiling of subsidy per annum Up to 1.0 MW 30 per cent ₹ 10.00 lakh above 1.0 MW 25 per cent 25.00 lakh
- 50 per cent of the cost incurred on linking of power from the main line to the factory shed will be subsidised for unit which are not provided land in developed industrial areas. For EOUs and units using raw materials produce from organic farm and Weaker Section the rate of subsidy shall be provided up to the extent of 55 per cent per unit.
- 30 per cent Subsidy will be admissible for purchase of Diesel Generating sets of 10 H.P. or more for the enterprises in the fold of Micro and Small manufacturing sector and the enterprises in the fold of Micro, Small and Medium enterprises service sector which will be listed under notification by the State Government. For EOUs, units using raw materials produce from organic farm and Weaker Section the rate of subsidy shall be provided up to the extent of 35 per cent.

12. *State Transport Subsidy:*

- The State Government will endeavour to provide transport subsidy at the rates to be notified categorically from time to time for transportation of raw materials and finished products. The subsidy will be provided to supplement and cover such areas where subsidy provided under the Transport Subsidy Scheme, 1971 (as amended from time to time) of the Government of India has not provided. The rates of subsidy will be as prescribed under the Transport Subsidy Scheme, 1971 (as amended from time to time) of the Government of India except where specifically mentioned under this policy. The transport subsidy will be available for a period of 5 years from the date of commercial production.

- The transport subsidy will be provided for another 5 years after expansion/diversification for Micro and Small enterprises only at the prescribed rates as available under the Transport Subsidy Scheme, 1971 (as amended from time to time) of the Government of India.
- (i) Transport subsidy will be provided for movement of raw materials and finished goods within the State.
  (ii) Subsidy @ 90 per cent will be admissible for transportation of raw materials by surface/waterways from any place of the State exceeding a distance of 50 kms. by shortest roadways/waterways or combined together with waterways and roadways, up to the premises of the factory.
  (iii) Subsidy @ 50 per cent will be admissible for transportation of finished products by surface/waterways from the enterprise to any place of the State exceeding a distance of 50 kms. by shortest roadways/waterways or combined together with waterways and roadways on a case by case basis.
- (i) The State Government will endeavour to provide transport subsidy to the enterprise eligible and availing subsidy under the Transport Subsidy Scheme, 1971 (as amended from time to time) of the Government of India @ 90 per cent for transportation of raw materials by surface in between the railhead nearest to source of raw material located outside the NE Region up to Siliguri.
  (ii) The State Government will endeavour to provide transport subsidy to the enterprise eligible and availing subsidy under the Transport Subsidy Scheme, 1971 (as amended from time to time) of the Government of India @ 90 per cent for transportation of finished products by surface in between the railhead nearest

to destination of finished products located outside the NE Region from Siliguri.

- (i) Subsidy to the extent of 75 per cent for air transport (maximum of ₹ 5.0 lakhs by air cargo per annum) for participation in Exhibition, Trade Expo, Trade Fairs, etc. outside the country, for a period of five years from the date of commercial production.

  (ii) Subsidy to the extent of @ 90 per cent by surface transport (maximum of' 2.0 lakhs per annum) will be available for the transportation of products/items, for participation in Exhibition, Trade Expo, Trade Fairs, etc. within the country, for a period of five years from the date of commercial production.

  (iii) Subsidy to the extent of @ 50 per cent by surface transport will be available for the transportation of products/items, for participation in Exhibition, Trade Expo, Trade Fairs, etc. within the State, for a period of five years from the date of commercial production.

13. *Reimbursement of Fee/Registration fee/Renewal Fee for registering with the Office of the Controller General of Patents, Designs and Trade Marks (CGPDTM):* Micro, Small and in the case of service sector up to Medium scale Enterprises/Individual/ Organisation/Association, etc. will be reimbursed in full for the amount paid towards Fee/Registration Fee, for getting certificate from the Office of the Controller General of Patents, Designs and Trade Marks (CGPDTM), Government of India.

14. *Reimbursement of Registration Fee/Renewal Fee for obtaining BIS, ISI, ISO Series and FPO:* Micro, Small and in the case of service sector up to Medium scale Enterprises will be reimbursed in full of the amount paid for the Registration fee/Renewal fee in getting, BIS/ISI, ISO, AGMARK and FPO etc. for a period of five years.

15. *Reimbursement of Stamp Duty and Registration*: Micro, Small, Medium enterprises and other category of Industries will be reimbursed in full of the amount paid towards Stamp Duty and Registration Fee for securing loans and other incentives from financial institutions including mortgage of fixed assets. The reimbursement will be admissible after disbursement of loan by Financial Institutions/Banks and will be subject to condition that the assets mortgaged would not be transferred for a period of 5 years.

16. *Quality Control*: For purchase of testing equipment, 75 per cent subsidy will be admissible to Micro, Small Enterprise. Subsidy will be 80 per cent in case of Weaker Section and EOUs in the fold of Micro and Small Enterprise.

17. *Subsidy for Substantial Expansion/Modernisation/Upgradation/Diversification:*

(a) State Capital investment subsidy on Substantial expansion/Modernisation/Diversification will be given to units in the fold Micro, Small Enterprise and in the case of service sector including Medium scale Enterprise, on the following condition:

 (i) effecting "an increase by not less than 25 per cent in the value of fixed capital investment in plant and machinery and equipment" against the installed value of fixed capital investment in plant and machinery at the commencement of commercial production of the enterprise,

 (ii) Utilisation of at least 60 per cent of the installed capacity of the enterprise is necessary to qualify "Diversification". The Subsidy for Substantial expansion/Modernisation/Diversification will be given at the rate of 20 per cent will be admissible for Micro, Small Enterprises, for the purchase of machinery and equipment. The subsidy will be admissible for the expanded, modernized and diversified portion only.

(b) Interest subsidy on Substantial expansion/Modernisation/Diversification, will be given to units in the fold of Micro, Small Enterprise and in the case of service sector including Medium scale Enterprise, up to 4 per cent per annum on term loan and 3 per cent working capital taken from Bank and Financial Institution, for a period of 5 years from the date of expansion/modernisation/diversification on the condition provided under Para 17(a)(i)(ii). The subsidy for Substantial Expansion/Modernisation/Diversification will be extended on the recommendation of a Committee constituted by the State Government.

18. *Exclusive Purchase Programme*: The State Government, undertakings, including organisations, and institute, getting grants,

and beneficiary of the state Government will commit to purchasing the products of Micro, Small enterprise located in the State subject to fulfilment of the quality, standards and specification. The Department of Commerce and Industries will circulate a list of locally manufactured products to all the offices of the State Government, and to all concerned from time to time.

19. *Price Preference:* The State Government will provide Price Preference, where under purchases by State Government Department/Office/State Government undertakings/Public Sector undertakings/State Government Company/Corporation/ Autonomous Board/Local self-Government Office/Semi-Government Organisation/Grant-aid-Institutions/Non-Governmental Organisation getting assistance from the State Government, etc. will accord first priority to products manufactured by Micro and Small Enterprise established in the State, for the item/items for which they filled Part-II of the "Entrepreneurs Memorandum"(EM) under the provision of the Micro, Small and Medium Enterprises Development Act, 2006, with the District Industries Centre. All other things being equal, such enterprise will be given a price preference up to 15 per cent over the lowest technically and commercially viable rate offered by others outside the State, including Medium and Large Scale of industries established in the State.

20. *Tax Incentives*: All eligible units, which manufacture goods in Manipur, will be entitled to exemption of 99 per cent of tax payable under the Manipur Value Added Tax Act, 2004, the Central Sales Tax Act, 1956, subject to the limit mentioned below: Category Year Term of Exemption Micro, Seven years subject to maximum of 200 per cent of fixed capital investment. Small, Seven years subject to maximum of 150 per cent of fixed capital investment. Medium and Large, Seven years subject to maximum of 100 per cent of fixed capital investment. Fixed capital investment means investment in plant and machinery or additional investment in plant and machinery (for expansion units) and building connected directly with manufacturing process. The Finance Department of the Government of Manipur will bring out a separate notification in this regard.

21. *Special Incentives for Mega Projects*: (a) Project with large capital investment with a minimum of ₹ 100 crore or generating a minimum of 1000 regular employment and having potential for

development of ancillary industries based on their products will be given Mega project Status.

(b) To encourage the establishment of Mega Projects, all incentives including land allotment, subsidy and tax concessions under the Policy will be relaxable on case to case basis to be decided by a High Power Committee specially constituted by the State Government for the purpose.

Challenges and Opportunities of Micro-enterprise

Microfinance and Micro-enterprise Opportunities in India FSD partners with several community-led organizations in the Udaipur and Jodhpur regions to increase economic opportunity for underserved populations. These grassroots initiatives offer thousands of marginalized groups the training, financial resources, and job opportunities needed to rise out of poverty.

To read about employment and Microfinance and Micro-enterprise issues in India. Interns, volunteers, and donors work with FSD to provide support for programmes that:

- Initiate and maintain of Self-Help Groups (SHG) that offer financial guidance and credit, promote savings, free members from unfair debt burdens, and create collective action opportunities that minimize exploitation of women and other marginalized groups.
- Offer skills training and capacity-building workshops to increase economic independence, empowerment, and local employability of women and other underserved groups.
- Develop small businesses that produce sale able goods, such as traditional handicrafts.
- Consult start-up microfinance programmes that struggle with operational, financial, or institutional sustainability.
- Provide entrepreneurial skills training to conduct feasibility studies, perform cost/benefit analyses, write business plans, acquire financing, and initiate start-ups.
- Research and analyse numerous topics that include local economic conditions, migration patterns, obstructions to economic growth, and efficacy of microfinance programmes.
- Increase the productivity and distribution of local farmers'

goods while providing drought relief to vulnerable families.

- Expand and increase exposure of microfinance programmes to outlying villages.
- Offer marketing, distribution, pricing, and management training to local micro-enterprises.

Read more about Microfinance and Micro-enterprise programmes and opportunities initiated by our Community Partners in India. For a description of the opportunities available in each development subject addressed by FSD in India.

Summary

Manipur is one of the economically and industrially backward state of the country. MSME segment plays the important role in economic development of the state. Micro-enterprise's contribution to the economy is also minimal, due to lack of proper development of this segment. Despite of various incentives and other packages provided under NEIIP-2001 and IIPM 2011, the pace of development of micro-enterprise in the state is far behind the expectation level.

Microfinance has contributed a lot in the growth and development of micro-enterprise in the state. Under the scheme, it not only provide the financial support but also the technical support which leads to develop the micro-enterprise in the state.

EIGHT
Data Analysis and Interpretation

> "Microfinance recognizes that poor people are remarkable reservoirs of energy and knowledge. And while the lack of financial services is a sign of poverty, today it is also understood as an untapped opportunity to create markets, bring people in from the margins and give them the tools with which to help themselves."
>
> —*Kofi Annan*

Introduction

The present research work is basically of a national character. But it was felt that an indepth study at the field level will help in drawing conclusions for the entire country. The study is based on the collected data from 20 different MFI, 104 SHGs and 200 Micro-enterprises spreading in all the nine districts of Manipur. The Research team personally visited all the sources wherefrom the duly filled questionnaire were collected, classification of those collected data were made and on the basis of their response through questionnaire, analysis and interpretation were also made to derive the following outcome of the study. Needless to say that the observations and suggestions made based on the field study, will receive due attention of concerned authorities at the state, regional and national level organisations and agencies involved in the development of the microfinance.

District-wise number of MFI and SHG

Table 8.1 shows the number of district-wise microfinance institutions and SHGs which have been selected for the present study. For the present study it has covered 20 MFI which have been spread in all nine districts of the state and another 104 SHGs/ JLGs have been selected from this 20 MFI spreading all the nine districts. From the 104 SHGs/JLGs again 200 micro-enterprises have been selected who are starting their own micro-enterprise through microfinance for the study.

Manipur is located in the extreme northeastern corner of India, bordering with Mynamar in the east, Nagaland in the north, Mizoram in the south and Assam in the west. There are nine administrative districts in Manipur of which five districts are in the hills and remaining four districts are in the valley. Out of the total population 9/10th populations are settled in valley districts and 1/10th populations of the state are settled in hill districts. Socio-economically all districts of the state are not similar. Despite of different in their socio-economic, banking, and other development infrastructure, the present study is concentrated in all districts of the state.

Thus, a district-wise distribution of MFIs, SHGs and micro-enterprises shows a quite uneven due to different in number of functioning MFIs, SHGs and Micro-enterprises. Imphal East district is representing 6 MFIs, 18 SHGs, 30 MEs, Imphal West district is, 6 MFIs, 17 SHGs, 30 MEs, Bishenpur district account 3 MFIs, 12 SHGs, 20 MEs, Thoubal district data is collected from 4 MFIs, 17 SHGs, 27 MEs, among the hill districts, Ukhrul district represent the highest number of 3 MFIs, 14 SHGs, 26 MEs, followed by Tamenglong district with 2 MFIs, 10 SHGs, 20 MEs, remaining three districts represents Chandel 1, MFIs, 5 SHGs, 15 MEs, Senapati 1 MFIs, 5 SHGs, 15 MEs and Churachandpur 1 MFIs, 6 SHGs, and 17 MEs respectively.

Year-wise Establishment of NGO/MFI

All the 20 different NGOs operating microfinance activities in the state have started their microfinance programme in different years and some of them have started since their inception. Among these 20 MFI-NGO, Loyalam Bank Project (LBP) under Rural Development Organization (RDO) Lamsang, Manipur is the oldest one for extending microfinance programme in the state for the first time in the year 1992. After this, other microfinance institutions say Youth Volunteer Union (YVU), SEVA, Macha

Table 8.1: District-wise distribution of MFI and SHG for the study

Sl. No.	District	MFI	SHG	Micro-enterprise
1.	Imphal East	Machaleima	5	5
		Friendship	2	5
		Loyalam B Project	3	5
		Chanura Microfin	3	5
		ESWOSSA	2	5
		SEVA	3	5
2.	Imphal West	Loyalam B Project	3	5
		Chanura Microfin	3	5
		HDA	4	5
		URDA	2	5
		HASWA	2	5
		TCP-RNBA	3	5
3.	Bishenpur	Loyalam B Project	3	6
		ORI	6	9
		URDA	3	5
4.	Thoubal	YVU	5	10
		Loyalam B Project	4	6
		Leima Microfinance	4	5
		ORI	4	6
5.	Ukhrul	UDWIM-IFAD	7	11
		VVD	5	10
		DSSS	2	5
6.	Chandel	REACH-M	5	15
7.	Senapati	WCWA	5	15
8.	Tamenglong	TCP-RNBA	8	16
		DSSS	2	4
9.	Churachandpur	RAS	6	17
	Total		104	200

Source: Field data.

Leima, Chanura Microfin, REEP, WSDS, etc. have been adopting microfinance activities along with other activities of the NGOs. It is also found that out of the total NGO/MFIs only four of them have started simultaneously with the activities of Microfinance whereas the remaining 16 NGO/MFIs have started microfinance activities much after the establishment of their main NGOs activities. A year-wise establishment of SHPI/NGO-MFI and year of undertaking microfinance activities are shown in Table 8.2.

Bank Linkage Programme

Figure 8.1 in the form of Pie chart shows the number of NGOs which have been providing bank linkage programme to their microfinance SHGs beneficiaries. From this figure it is clearly understood that only 25 per cent of the NGOs has facilitated bank linkage programme to their beneficiaries and micro-enterpreneurs and maximum of them i.e., 75 per cent of them have providing no bank linkage programme to their microfinance beneficiaries. Further, it can be said that the present initiative taken by the government for financial inclusion target is far behind the expectation. Here, government should undertake more stringent action for inclusion of finance with this micro-entepreneurs who are deals with economic oriented activities.

Table 8.2: Year-wise Establishment of SHPI/NGO/MFI

Name	*YOE*	*YOMF*
LBP	1975	1992
YVU	1972	1996
SEVA	1991	1996
Macha Leima	1969	1997
Friendship centre Manipur	1988	1997
TCP-RNBA	1981	2000
ESWOSSA	1988	2000
RAS	1995	2001
HAD	2003	2003
REEP-ORI	2003	2003
HASWA	1990	2004
WCWA	1999	2004
DSSS	1981	2005
URDA	1986	2006
VVD	1982	2007
Leima Microfin	2006	2007
UDWIM	2007	2007
Chanura Microfin Manipur	2007	2007
RCN-REACH-M	1991	2008
WWAG	1958	2010

Source: Compiled from the official record of all NGO-MFIs deals with microfinance activities.
YoE — Year of establishment XoMF — Year of Microfinance

Reasons for Not Bank Linkage

There are many reasons behind for not providing bank linkage programme by the NGO/MFIs to their microfinance beneficiaries

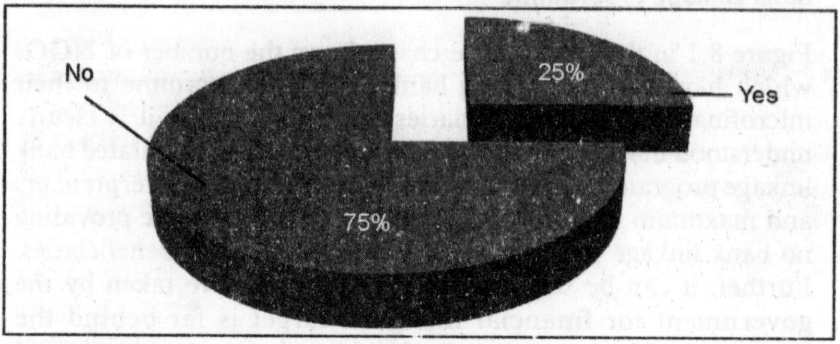

Source: Field data.

Fig. 8.1: Providing Bank Linkage

which has been shown in Table 8.3. From the response of NGOs/MFIs, the reasons have been classified into six different areas. Of the total six different reasons 28.6 per cent each of the NGOs/MFIs express that the process of bank linkage is a problem and bank linkage programme is out of their programme and objectives respectively. Another 14.3 per cent each have also responded that they were in process, and no bank branches are operating in the rural areas and also beneficiaries are not willing to link with bank etc.

Table 8.3: Reason for not linkage

Reasons	*No of Respondents*	*%*
In process	2	14.3
No bank branches in the rural areas and Beneficiaries are not willing to link with bank	2	14.3
Process is a problem	4	28.6
It is out of our programme	4	28.6
Banking services are very poor	1	7.1
Due to small scope of the programme	1	7.1
Total	14	100.0

Chi-Square = 4.000
Df = 5
P >0.05

Source: Field data.

Bank Where Linkage with Beneficiaries

From Fig. 8.1 it is understood that only 25 per cent of NGO/MFIs have provided bank linkage to their clients. Below Table 8.4 shows the names of the banks where 25 per cent linkage programme have been made. It is found that major four different bank branches where linkage have been made. Among these four bank branches 40 per cent of the NGO/MFIs have linked with State Bank of India and other three bank branches have 20 per cent each of bank linkage programme with NGOs/MFIs in the state.

Table 8.4: Name of the Bank where Linkage with beneficiaries

Name	*No of Respondents*	*%*
MRB	1	20
IUCB	1	20
SBI	2	40
UBI	1	20
Total	5	100
	Chi-Square = 0.600 Df = 3 P >0.05	

Source: Field data.

Year-wise Number of Active SHG/JLG

Table 8.5 shows the number of SHGs/JLGs which have been formed and active upto the end of March of respective year. Data which have been shown in this table are retrieved from the information of 20 selected microfinance NGOs/MFIs for the present study and the information are not represent for all SHGs/JLGs of the state. As on 31st March 2010-11, there were 10,755 SHGs/JLGs registered under the selected 20 NGOs/MFIs in the state of which 10,278 SHGs/JLGs are active and performing their day-to-day microfinance activities. From Table 8.5 it has clearly shows that majority of the SHGs/JLGs are active and only a few of them are not performing their activities.

Table 8.5: Year-wise Cumulative total of SHG/JLG

Year	*No SHG/JLG*	*Active SHG/JLG*	*% of Active SHG/JLG*
2000-01	1745	1736	99.48
2001-02	2801	2790	99.61
2002-03	3749	3734	99.60
2003-04	4224	4210	99.67
2004-05	4558	4545	99.71
2005-06	5093	5075	99.65
2006-07	4288	4271	99.60
2007-08	6357	6299	99.09
2008-09	7795	7660	98.27
2009-10	9295	9085	97.74
2010-11	10755	10278	95.56

Source: Field data.

Fig 8.2 shows the number of NGOs/MFIs getting financial assistance from the different funding agencies. Of the total SHGs/JLGs 80 per cent of them have received financial assistance and remaining 20 per cent of them have not getting any financial assistance and hence they are either running from their own sources or they are not getting from any other sources.

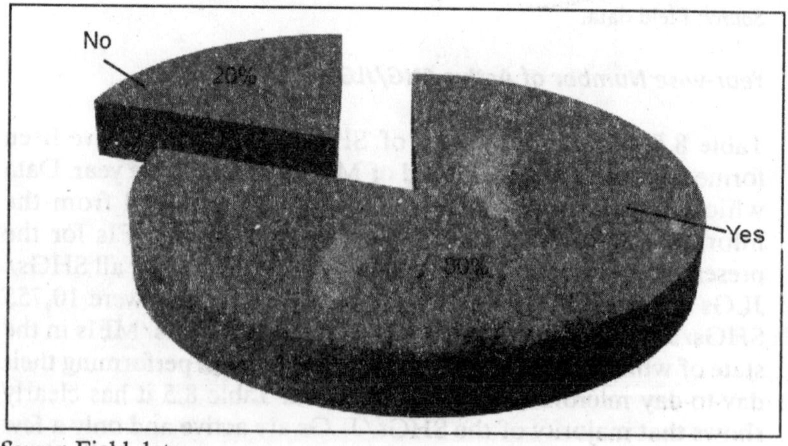

Source: Field data.

Fig. 8.2: NGO/MFIs Getting financial Assistance from Funding Agencies

Interest of Rate Against Microfinance Funds

Table 8.6 represents the different rate of interest charged by microfinance funding agencies such as RMK, RGVN, IGS, NEDFi, SIDBI, FWWB, BASIX, ANANYA, CORDAID and Missorireo to NGO-MFI operating in Manipur. Out of 20 NGO-MFI who received loan from funding agencies, there is only one such agency who charge a nominal rate of 0.5 per cent per annum. Other rate of interest range from 8 per cent per annum to 19.2 per cent per annum from 15 NGO-MFI operating in Manipur by the funding agencies. One NGO received in the form of grant in aid and three others have not received any grants or aid from the funding agencies, but from their own sources of financing.

It is also seen from Table 8.6 that one NGO-MFI who received loan at the rate of 19.2 per cent interest, which is quite high in comparison with other rate of interest fixed by the government. There are seven such NGOs who got loan from the funding agencies less than 10 per cent rate of interest.

Table 8.6: Rate of Interest against Microfinance Funds

Interest Rate per annum	*No. of Respondents*	*%*
0.5	1	6.2
8	2	12.5
9	1	6.2
10	3	18.8
11.75	2	12.5
12.25	1	6.2
12.5	1	6.2
13	1	6.2
13.5	2	12.5
15	1	6.2
19.2	1	6.2
Total*	16	100

Chi-Square = 3.250
Df = 10
P >0.05

* One NGO received fund as grant and 3 are not getting any microfinance fund.

Mode of Lending

Figure 8.3 depicts the mode of lending to Microfinance beneficiaries by the NGO-MFIs selected for study. No NGO-MFI

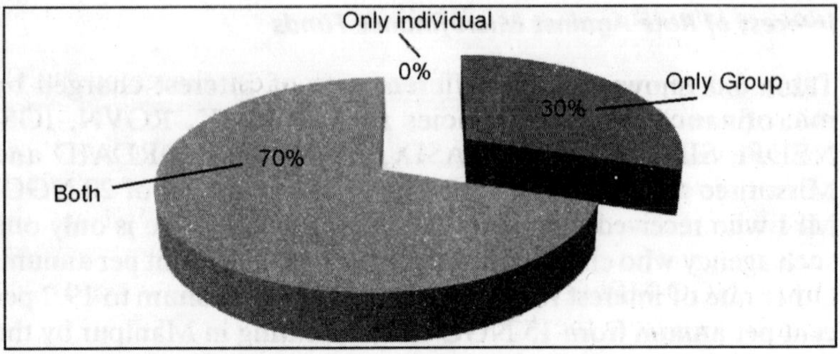

Fig. 8.3: Type of lending

provide microfinance loan only to individual from the information of 20 selected microfinance NGOs/MFIs for the present study and the information are not represent for all SHGs/JLGs of the state. As on 31st March 2010-11, there were 10,755 SHGs/JLGs registered under the selected 20 NGOs/MFIs in the state of which 10,278 SHGs/JLGs are active and is found out of the total whereas 70 per cent of them provide loan to both individual and groups and remaining 30 per cent provide loan to group only.

Average Loan given to the Groups

Table 8.7 given spread the average loan size given by NGO/MFIs to the SHGs. There were 4 NGOs/MFI each who have extended loan facilities to the SHGs to the maximum of ₹ 1,00,000 and ₹ 25,000 respectively. Followed by another 3 NGOs/MFIs each with an average loan facilities of ₹ 15,000 and ₹ 50,000 respectively.

Table 8.7: Average Loan Size to the Groups

Amount in ₹	*No. of Respondents*	*Percentage*
10000	1	5.0
15000	3	15.0
25000	4	20.0
40000	2	10.0
45000	2	10.0
50000	3	15.0
60000	1	5.0
100000	4	20.0
Total	20	100.0

Source: Field Study.

Rate of Interest Charge per Month

Table 8.8 shows the different rate of interest charge by NGO-MFI from SHGs and individual entrepreneurs. It is found that on face value the rate of interest are range from 1 to 3 per cent per month. It comes to 24 per cent and 36 per cent per annum which is quite high in comparison with bank interest rate. Further, the rate is again exorbitantly high due to flat rate of interest charge by the NGO-MFI from the SHGs and micro-entrepreneurs which can be seen from the Appendix-V.

Table 8.8: Rate of Interest Charge Per Month

Interest Rate	*No. of Respondents*	*%*
1.00	1	5.0
1.12	1	5.0
1.25	1	5.0
1.50	3	15.0
1.60	1	5.0
1.66	1	5.0
1.75	2	10.0
2.00	6	30.0
2.17	1	5.0
2.25	1	5.0
2.40	1	5.0
3.00	1	5.0
Total	20	100.0
	Mode = 2.00	

Source: Field data.

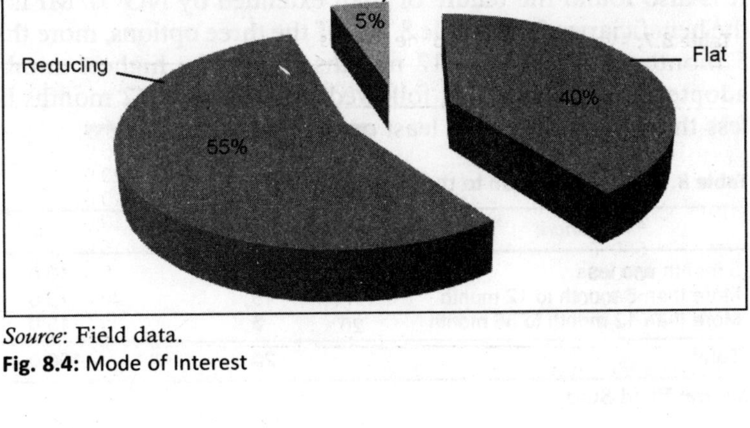

Source: Field data.

Fig. 8.4: Mode of Interest

Table 8.9 carries the mode of recovery of loan collected by NGOs-MFIs from clients SHGs. There are good number of options given to the clients by the MFIs such as daily, weekly collection which is more client's friendly than the lender. Clients are easy to repay back with minimum instalment whereas it will be difficult task for the lender as they have to collect daily or weekly and also with a small amount with proper maintenance of accounts. Among the different mode of collection, monthly collection is the best choice from the NGOs/MFIs side because it facilitates the collection of monthly as well as a moderate amount of instalments. But from the clients side it is totally differ which can been seen in later.

Table 8.9: Mode of Recovery

Mode	*No. of Respondent*	*%*
Daily	1	5.0
Weekly	6	30.0
Fortnightly	1	5.0
Monthly	9	45.0
Quarterly	1	5.0
Fortnightly and monthly	1	5.0
All	1	5.0
Total	20	100.0
	Mode = Monthly	

Source: Field Study.

Duration of Loan Facilities to Beneficiaries

It is also found the tenure of loan extended by NGOs/MFIs to the beneficiaries from Table 8.10. Of the three options, more than 5 months and less than 12 months stands the highest number adopted by NGOs/MFIs, followed by more than 12 months but less than 36 months. The least one is 5 months and less.

Table 8.10: Tenure of loan to the beneficiaries

Tenure	*No. of Respondent*	*%*
5 month and less	2	10.0
More than 5 month to 12 month	15	75.0
More than 12 month to 36 month	3	15.0
Total	20	100.0

Source: Field Study.

Forward and Backward Linkage

Figure 8.5 shows the NGO-MFIs providing forward and backward linkage to SHGs/micro-entrepreneurs. Only 20 per cent of the NGO-MFIs extend this services whereas 80 per cent do not provide this services.

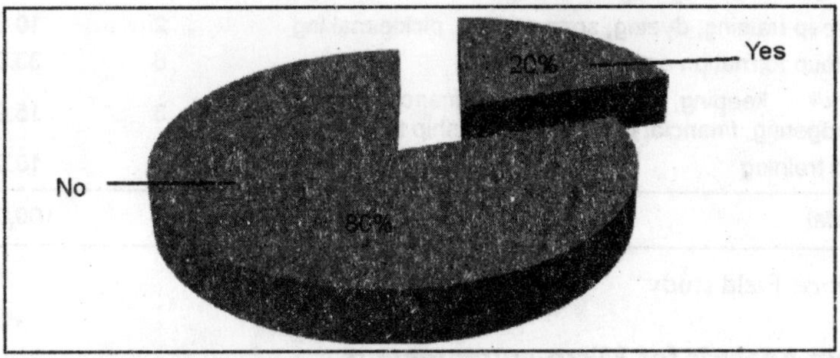

Fig. 8.5: Giving forward backward linkage

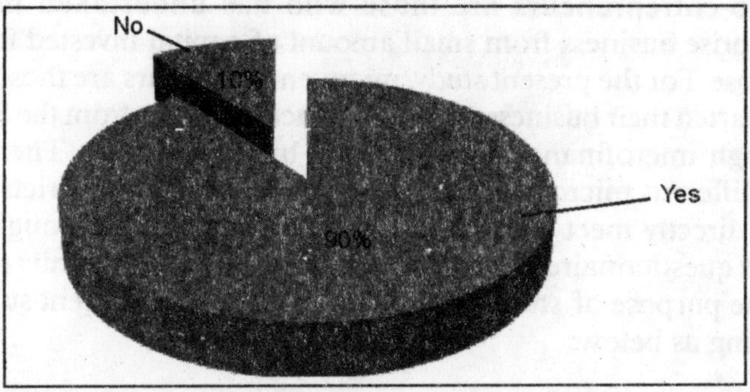

Fig. 8.6: Giving Training to the Beneficiaries

Training to Beneficiaries

Figure 8.6 covers the training facilities provides by NGO-MFIs to clients beneficiaries. It is found that 90 per cent of them had provide training facilities of financial literacy, financial planning and accounting practices in addition to provide loan facilities to their clients. The details of training and education facilities extended by NGO-MFIs are also represented in Table 8.11.

Table 8.11: Training and Education Facilities

Types of training	*No. of Respondent*	*%*
Account and Apiculture	2	10.0
Book keeping and income generating activities	4	20.0
Apiculture and dyeing workshop	1	5.0
Group training, dyeing, soap making, pickle making	2	10.0
Group formation and management	6	30.0
Book keeping, accounting, financial literacy, budgeting, financial planning, leadership training	3	15.0
No training	2	10.0
Total	20	100.0

Source: Field study

Data Analysis for Micro-entrepreneurs

Micro-entrepreneurs are those who has undertaken micro-enterprise business from small amount of capital invested for the purpose. For the present study, micro-entrepreneurs are those who has started their business with the financial support from the SHGs through microfinance support given by NGO-MFIs. There are 200 different micro-enterprises from nine different districts have been directly meet and relevant data were collected through pre-tested questionnaire. They are analysed, discussed and interpreted for the purpose of study. It has been analysed in different suitable heading as below:

Year-wise Establishment of Microenterprise

Table 8.12 shows the number of micro-enterprises which have been establishing in different years. These enterprises have taken microfinance loan for their micro business from their parent SHGs or indirectly from some other MFIs who use to provide such financing to micro-entrepreneurs directly.

From Table 8.12 it is found that maximum numbers of micro-entrepreneurs have been setting up their units in the year 2009. It is also seen that 80 per cent of the total enterprises have been established after 1999 (i.e., 21 in 2000, 19 in 2005, 18 in 2001).

Table 8.12: No. of Micro-enterprises Established in Different Year

Year of Establishment	*Number of Respondents*	*%*
1970	3	1.5
1981	4	2.0
1989	3	1.5
1990	6	3.0
1991	12	6.0
1996	3	1.5
1998	7	3.5
1999	4	2.0
2000	21	10.5
2001	18	9.0
2002	10	5.0
2003	3	1.5
2004	12	6.0
2005	19	9.5
2006	9	4.5
2007	15	7.5
2008	3	1.5
2009	24	12.0
2010	18	9.0
2011	6	3.0
Total	200	100.0
	Mode of year = 2009 Std. deviation = 7.659	

Source: Field data.

It is also seen that most of the micro-enterprise units were established before getting microfinance loan and only few of them started their units after getting microfinance loan. The amount of microfinance loan were utilised for their expanision of units.

Age Group of Entrepreneurs

Following Fig. 8.7 shows the different age-groups of entrepreneurs. For the present study the age-group of the entrepreneurs have been classified into five different categories. It is understood that maximum number of entrepreneurs fall under the age-group between 36 to 45 years followed by age-group between 46 years to 55 years. It covers the 38 per cent of the total study population. Least number of entrepreneurs falls under the age group of below 25 years and it is only 1.5 per cent of the total population. It is also seen that only 14 micro-entrepreneurs out

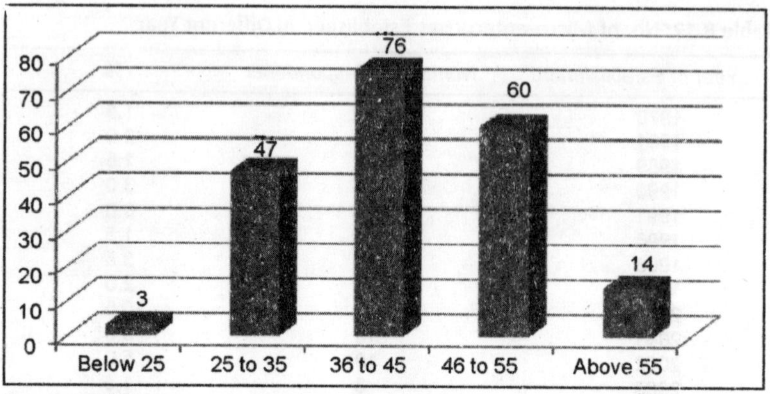

Source: Field data.

Fig. 8.7: No. of Entrepreneurs in Different Age-Group

of 200 are falls under the age-group of 55 and above. By analysing these data it can be concluded that the age-group of "36 to 45" years have taken more economic responsibility in a family as well as in the society and the age-group of "below 25" years have taken less economic responsibility.

Sex Ratio

The sex ratio of micro-entrepreneurs has been shown in Fig. 8.8. It shows nearly 90 per cent of the micro-entrepreneurs are female

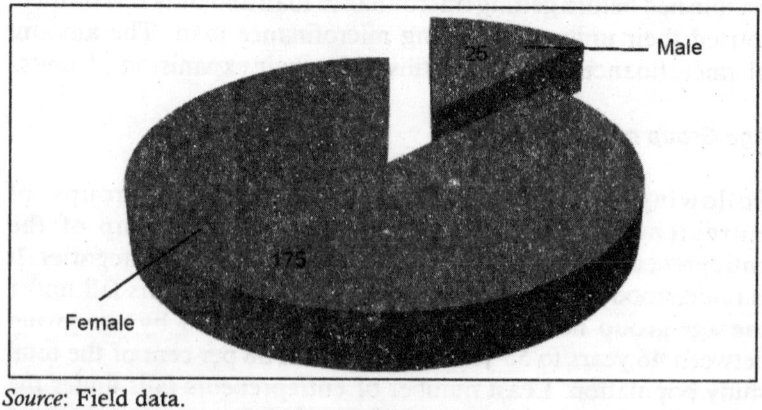

Source: Field data.

Fig. 8.8: Sex-Ratio of Micro-entrepreneures

and only 10 per cent have been found as male entrepreneurs. This data indicate that women are active participation in the micro-enterprise business than their counterpart. It is also correlated with other economic oriented activities undertaken by the women folk in Manipur.

Marital Status of Micro-entrepreneurs

Among the selected micro-entrepreneurs for present study only 1.5 per cent are unmarried persons and remaining are married. It is also found that 6 per cent of the total populations are widow. From this data it can be concluded that married person have been taking more economic responsibility than unmarried one. It has been shown in the following Table 8.13.

Table 8.13: Marital Status of the Micro- entrepreneurs

Marital Status	*No. of Respondents*	*%*
Married	185	92.5
Unmarried	3	1.5
Widow	12	6.0
Total	200	100.0

Source: Field data.

Occupation of Spouse

Out of the total 200 micro-entrepreneurs 185 are married persons so the occupations of their spouse have been presented in Table 8.14. From this table it is understood that maximum number of spouse have been doing their own business and this category covered 42.2 per cent of the total population. Next to business 22.2 per cent of them have joint to the same business. It is also found that 12.4 per cent of them have fall under "government employee" category. Among them least number are fall under the categories of "quasi-govt" and "taxi service"; it covered 3.2 per cent each of the total population. From this information it can be inferred that all the micro-entrepreneurs who have getting microfinance facilities in the state are not only poor family because some of their spouse have been doing government service.

Table 8.14: Occupation of the Spouse of the Micro-Entrepreneurs

Occupation of Spouse	*No. of Respondents*	*%*
Farmer	14	7.6
Business	78	42.2
Govt. employee	23	12.4
Employed in Pvt. sector	8	4.3
Quasi-Govt.	6	3.2
Joint to the same business	41	22.2
Housewife	9	4.9
Taxi service	6	3.2
Total	185	100.0

Chi-square = 191.519
df = 7
P < 0.01

Source: Field data.

Educational Qualification

Educational qualification of micro-entrepreneurs have been shown in Table 8.15. This Table 8.15 shows that only 17.5 per cent of the total population are illiterate and rest are literate.

Table 8.15: Qualification of the Micro-Entrepreneurs

Qualification	*No. of Respondents*	*%*
Illiterate	35	17.5
Below HSLC	33	16.5
HSLC	35	17.5
HSSLC	62	31.0
Graduate	29	14.5
Master and above	3	1.5
No response	3	1.5
Total	200	100

Chi-square = 88.470
df = 6
P < 0.01

Source: Field data.

Against the literate population maximum numbers have completed their class XIIth standard; which represent the 31 per cent of the total population. Interestingly there are some graduate and post-graduate holders among them who remain unemployed educated youth. Therefore, in brief, we can conclude that the microfinance beneficiaries in Manipur are educated unemployed people.

Transaction with Banks

Table 8.16 shows the banking status of micro-entrepreneurs of the present study population. Out of the 200 micro-entrepreneurs less than 50 per cent of them have open their own bank account. It accounts 48.5 per cent of the total population. From this information it can be concluded that maximum number of microfinance beneficiaries are out of financial inclusion which is against the government policy of inclusion of more under banking services.

Table 8.16: Banking Status of the Micro-Entrepreneurs

Having Bank Account	*No. of Respondents*	*%*
Yes	97	48.5
No	103	51.5
Total	200	100

Source: Field data.

Timing of Account

From the previous Table 8.16 it is understood that out of 200 entrepreneurs 97 have been opening their own bank account. Among the entrepreneurs who have opened their own bank account 37 per cent have opened their account before starting their business and 63 per cent of them have opened their bank account after starting their business. These have clearly shown in Fig. 8.9. From this Figure it can be inferred that maximum number of micro-entrepreneurs has opened their bank account after starting their business.

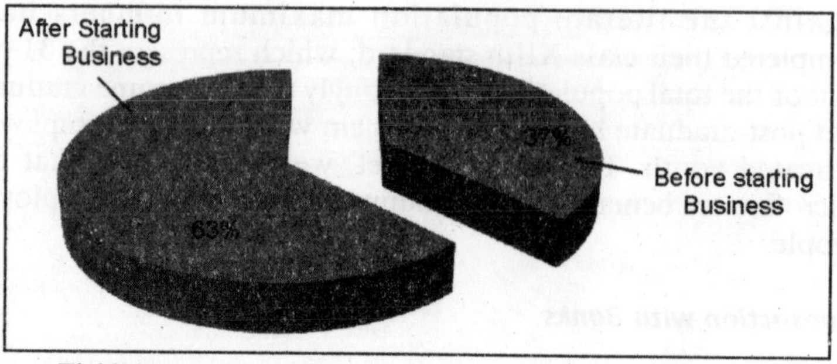

Source: Field data.

Fig. 8.9: Timing of Account Open

Banks where Beneficiaries Open their Account

Table 8.17 shows the number of entrepreneurs and name of bank where they open their account. It is found that in 5 different banks the entrepreneurs have opened their own account against the 20 scheduled commercial banks operating in the state. Among these banks UBI has the maximum number of account from micro-entrepreneurs, it account 35.1 per cent of the total entrepreneurs who have opened their own bank account. Next to this MRB stood in the second position with 34 per cent and SBI in third with 15.5 per cent. From this information it can be said that among the bank UBI and MRB have more friendly to open the bank account for micro-entrepreneurs in the state.

Table 8.17: Banks where Accounts are Open for Micro-entrepreneurs

Name	No. of enterprise	%
SBI	15	15.5
UBI	34	35.1
MRB	33	34.0
Urban Cooperative Bank	6	6.2
MSCB	9	9.3
Total	97	100.0
	Chi-Square = 36.351 df = 4 P < 0.01	

Source: Field data.

Year-wise Bank Account

The year-wise bank account open by the different micro-entrepreneurs have been shown in Table 8.18. This table shows maximum number of entrepreneurs have opened their account in the year 2008. Only one person each of them has opened their account in the year 1999 and 2001.

Table 8.18: Year-wise Bank Account Open

Year	*No. of entrepreneurs*	*%*
1990	4	4.1
1991	3	3.1
1992	3	3.1
1998	3	3.1
1999	1	1.0
2000	5	5.2
2001	1	1.0
2002	9	9.3
2003	3	3.1
2004	2	2.1
2005	7	7.2
2006	8	8.2
2007	9	9.3
2008	19	19.6
2010	5	5.2
2011	9	9.3
2012	6	6.2
Total	**97**	**100.0**

Source: Field data.

Mode of Business Started

To know how to start their business the study made a question and from their answer Table 8.19 has been prepared. From this table it is clear that the mode of starting their business by 200 different entrepreneurs have been found in different reasons. Maximum number of entrepreneurs has started their business by their own fund; it covered 76.5 per cent of the total population. A moderate rate on micro-entrepreneurs also shows that their business have started with the loan from local moneylenders. The least number of entrepreneurs i.e., 1.5 per cent of the total population have started their business with the fund from bank loan. Fund from moneylender stood in second position.

From this information it is understood that at the beginning of their enterprises the maximum entrepreneurs did not have taken loan from microfinance except only 6.5 per cent of the micro-entrepreneurs.

Table 8.19: Mode of Business Started

Mode	*No. of Respondents*	*%*
Loan from microfinance	13	6.5
Loan from friends and relatives	13	6.5
Loan from moneylender	18	9.0
Loan from bank	3	1.5
Own fund	153	76.5
Total	200	100.0

Source: Field data.

Benefit of Microfinance

To know how far microfinance gave benefit to the micro-entrepreneurs, the present study has asked a question to the beneficiaries (micro-entrepreneurs) and from the question, Table 8.20 has been prepared. This table present that 43.5 per cent of the entrepreneur's response microfinance has gave very significant help to them. Next to this 37.54 per cent of them have response that microfinance has given significant help to their business. 6.5 per cent each of them said that microfinance help to

Table 8.20: Usefulness of Microfinance in the Micro-Enterprise

Degree of helping to the business	*No. of Respondents*	*%*
Great extent	13	6.5
Very significant	87	43.5
Significant	75	37.5
Less significant	13	6.5
No response	12	6.0
Total	200	100.0

Chi-Square = 141.900
df = 4
P < 0.01

Source: Field data.

their business at a great extent and less significant respectively. Among these 200 respondents, 6 per cent of them have given no response. From this response it can be concluded that microfinance help to the micro-enterprises in the moderate way.

Investment Amount to the Business

Investment amount of micro-entrepreneurs before and after getting microfinance loan has been shown in Fig. 8.10. The blue colour indicates the investment before getting microfinance and red colour indicate the investment amount after getting microfinance loan. From Fig. 8.10 it is clearly understood that up to the investment amount of ₹ 15,000 the number of entrepreneurs before microfinance loan is more than the number of entrepreneurs after getting microfinance loan. Just opposite to this the number of entrepreneurs after getting microfinance is more than number of entrepreneurs before getting microfinance loan in case of investment amount which is above ₹ 15,000. It means

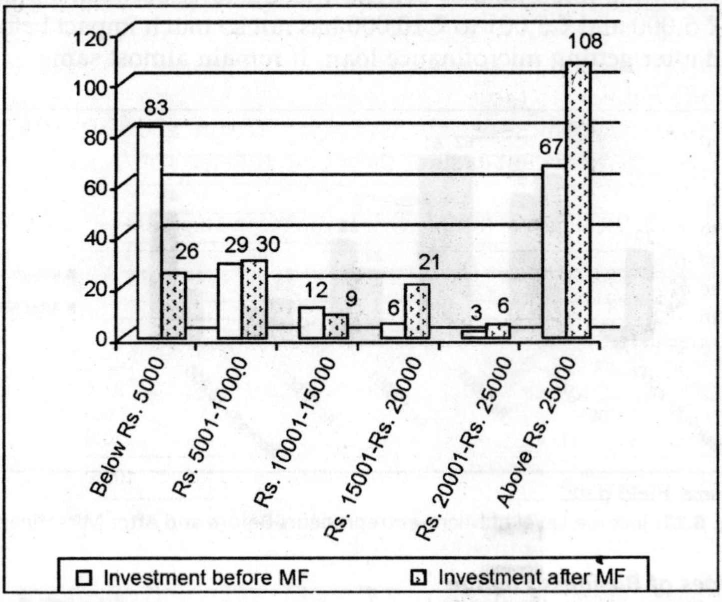

Source: Field data.

Fig. 8.10: Investment Amount Income of the Micro-Enterprises

the investment amount of existing micro-enterprises have been increasing after getting microfinance loan.

Income Level of Micro-enterprises

The income level of micro-enterprises before and after getting microfinance benefit has been shown in Fig. 8.10. For the clear and precise presentation, the income level has been classified into six different categories i.e., "Below ₹ 1,000", "₹ 1,001 to ₹ 5,000", ₹ 5,001 to ₹ 10,000", "₹ 10,001 to ₹ 15,000", "₹ 15,001 to ₹ 20,000" and "Above ₹ 20,000". From Fig. 8.11 is found that in the income level of below ₹ 1,000 there were 30 micro-entrepreneurs before getting microfinance loan but it reduce to 4 after getting microfinance loan. It means from 15 per cent to 2 per cent. For the income level of above ₹ 20,000 there were only 16 entrepreneurs before getting microfinance loan but it increases to 43 which shows the increases from 8 per cent to 21.5 per cent. It means the income level of entrepreneurs have been increasing after getting microfinance benefit. Income level between ₹ 1,001 to ₹ 5,000 and ₹ 5,001 to ₹ 10,000 has not so much impact before and after getting microfinance loan. It remain almost same.

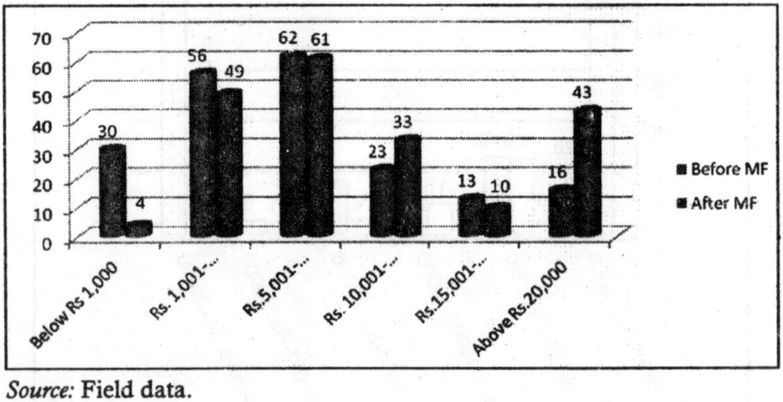

Source: Field data.

Fig. 8.11: Income Level of Micro-entrepreneurs Before and After Microfinance

Types of Business Engage

Different micro-entrepreneurs have run different nature of their business or enterprises. For the present study the type of business run by them has been classified into 20 different categories and it has been shown in the following Table 8.11. Among the different types of business grocery and vegetable vending are the highest in number and it cover 15 per cent each of the total population. Among the cloth selling in the valley districts maximum of them have sale *chadar* (particularly thin local shawl i.e., Wangkhei phee and Rani phee) and mekhala but in the hill districts mostly they have sold second hand clothes. Livestock includes poultry, duckery and piggery etc. For the vegetable vending they have sold vegetable from time to time and they also sell *soibum* (bamboo shoot) which they have prepared themselves.

Table 8.21: Types of Business Engage by Entrepreneurs

Nature of Business	*No. of Respondent*	*%*
Shoe vendor	3	1.5
Food processing units	20	10.0
Weaving	6	3.0
Embroidery and knitting	6	3.0
Grocery	30	15.0
Livestock	9	4.5
Fruit vendors	6	3.0
Fishery	3	1.5
Jewellery	6	3.0
Fuel oil selling shop	3	1.5
Cloth selling	23	11.5
Departmental store	6	3.0
Electronics items	1	.5
Vegetable vendor	29	14.5
Pan ki dukan	10	5.0
Agarbati making	3	1.5
Toy making	3	1.5
Toy and ornamental item selling	8	4.0
Bamboo mat making	16	8.0
Other*	9	4.5
Total	200	100.0

Chi-Square = 147.800a
df = 19
P< 0.01

* Others include blacksmith, pharmacy, charcoal selling, book store, cassette parlour, fertilizer selling, etc.

Source of Raw Materials

To know the sources of raw materials of the micro-entrepreneurs, a separate questions has been asked to the micro-entrepreneurs. The present study has been dividing into six different sources for the precise presentation. It has been shown in Table 8.22 that 87 per cent of the entrepreneurs have collected their raw materials from the local market, 5 per cent from own and local market, 3.5 per cent from local and outside state market and 1.5 per cent each from own, outside the state and "outside the state and foreign" respectively. From this data it is easily understood that local market is the main sources of their raw material and the least number of them have only from their own source.

Table 8.22: Sources of Raw materials

Sources	*No. of Respondents*	*%*
Own	3	1.5
Local market	174	87.0
Outside the state	3	1.5
Outside the state & Foreign	3	1.5
Local & Outside the state	7	3.5
Own & Local Market	10	5.0
Total	200	100.0
	Chi-Square = 713.560b df = 5 P < 0.01	

Source: Field data.

Training Availability

Maximum number of micro-entrepreneurs have not getting any training facilities for their business. From the collected data it is cleared that only 5 per cent have got training and rest 95 per cent were not receiving any training facilities. It has been shown in Fig. 8.12. Against the entrepreneurs those who get the training are also not from microfinance. They got training from others which are not related with microfinance and it has been shown in the following Table 8.23. From this table it is understood that 4 of the entrepreneurs learn about their business from others who have been running similar business. Next to this 3 of them have

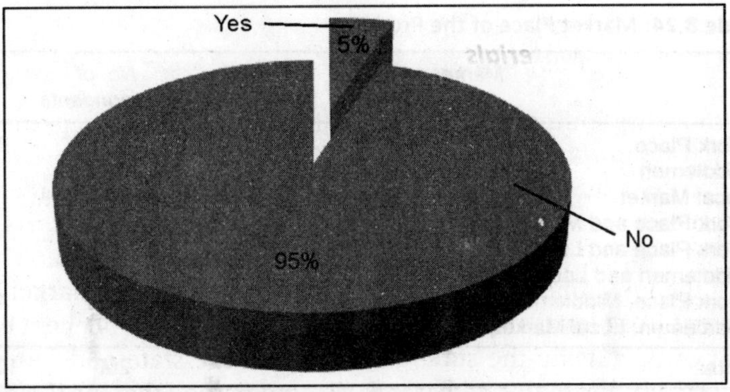

Fig. 8.12: Availability of Training

learned from their forefather as they were second generation entrepreneurs and rest of them have trained from ITI and nearby private institution by their own cost.

Table 8.23: Trainer from Where Micro-Entrepreneurs Get Training

Trainer	*No. of Respondents*	*%*
ITI Imphal	1	10.0
Learn from others	4	40.0
Nearby Pvt. institutions	2	20.0
Second generation	3	30.0
Total	10	100.0

Source: Field data.

Marketing of the Products

Table 8.24 shows the market place of different micro-entrepreneurs. It has been classified into 8 different market bases on their response. Among these market place maximum of the entrepreneurs i.e., 68.5 per cent of them have sale their product to their work place itselves. Least number of entrepreneurs have sold their product through "middlemen" and "local market", it account 3 per cent each of these two markets. Next to "work place" entrepreneurs sales their product through "work place, middlemen and local market" where found customers were available and it cover the 10 per cent of the total population.

Table 8.24: Market Place of the Products

Market	*No. of Respondents*	*%*
Work Place	137	68.5
Middlemen	3	1.5
Local Market	3	1.5
Work Place and Middleman	11	5.5
Work Place and Local Market	10	5.0
Middlemen and Local Market	9	4.5
Work Place, Middlemen and Local Market	20	10.0
Middlemen, Local Market, Exhibition, Outside the State	7	3.5
Total	200	100.0

Chi-Square = 581.520c
df = 7
P < 0.01

Source: Field data.

Microfinance Loan Received

Micro-entrepreneurs have received different ranges of microfinance loan from the microfinance institutions and started their suitable enterprises. Base on the data collected from the entrepreneurs it has been classified into 5 different ranges i.e., "below ₹ 10,000", "₹ 10,001 to ₹ 20,000", ₹ 20,001 to ₹ 30,000", ₹ 30,001 to ₹ 40,000", "₹ 40,001 to ₹ 50,000" and "above ₹ 50,000". The maximum number of the entrepreneurs have received an amount range of "below ₹ 10,000" it accounts 41.5 per cent of the total population. Least number of the entrepreneurs i.e., only 4 per cent of them have received the highest ranges of

Table 8.25: Loan Amount from Microfinance

Amount	*No. of Respondents*	*%*
Below ₹ 10000	83	41.5
₹ 10001 – ₹ 20000	45	22.5
₹ 20001 – ₹ 30000	12	6.0
₹ 30001 – ₹ 40000	24	12.0
₹ 40001 – ₹ 50000	28	14.0
Above ₹ 50000	8	4.0
Total	200	100

Source: Field data.

amount i.e., "above ₹ 50,000". From this data it is understood that average entrepreneurs receives the microfinance loan amount below ₹ 20,000.

Interest Paid by Entrepreneurs

Entrepreneurs have paid different rate of interest against their loan amount according to their loan amount and loan providers. These different rates of interest have been shown in Table 8.26. According to entrepreneur's response it has found nine different rate of interest. The lowest rate of interest is 1 per cent per month and highest rate of interest is 8 per cent per month. From this table it is understood that least number of beneficiaries i.e., only one beneficiary has given lowest rate of interest and 9 beneficiaries has given highest rate of interest. It is also understood that maximum number of beneficiaries (entrepreneurs) have given interest of 2 per cent per month and it account the 51.5 per cent of total population. Therefore, it can be concluded that in an average microfinance beneficiaries have given an interest rate of 2 per cent per month against the microfinance loan. If it is calculated on flat basis it is more than 50 per cent in a year. It means maximum number of microfinance beneficiaries has given higher interest compared with bank loan.

Table 8.26: Interest Paid Against Loan Per Month

Rate of interest %	*No. of Respondents*	*%*
1.00	1	0.5
1.12	15	7.5
1.30	21	10.5
1.60	10	5.0
1.90	15	7.5
2.00	103	51.5
2.17	10	5.0
2.40	15	7.5
8.00	9	4.5
No response	1	0.5
Total	200	100
	Mode = 2 per cent	

Source: Field data.

Tenure of Loan

Entrepreneurs have taken microfinance loan from different providers and at different schemes. So the tenure of these loans are different and based on data collected from them it has been classified into eleven different ranges and it has been shown in Table 8.27. The minimum period is 105 days and maximum period is presented as more than 1 year. From this table it is cleared that only one beneficiary get the loan tenure which is more than one year. Among these eleven different ranges of tenure 37.5 per cent of the total population has fall under the period of 50 weeks, it means in an average microfinance beneficiaries have received the loan of the tenure 50 weeks. By studying this data it can be concluded that maximum number of the entrepreneurs have received the microfinance loan with the tenure of ranges from 10 month to 12 month.

Table 8.27: Tenure of Loan

Period	*No. of Respondents*	*%*
105 days	15	7.5
110 days	2	1.0
112 days	4	2.0
120 days	9	4.5
150 days	6	3.0
180 days	6	3.0
245 days	9	4.5
300 days	33	16.5
350 days	75	37.5
365 days	33	16.5
More than 1 year	1	0.5
No response	7	3.5
Total	200	100.0
	Mode = 50 weeks	

Source: Field data.

Change of Income

How far microfinance change the income level of micro-entrepreneurs have been shown in Table 8.28. For the present study the level of income changes have been classified into four different levels. According to the response of beneficiaries it has been presented in table form as under. From this table it is understood that around 50 per cent entrepreneurs have selected second option of "increase" and next to this 24.5 per cent of them have selected the third option of "little increased" and so on. By their response it is understood that 90 per cent of them have increased their income after getting microfinance loan and rest 10 per cent could not increase their income. According to their experience the main reasons for not increase their incomes were the loan amount is small and repayment of existing borrowed amount from moneylender by this microfinance loan.

Table 8.28: Changes of Income Level After Business

Level	*No. of Respondents*	*%*
Increased at a great extent	31	15.5
Increased	99	49.5
Little increased	49	24.5
No increased	21	10.5
Total	200	100.0

X2 = 72.080
df = 3
P < 0.01

Source: Field data.

Level of Poverty Reduction

Around 60 per cent of the beneficiaries said microfinance reduces their poverty at the reasonable way and minimum number of them i.e., around 6 per cent of them response that it reduce their poverty at great extent. It has been shown in Table 8.29. Some of the beneficiary response that microfinance could not reduce their poverty, they say that the amount received from microfinance is minimal and it cannot be effective to their economic oriented activities.

Again it is also found that some of the beneficiaries opined that it cannot increased their income but at least they get relief from moneylenders which is more important to leave in peaceful life.

Table 8.29: Reduction of Poverty by the Income

Level of reduction	*No. of Respondents*	*%*
Reduced at a great extent	13	6.5
Reduced	119	59.5
Little reduced	53	26.5
No reduced	15	7.5
Total	200	100.0

$X2 = 147.280$
$df = 3$
$P < 0.01$

Source: Field data.

Way of Empowerment

To know how microfinance empowering to the beneficiaries after getting both financial and technical support from the microfinance institutions. According to the response given by the entrepreneurs, it has found that 73.5 per cent of them can get the self-decision-making and next to this 21 per cent of them response that they can participate in decision-making as well as they can take their own decision. It is also found that microfinance has given the chance to attain the fair and exhibition, it also given them the empowerment. Out of these 200 beneficiaries 1.5 per cent of them have response that microfinance has not given any empowerment to them directly.

Table 8.30: Way of Empowerment to the Entrepreneurs

Ways	*No. of Respondents*	%
Participation in decision-making	7	3.5
Participation in fair/exhibition	1	.5
Self-decision-making	147	73.5
Participation in decision-making and self-decision-making	42	21.0
No empower	3	1.5
Total	200	100.0

$X^2 = 385.800$
$df = 4$
$P < 0.01$

Source: Field data.

Reasons Behind the Selection of Business

Different entrepreneurs have opined different reasons for choosing their business. Base on their response, it has been classified into 12 different reasons for the present study. It has been shown in Table 8.31. Among the different reasons for choosing their own business, maximum number of entrepreneurs select "profit" is the main reason and it account 26 per cent of the total population of study. Which is quite relevant because, without profit none of the business can survive, prosper and growth.

Next to this, second generation is the reason behind the selection of business. In this factor, most of the entrepreneurs continue business as their parents and forefathers had run the same business. Which is quite a common nature that maximum of todays successful business are generation business. Market demand and easy availability of raw materials are other reasons behind the selection of their business. Least number of entrepreneurs has selected their business due to confidence in the products or services offered.

Table 8.31: Reasons for Choosing the Present Business

Reasons	*No. of Respondents*	*%*
Profitable	52	26.0
Want for Control and Freedom to Make My Own Decision	9	4.5
Self-Achievement	6	3.0
Confidence in the Products/Services Offered	3	1.5
Having Technical Skills for Manufacturing Products	12	6.0
Easily Available for Raw Materials	24	12.0
Market Demand	25	12.5
Second Generation Business	33	16.5
Remain at Home	9	4.5
All Excluding 6 and 11	12	6.0
Profitable and Remain at Home	9	4.5
Low Investment	6	3.0
Total	200	100.0

$X^2 = 136.360$
df =11
$P < 0.01$

Source: Field data.

Problem Faced

Table 8.32 shows the different problems faced by different entrepreneurs. These problems have been broadly classified into 5 different sub-headings they are, financial problems while taking loan, financial problems while management, marketing problem, management problem, and training problem etc. From the information of the respondent it is understood that while taking microfinance loan maximum of them have no problem, they can access the loan very smoothly. But 9 per cent of them opined that the interest charged by the microfinance is high and 14 of them said that the process of taking loan is lengthy and it wastage their time.

In case of financial management problem 40 per cent of the entrepreneurs said that they have the lack of financial management knowledge and skill, 30.5 per cent and 6.5 each of them opined that they have lack of accounting knowledge and lack of credit management policy respectively. It is also found that 23 per cent of them have response that they have no problem in financial management. From this data it can be concluded that maximum of the microfinance beneficiaries faced the financial management problem.

For the market problem more than 50 per cent of entrepreneurs opined that they have faced the problem of fluctuation in demand and it reduces their income at the time of lean and thin season. In this period sometime it is hard to maintain the family. Among the entrepreneurs 35 per cent of them have no problem in their market.

Testing of Hypotheses

Hypothesis testing or significance testing is a method for testing a claim or hypothesis about a parameter in population using data measured in a sample. In this method some hypothesis has been tested by determining the likelihood that a sample statistic could have been selected, if the hypothesis regarding the population parameter were true. Hypothesis testing is used to help make a judgment about a claim by addressing the question, can the observed difference be attributed to chance?

Table 8.32: Problem Faced by the Entrepreneurs

Problems	*Types*	*No. of Respondents*	*%*	
Financial Problems while taking loan	High rate of interest	18	9.0	$\chi^2 = 172.360^h$ Df = 2 P < 0.01
	Lengthy in process	28	14.0	
	No problem	154	77.0	
Total		200	100.0	
Financial Problems while management	Lack of accounting knowledge	61	30.5	$\chi^2 = 48.120^e$ Df = 3 P < 0.01
	Lack of credit Management/ policy	13	6.5	
	Lack of financial management skill	80	40.0	
	No problem	46	23.0	
Total		200	100.0	
Market Problems	Price fixation of the product	3	1.5	$\chi^2 = 165.560^e$ Df = 3 P < 0.01
	Fluctuation in demand	115	57.5	
	Competition	12	6.0	
	No problem	70	35.0	
Total		200	100.0	
Management Problems	To get suitable personnel	3	1.5	$\chi^2 = 253.523^i$ Df = 3 P < 0.01
	Lack of proper management technique	6	3.0	
	Collision of family and Business work	48	24.0	
	No problem	143	71.5	
Total		200	100	
Training	No training facility	28	14.0	$\chi^2 = 103.680^j$ Df = 1 P < 0.01
	No problem	172	86.0	
Total		200	100.0	

Source: Field Study.

Steps of Significance Testing

There are some steps for testing the significance/hypothesis, it can be broadly classify into four. They are:

- ***Step-I: Null and Alternative Hypotheses:*** The first step of hypothesis testing is to convert the research question into null and alternative hypotheses. It is normally started with the **null hypothesis (H_0)** and it can be symbolically represented as, H_0: $\mu_0 = \mu$. The null hypothesis is a claim of "no difference". When the null hypothesis fails to hold the **alternative hypothesis (H_1)** arises and it can be symbolically stated as, H_1: $\mu_0 \neq \mu$. The alternative hypothesis is a claim of "a difference in the population". These hypotheses reference the population values and not the observed statistics.

- ***Step-II: Test Statistic:*** The test statistic has been calculated from the data available. There are different types of test statistics but for the present study chi-square test has been introduced. And it is to be computed under the null hypothesis.

$$\chi^2 = \Sigma\,(O - E)^2/E$$

- ***Step-III: P Value and Conclusion:*** The test statistic is converted to a conditional probability called a *p*-value. The *p*-value answers the question "if the null hypothesis were true, what is the probability of observing the current data or data that is more extreme?" Small *p*-values provide evidence against the null hypothesis because it say the observe data are unlikely when the null hypothesis is true.
- ***Step-IV: Decision:*** Alpha (α) is a probability threshold for a decision. If $P \leq \alpha$, the null hypothesis will be rejected otherwise it will be retained for want of evidence. For the present study the following two decision have been taken:
  (i) When *p*-value >0.05, the observed difference is "not significant" and hence the null hypothesis is accepted.
  (ii) When *p*-value $\leq$ 0.05, the observed difference is "significant" and hence the null hypothesis is rejected.

Here the term *"significant"* means "*the observed difference is not likely due to chance*". It does not mean of "*important*" or "*meaningful*".

Testing of Hypothesis – I

H_0: "there is no relationship between NGO/MFI and establishment of new micro-enterprises".

H_1: "NGO/MFI has taken important role to set up new micro-enterprises in the state". To prove the above hypothesis Table 8.33 has been developed on the basis of data collected from different micro-enterprises. From this table it is understood that only 6.5 per cent of enterprises have taken loan from microfinance as their initial capital of business. The maximum enterprises i.e., 76.5 per cent of them started their business with their own fund. From this available data the null hypothesis "there is no relationship between NGO/MFI and establishment of new micro-enterprises". It means establishment of new micro-enterprises in the state are not base on microfinance loan.

Table 8.33: Source of Initial Capital of Micro-Enterprises

Loan from whom	*Observed N*	*%*
Loan from microfinance	13	6.5
Loan from friends and relatives	13	6.5
Loan from moneylender	18	9.0
Loan from bank	3	1.5
Own fund	153	76.5
Total	200	100
	Mode = Own fund	

Source: Compiled from questionnaire.

Testing of Hypothesis – II

H_0: "there is no significant difference of the income level of micro-entrepreneurs before and after getting microfinance loan".

H_1: "after getting microfinance loan the income level of the micro-entrepreneurs have been increasing"

To test the above hypothesis the following Table 8.34 has been prepared by compiling the income level of 200 entrepreneurs before and after taking microfinance loan. The chi-square test has been applied for testing the hypothesis.

Table 8.34: Income Level of Micro-Entrepreneurs

Level of Income	*Income of Entrepreneurs*		*Total*
	Before taking microfinance loan	*After taking microfinance loan*	
₹ 1000 and less	30	4	34
₹ 1001 – ₹ 5000	56	49	105
₹ 5001 – ₹ 10000	62	61	123
₹ 10001 –₹ 15000	24	33	57
₹ 15001 – ₹ 20000	12	10	22
₹ 20001 and above	16	43	59
Total	200	200	400

Source: Compiled from questionnaire.

Base on the frequencies found in the table—the expected frequencies have been developed by using the formula of "*Expectation of (AB) = [(A) × (B)] ÷ N*" in the following table as:

E.g., E_{11} = [200 × 34] ÷ 400 = 17; E_{12} = [200 × 105] ÷ 400 = 52.5 *etc....*

17	17	34
52.5	52.5	105
61.5	61.5	123
28.5	28.5	57
11	11	22
29.5	29.5	59
200	200	400

Applying chi-square (χ^2) test:

Observed (O)	Expected (E)	$(O-E)^2$	$(O-E)^2/E$
30	17	169	9.94
56	52.5	12.25	0.23
62	61.5	0.25	0.01
24	28.5	20.25	0.71
12	11	1	0.09
16	29.5	182.3	6.17
4	17	169	9.94
49	52.5	12.25	0.23
61	61.5	0.25	0.01
33	28.5	20.25	0.71
10	11	1	0.09
43	29.5	182.3	6.17

$X^2 = \Sigma [(O-E)^2/E] = 34.32$
df = (r–1) (c–1) = (2 –1) (6 –1) = 5
[where the table value of χ^2 at 5 df at 5 per cent = 11.1]

The calculated value of χ^2 is much significant i.e., very much greater than the table value. Hence, the null hypothesis is rejected. Therefore, the alternate hypothesis "after getting microfinance loan the income level of the micro-entrepreneurs have been increasing" has been accepted.

Testing of Hypothesis–III

H_0: "there is no relationship between microfinance and poverty reduction of microfinance beneficiaries".

H_1: "microfinance beneficiaries have been reduced their poverty after getting microfinance loan".

For testing the above hypothesis the pre-set study have collected some information from the entrepreneurs regarding poverty reduction by their income and it has been presented in Table 8.35. By using SPSS these data has been processed and calculated the value of Chi-square.

Only 7.5 per cent of the entrepreneur's response that microfinance could not reduce the poverty and rest 92.5 per cent response that microfinance reduced their poverty at different degree. The calculated value of chi-square = 147.280, df = 3 and P < 0.05 also reject the null hypothesis "there is no relationship between microfinance and poverty reduction of microfinance beneficiaries", therefore, the alternate hypothesis "microfinance beneficiaries have been reduced their poverty after getting microfinance loan" is true.

Table 8.35: Degree of Poverty Reduced by Microfinance

Degree of reduced	*Observed N*	*Expected N*	*Residual*
Reduced at a great extend	13	50.0	–37.0
Reduced	119	50.0	69.0
Little reduced	53	50.0	3.0
No reduced	15	50.0	–35.0
Total	200		

Test Statistics	
	Degree of poverty reduced by MF
Chi-Square	147.280
Df	3
Asymp. Sig.	.000

a. 0 cells (.0 per cent) have expected frequencies less than 5. The minimum expected cell frequency is 50.0.

NINE
Findings, Recommendations and Conclusion

"When combined with information and communication technologies, microcredit can unleash new opportunities for the world's poorest entrepreneurs and thereby revitalize the village economies they serve."

— *Madeleine K. Albright and John Doerr*

Introduction

It is very necessary to determine few important points as finding of the study after the length and breadth of a study. Both primary and secondary data collected for the study have been put up, arranged, analysed and interpreted with the help of suitable statistical tool and techniques where found necessary outcome of the study is given below:

Findings of the Study

The finding of the study is classified into two i.e., (i) finding from Microfinance institutions and (ii) finding from micro-entrepreneurs.

Finding from Microfinance Institutions

- Microfinance is started in Manipur in the year 1992 when Loyalam Bank Project-RDO started its project in the state.
- It is found that 80 per cent of the total NGOs which have been working with microfinance in the state started their microfinance after some gap of starting their organizations.

- Out of the 20 microfinance-NGOs only six are based on hill districts, and remaining are from valley districts. It means maximum of the microfinance NGOs have been working in the valley districts.
- It is also found that 75 per cent of the NGOs started their microfinance programme very late in the state i.e., after 2000 only.
- Only 25 per cent of the NGO have given the bank linkage facilities to their beneficiaries and 75 per cent of them do not provide the bank linkage facilities due to different reasons such as lack of bank branches in the rural areas, lengthy process of banking and geographical isolation from the mainstream, etc.
- Maximum NGOs working microfinance in Manipur have been getting financial assistance for microfinance from different funding agencies. The number of NGOs which have been running microfinance only by their own fund is very less. From the present study it has been found that only 20 per cent of the NGOs have been running microfinance only by their own fund. The rest 80 per cent of the NGOs have been running microfinance only by outside funds i.e., received from funding agencies.
- Average number of NGOs have given the interest rate of more than 11 per cent per annum against the microfinance fund received from funding agencies. Even some of them have given more than 19 per cent per annum. It may be one of the reason behind the increase in interest rate for microfinance loan given to their beneficiaries.
- The two model of lending of microfinance loan to the beneficiaries have been found in this present study i.e., only to the group and individual. 70 per cent of NGOs have been lending their microfinance loan to both group as well as individual and only 30 per cent of them have been investing only to the groups.
- The average loan size of the NGOs to the group is found from ₹ 10,000 to ₹ 1,00,000 but maximum number of the NGOs have lend an average loan amount of ₹ 25,000 in a group.
- The interest rate charged by the NGO is found in different rate and the minimum rate is 1 per cent per month and

maximum is 3 per cent per month. But maximum number of them has charged an average of 2 per cent per month as interest against the microfinance loan extended to their beneficiaries.

- Against the mode of interest charged the study also found two methods one is *flat method* and another is *reducing balance method*. From the study it is found that 55 per cent of them have followed reducing method, 40 per cent of them have followed flat method and rest 5 per cent of them has followed both flat and reducing method as per the convenient of the MFI_NGOs.
- It has been found that the mode of recovery of loan is provided in different form as per the suitability and convenient of the clients. Most of the NGOs-MFIs have followed the *weekly* and *monthly* mode of collection and it account 75 per cent of the total NGO-MFIs.
- For the tenure of the loan to the beneficiaries, 75 per cent of the NGOs-MFIs have given the loan period of 5 months to 12 months range and rest have given the tenure of less than 5 months and more than 12 months respectively.
- It is also found that only 20 per cent of the NGO-MFIs have given forward and backward linkage services to their beneficiaries.
- NGO are not only giving loan to their beneficiaries they also giving training facilities to their beneficiaries. From the present study it is found that 90 per cent of the NGOs-MFIs have given training to their beneficiaries and only 10 per cent have given loan to their beneficiaries.
- The training given by the NGOs are different but mainly they have given training in the area of book keeping, accounting, financial literacy, group formation and management, etc.

Finding from Micro-enterpreneurs

- Around 80 per cent of the enterprises established after the year 2000 and rest 20 per cent have started before the year 2000.
- From the present study it is understood that the age-group

of 36 to 55 years have taken more economic responsibility in the family as well as in the society. 70 per cent of the entrepreneurs have fall under this age-group.

- It is also found that maximum numbers of micro-enterprises are running by women. For the present study 88 per cent of entrepreneurs are women. It means microfinance is more favourable to the women than men.
- Again it is also understood that married person have taken more economic responsibility than unmarried one because in this study only 1.5 per cent of the entrepreneurs are unmarried and rest are married persons.
- The spouse of the micro-entrepreneurs has been engaging different occupation but more interestingly 22 per cent of them have joint the same enterprise where his/her spouse is engaging business. And it is the second highest number of spouse who has been engaging different occupation.
- Around 80 per cent of the entrepreneurs are literate among them some have been completed their graduate and master degree. Maximum number of them has completed higher secondary education and it account 31 per cent of the total entrepreneurs. Overall the educational qualification of the micro-entrepreneurs are very high.
- It is found that more than 50 per cent of micro-entrepreneurs have their own bank account, it means still 50 per cent are out of financial inclusion which far lagging behind the 100 per cent financial inclusion target of the government.
- Among the entrepreneurs who have their own bank account 37 per cent of them have opened their account before starting their business and rest are after starting their business. Thus, opening of account and business are not correlated.
- The maximum number of micro-entrepreneurs bank account have been open to UBI and MRB, it accounts around 70 per cent of the total account open entrepreneurs.
- While studying the mode of starting their enterprise it has been found that around 76 per cent of them have started their business with their own fund and only around

6 per cent of them have started with microfinance loan and rest have been started with other sources. This mean that in Manipur microfinance normally looking for assisting to the existing entrepreneurs instead of the person who have the dream to set up their own micro-enterprise but have no capital.

- Maximum beneficiaries opined that microfinance is moderately helpful to their business and around 6 per cent of the total entrepreneurs opined that microfinance has given a great extent to help their business.
- It is also found that after getting microfinance loan beneficiaries has increased their investment amount to their enterprises. Before taking microfinance loan only 67 entrepreneurs out of 200 has been invest an amount of above ₹ 25,000 to their enterprises but it has increased to 108 entrepreneurs after getting microfinance loan. It means microfinance is more positive impact on increasing investment amount by the micro-enterprises.
- In case of entrepreneurs income level, maximum of them have increased their income after getting microfinance loan. Before getting microfinance loan only 16 entrepreneurs can earn ₹ 20,000 and above in a month but it has increased to 43 entrepreneurs after getting microfinance loan. Again before getting microfinance loan the number of entrepreneurs who earn less than ₹ 1,000 per month were 30 but it has reduced to only 4 it means 26 of them has increased their income level after getting microfinance loan.
- Different micro-entrepreneurs have engaged different type of business but maximum number of them has found to engage grocery and vegetable vending as their business it account around 30 per cent of the total entrepreneurs.
- It is also found that the main sources of the micro-enterprises raw material have been found from local market it account 87 per cent of the total sources. Rest of them is from other sources like outside the state even foreign market.
- 95 per cent of the total entrepreneurs have not been getting proper training regarding their business. Only 5 per cent have found to get training regarding their business but it is not given by the microfinance institution.
- From the study it is also understood that 68 per cent of

the micro-enterprises sales their product to their work place and rest have sale their product through middlemen, nearby market, exhibition etc.

- Around 40 per cent of entrepreneurs have been getting microfinance loan below ₹ 10,000 and only 4 per cent of them have been getting the loan amount of above ₹ 50,000. It means maximum number of beneficiaries have been getting microfinance loan with an amount ranging from ₹ 10,000 to ₹ 50,000.
- It is also found that around 51 per cent of the microfinance beneficiaries have given interest rate of 2 per cent per month for getting loan from NGO-MFIs. The interest rate which is given by the beneficiaries against microfinance loan is ranges from 1 per cent to 8 per cent per month.
- In case of microfinance loan tenure around 37 per cent of entrepreneurs have getting the loan period of 52 weeks and only 0.5 per cent of the total population have getting the maximum loan tenure of more than one year.
- More than 73 per cent of the entrepreneurs opined that by running their own micro-enterprises empower them in self-decision making. 3 per cent of them opined that it could not empower them and rest of them opined it empower them in different areas like participation in decision-making, participation in fair and exhibition, etc.
- For choosing their own business around 67 per cent of the entrepreneurs opined that they have chosen their business due to, profitability, easily available of raw materials, market demand and second generation business.
- It is also found that more than 70 per cent of the micro-enterprises do not maintain proper financial record for their business. This may be one of the reason for inability to show the exact figure of their financial position.
- While taking the microfinance loan 77 per cent of the beneficiaries opined that they have faced no problem but 9 per cent opined the rate of interest is high and rest 14 per cent opined that the process are lengthy.
- Only 35 per cent of the entrepreneurs have no problem for their market but 65 per cent of them said they have faced the problem of price fixation of the product, fluctuation in demand and increased competition.

- Around 71 per cent of the entrepreneurs opined that there has no problem while managing their business but around 28 per cent opined that they have faced the problem of unavailability of suitable person, lack of proper management technique and collision with family work.
- It is also found that 14 per cent of the total enterprises opined that they need training regarding their business but they have not receiving any training facility and rest 86 per cent opined that they need no training regarding their business.

Issues of Microfinance in India

After considering the various finding of the study, following points have been developed as main issues of microfinance in India, they are–

- *Legal Issues*: No Microfinance act has passed despite of several attempt made by the government in the last few years. Further, State government should also come forward and making their own state microfinance act as early as possible.
- *Gender Issues*: More than 95 per cent of SHGs members are women and only 5 per cent are men. It is more women dominant scheme. Major share of the men population are remain untouched by this sector.
- *Rate of interest*: Different rates were charged by the MFI to SHGs and even SHGs to its members. It has exploited the ultimate users of microfinance services by the poor.
- *Imbalanced Geographical Growth*: Microfinance is growing along with geographical imbalance of a state or a region. For instance, microfinance is more significant in southern state of the country. Likewise, microfinance in the valley is more significant than hills in Manipur.
- *Choice of Productive Activities*: Microfinance is not being effectively used for productive activities. Rather it is being used for consumable and other domestic purpose.
- *Assessment of Demand*: Assessment of demand for microfinance will be a difficult task for microfinance promotion institutions. Without assessing proper demand

for microfinance, microfinance development scheme and policy can not implement effectively.

- *Subsidy*: Subsidy provided for formation of SHGs and JLGs are misdirected and it should be bring into proper direction with guidance.
- *Capacity building*: Microfinance should give more emphasis on capacity building of the members of SHGs other than providing financial assistance. It will help in making their own venture of economic oriented activities effectively.
- *Records Maintenance*: Most of the SHGs, JLGs, micro-entrepreneurs and even NGO-MFIs were poor in maintenance of record and financial statement. Without proper maintenance of record and accounts, none of the enterprise can growth and prosper.
- *Auditing*:Auditing and internal checking of account and other information is very much lacking in microfinance system.
- *Transparency*: Transparency of accounts, confidential information among the members of SHGs, JLGs is very much lacking.
- *Absence of Policy*: Even concerted efforts by the government, Microfinance Act is still pending in the Parliament. It need to be passed without delay giving more teeth to control the microfinance in the country.
- *Absence of information/statistics*: After almost 30 years of its presence in the country, still there is lack of information and statistics related to microfinance.

Recommendations of the Study

On the basis of the length and breadth of the study, finding of the study, following few points have been suggested to overcome the problems faced and further strengthening the microfinance activities in the state in particular and region and country in general.

- The long pending Microfinance bill should be passed and converted into act so that a stringent measure for controlling microfinance activities can be started as early as possible.

- There is need to streamline government programmes and to ensure convergence of schemes, so that officials' support for skill training, extension support, credit and other enterprise related services may be accessed easily.
- Microfinance programmes must include strategies and budgetary allocation for building the capacity of SHGs, their members and federation of SHG to manage savings and credit, augment vocational skills and promote enterprise. Skill training programmes should be linked with market analysis, credit provision, income generating activities and market exposure.
- Designing wide range of financial products and services is the need of the hour. SHGs have different kinds of credit needs and thus, the credit needs should be classified into different categories such as livelihoods, income generating activities, investment in education, health, consumption, household needs, marriages, death ceremonies and products for social security.
- There is urgent need to streamline the procedure for applying, seeking and releasing of credit from the banks. The procedural difficulties are one of the major impediments which are denied by women for getting financial benefits from the banks. Therefore, the procedure for credit access to beneficiaries should be making more easy and simple.
- Microfinance Institutions need proper regulation and operation of business transaction. Thus, RBI, NABARD, SIDBI and other microfinance development agencies should evolve proper mechanism for monitoring, supervision, direction, appraisal and evaluation of microfinance institutions as well as self-help promotion institutions.
- A proper mechanism should be evolved to prepare database on SHGs, SSPs, MFIs, etc. A census of SHGs may also be undertaken for ensuring effective regulation of microfinancing activities and examining their problems. MIS with good management backing needs to be developed to achieve sustainability of microfinancing institutions.
- Transformation of the repayment culture is required. Any expansion of microfinancing services will need not only

appropriate and efficient micro-products on a very large scale, but also customers who can willingly to pay the full cost of those services. Bankers must change their attitude towards small loans to poor people, including women, as a social obligation of treating them as potential business entrepreneurs and also to fulfilling the target of 100 per cent financial inclusion.

- Majority of the women members have joined SHGs by self-motivation, motivation by SHG promoters, peer pressure and also from family members. Most of the beneficiaries reported that the frequency of group meetings is monthly. More than half of the beneficiaries said that all the members participate in such meetings. They also reported that decisions in the meetings are taken by the majority of the members.
- The impact of SHGs on women's empowerment has been seen in increased mobility, recognition in family, community and interaction with outsiders, access to health, immunization, and medical services, and increased participation in decision-making and development process.
- Micro credit should be made available not only for income generation activities but also for consumption needs arising out of emergencies, crisis, as also for housing, sanitation and provision of basic amenities. Micro credit should be provided in the form of revolving funds so that local communities can identify priorities and not be restricted by any predetermined activities.
- Government support is required to start income generating activities. More training in income generating activities is required. Training programmes should be organized as per market demand and feasibility studies are undertaken. Marketing facilities need to be provided to the SHGs.
- All record keeping of MFI NGOs has been done manually and it is very time consuming. Thus, a computer and a computer assistant for the programmes would go a long way in maintenance of records, accounts, correspondence and updating the same periodically.
- Proper monitoring of SHGs, SHG promoters, PIAs and other development functionaries should be ensured on part of State Government and Central Government agencies.

The ad-hoc arrangement of supervision, monitoring and regulation of projects should be discouraged.

- Development strategies for SHGs must be planned with an empowerment perspective. Consolidation of SHGs at high levels enables access to large funding.
- Marketing centres may be provided within the village to ensure better selling of products. Quality control of products is needed. There should be more budgetary allocation on market development in order to provide an effective platform for marketing of SHG products.
- The SHG members should be inculcated the feeling of collective development, social harmony and active role in development process and governance. The members should be mentally prepared for starting income generating activities and their sustainability.
- Women have varied credit requirements which current microfinance programmes do not meet. Most of the financial institutions provide micro-credit only for income generating activities and livelihood developments, however, women have to depend on non-institutional credit sources for meeting out their credit needs other than income generating activities.

Conclusions

Microfinance has been providing as an important tool for alleviation of poverty over the last few decades despite of its regulations passed in the Parliament. It has served as an important financial support to micro-entrepreneurs where commercial banks and other financial banks fail to provide. The scheme introduced by the government through NABARD has played an important role for socio-economic development of the people living in rural areas. Despite of having its significant role, it has been considered as bane for the poor people due to high rate of interest, flat rate of interest calculation and lack of proper guidelines to control the microfinance predator.

Case Studies of Select Micro-enterprises

Case 1

Type of Business: Hotel
Proprietor: Ramtawon
Age: 40 years
Sex: Female
Year of Estd: 2005
Education: Below HSLC
Address: Phunghidang, Ukhrul
MFI: VVD

She started her business with only ₹ 270. Ramtawon has two daughters and 1 son. Her husband is carpenter. Since 2005, she runs her own hotel at Phunghidang, Ukhrul just adjacent to her home. At that time she can earn ₹ 500 per day. Now she got ₹ 10,000 loan amount from VVD Ukhrul in 2007 and after getting loan, she has invested more amount to her business. Her income per day is ₹ 1,000 to ₹ 1,500 after deducting all the expenditure today. All of her day-to-day expenditures for family as well as children education has been maintained by the income from the hotel. She expressed that the microfinance has helped her to a great extent to solve the problems of her family.

Case 2

Type of Business: Tea and Snack Stall
Proprietor: W. Maimu Devi
Age: 56 years
Sex: Female
Year of Estd: 2004
Education: Illiterate
Address: Thoubal Awang Leikai
MFI:YVU

Since 2004 she has been running her business at Thoubal Bazar. She had chosen the existing business due to low investment. At the beginning she has invested only ₹ 1,000 per day for acquiring raw materials and can earn ₹ 200 to 250 per day from the business. Since the investment was less in those days profits were also very less. But today after taking microfinance loan a sum of ₹ 30,000 from YVU microfinance, she has been investing more and started earning more profit than before. With this business, she has financed for her sons marriage and also maintain her family better than before.

Case 3

Type of Business: Electronic Repairing Service
Proprietor: Ak. Gyaneldro Singh
Age: 42
Sex: Male
Education: Graduate
Address: Thoubal Wangmataba Sorok Makha

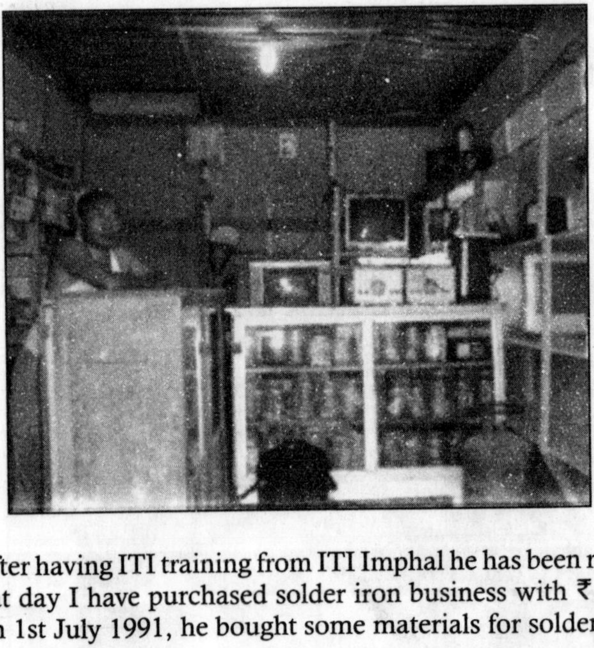

After having ITI training from ITI Imphal he has been running his that day I have purchased solder iron business with ₹ 500. It was on 1st July 1991, he bought some materials for soldering the electronics items. During those days, he could earn ₹ 400 to ₹ 500 per day by repairing the electronics items like Radio, Tape Recorder and T.V. After taking microfinance loan from YVUMF as sum of ₹ 20,000 his business has been growing. The current investment amounts to his business has increased to around 2 lakh rupee. Today, he can earn ₹ 2,000 to ₹ 3,000 per day in an average. He has two divisions of his business, one for sales and another for servicing division and also employed one person for his business.

Case 4

Type of Business: Shoe stall
Name: Y. Dasumati Devi
Age: 47
Sex: Female
Education: Illiterate
Address: Thoubal Bamon Leirak

Since 10 years, she has been selling shoes at Thoubal bazaar, Thoubal district. At the beginning, she has invested ₹ 5000 as capital. During those days due to less number of vendors, she could earn ₹ 1000-1500 per pay.

But now the number of shoe vendors has increased so it is hard to earn ₹ 600 in a day. On the other hand the capital amount invested today is also increased as compared with in the beginning. Today she has been investing ₹ 40,000 to her business with taking loan amount of ₹ 20,000 from YVUMF.

The income earn from her business maintain her six members family smoothly without facing much difficulty which she encountered once before starting her business of shoe vendor.

Case 5

Type of Business: Vegetable Vending
Name: R. Kanmila
Age: 50
Sex: Female
Education: Below HSLC
Address: Ngaimo Village, Ukhrul

Since 2000 she has been selling vegetables at Ukhrul mini secretariat opposite. At the beginning she had started her business with ₹ 2000 and in those days she could earn in an average ₹ 100 per day.

She took ₹ 5,000 loan from VVD Ukhrul for expansion of her business in 2005 and earning from her business she has timely repay the amount of loan to VVD. As second time loan she got another ₹ 12,000 from VVD microfinance loan. Today she has been investing around ₹ 20000 to her business and could earn ₹ 600 to ₹ 700 per day.

Case 6

Type of Business: Secondhand Cloth Vendor
Name: Rita Keising
Age: 35
Sex: Female
Education: 12th standard
Address: Chatric Khunou, Ukhrul

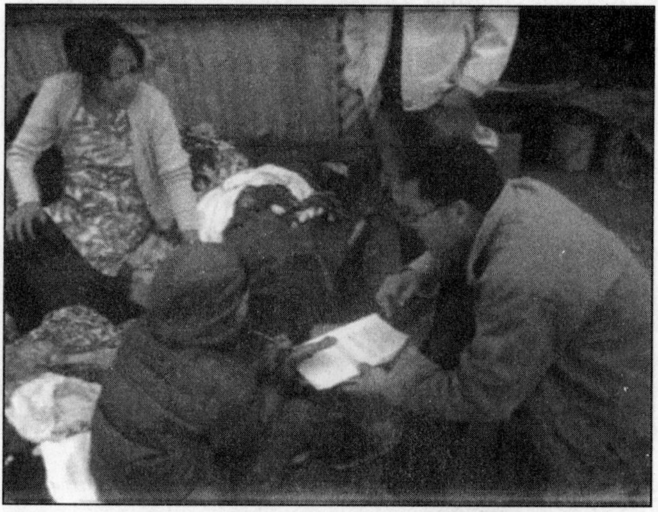

She had started her business from 2010 onwards. This has been one of the most profitable business at Ukhrul as there is high demand for warm clothes at low price. At the beginning she has invested around ₹ 20,000 for this business and could earn an average of ₹ 3,000 to ₹ 5000 per month after 2 to 3 rotation of business worth of ₹ 20,000. She got a loan amount of ₹ 50000 from UDWIM (microfinance NGO in Ukhrul) and invested in her business. Even though capital amount is increased the profit cannot increase much it is almost same as before. The main reason for unable to increase profit are, number of vendors have been increasing and the cost of product also increase.

Case 7

Type of Business: Dry flower making and Handicraft
Name: Pecha
Age: 60 years
Sex: Female
Education: Illiterate
Address: Ningthoupham, Senapati

She started making dry flower and handicrafts items making from bamboo and wooden piece.

Initially she had financially difficulties but now she and other members nearby form a SHG and getting financial assistance from MFIs and also from DIC Senapati. She had attended various trade fairs both domestic as well as international trade fair. One of the unique of her dry flower is making from different leaf, husk and reed. Now with her individual enterprise, maintain her family smoothly.

Case 8

Type of Business: Vegetable Vending
Name: Kajaibonli
Age: 65
Sex: Female
Education: High School level
Address: Noney

Since 1980 she has been doing her business. The main work for our place is making soibum (bamboo shoot).

Since the time immemorial this work has been done by our forefathers and still it is going on and it is one of the most profitable businesses. She sold both dry and wet soibum, chilli and other seasonal vegetables. She has invested around ₹ 40,000 taking microfinance loan TCP-RNBA, Longmei (Noney). After getting loan now my total capital investment amount may be ₹ 60,000, but the profit before and after taking loan is almost same even though investment amount is different. The main reason for not increasing profit is to increase the number of vendors and increases the cost price of the items. Now she can earn an average of ₹ 10,000 per month.

Appendices

Appendix I

Department of Commerce
Manipur University,
Canchipur, Imphal-795003, Manipur

QUESTIONNAIRE FOR MICROENTERPRISE

1. Name of the Enterprise/Business organization:............
2. Year of establishment:......... Year of Registration:.........
3. Name of the Entrepreneur: ....
4. (a) Age................................
   (b) Sex: Male/Female
   (c) Marital status: married/unmarried/widow/widower/single (never married)/divorce
5. If married what is the main occupation of your spouse? (a) Business (b) Government employee (c) Employed in the pvt. Sector (d) Others (specify).........
6. Could you please tell us your educational qualification? (Put a Tick)

(a) Illiterate	[ ]	(d) HSSLC	[ ]
(b) Below HSLC	[ ]	(e) Graduate	[ ]
(c) HSLC	[ ]	(f) Master and above	[ ]

7. Address...
   ... . Phone No. ....
8. Does your enterprise have the bank account? Yes/No, if yes

(a) Before starting enterprise
(b) After starting enterprise

Name of the Bank:....... Year of opening account:.......

9. How does your business started?
   (a) Loan from microfinance
   (b) Loan from friends and relatives
   (c) Loan from moneylender
   (d) Loan from bank
   (e) Others....................
10. Do you really feel that microfinance has helped in starting your business? If so, to what extent?
   (a) Great extent (b) Very significant
   (c) Significant (d) Less significant
   (e) Insignificant
11. Please give the following information.

Particulars	*Before getting microfinance*	*After getting microfinance*
No. of Male workers		
No. of Female workers		
No. of trained workers		
Investment amount	₹	₹
Monthly income	₹	₹

12. Nature of the business:
   (a) Food processing units
   (b) Handloom and handicraft
   (c) Embroidery and knitting
   (d) Grocery
   (e) Livestock
   (f) Fruit vendors
   (g) Vegetable vendors
   (h) Others........
13. Products produces: (in order of priority)
   1. .... 2. ....
   3. .... 4. ....

14. Where do you get the raw materials from?
    (a) Own source (b) Local market
    (c) Govt. supply (d) Outside the state
    (e) Foreign
15. Did you get any training for producing the items which you produce? If yes
    (a) From MFI (b) NABARD
    (c) DIC (d) NGOs
    (e) Others (please specify)...............
16. Where do you sale your products?
    (a) Work place (b) Middlemen
    (c) Local market (d) Exhibition/Mela
    (e) Outside the state (f) Foreign
17. Do you get any loan/fund? If yes, please specify the following.

Name of the funding agency	*Amount*	*Rate of interest*	*Tenure of loan with year*

18. Did your income changes after getting microfinance loan? If yes.......
    (a) Increased at a great extent
    (b) Increased
    (c) Little increased
    (d) Not increased
19. Whether the income earned from this business has reduced your poverty? If yes, how?
    (a) Reduced at a great extent
    (b) Reduced
    (c) Little reduced
    (d) Not reduced
20. Whether you have been empowered by this enterprise? If yes in which area? (Yes/No)
    (a) Participation in decision-making
    (b) Participation in fair/exhibition
    (c) Self-decision making
    (d) Others...........

21. What are the main reasons for starting this present enterprise?

Reasons	*put tick*
Generate income	
Want for control and freedom to make my own decision	
To maintain social status and recognition	
Self-achievement	
Confidence in the products/services offered	
Having technical skills for manufacturing products	
Easily available for raw materials	
Market demand	
Second generation business	
Remain at home	
Trained from micro-enterprise development agencies	
Getting ideas from other enterprise	

22. Problems faced by your business.
    (I) Financial problem: (while taking microfinance loan)
        (a) Lack of transparency
        (b) High rate of interest
        (c) Lengthy in process
        (d) Corruption
        (e) No problem
    (II) Financial problem: (while management)
        (a) Lack of accounting knowledge
        (b) Lack of credit management/policy
        (c) Lack of financial management skill
        (d) No problem
    (III) Market problem:
        (a) To establish contacts with customers
        (b) To find suppliers
        (c) Price fixation of the product

(d) Fluctuation in demand
(e) Competition
(f) No problem

(IV) Management problem:
(a) To deal with legal/government/administrative matters
(b) To get suitable personnel
(c) Lack of proper management technique
(d) Collision of family and business work
(e) No problem

(V) Training:
(a) No training facility
(b) Training place is very far
(c) Training fee is high
(d) No problem

23. Give your suggestion for solving the above cited problems.
(i)
(ii)

Thank you very much for having taken the time to complete this questionnaire. The information on your perceptions is a very important input for the evaluation of conditions in micro-enterprises through microfinance as well as for the formulation of policy advice. We would appreciate any thoughts you might like to add on the micro-enterprise and microfinance institutions, or comment on the questionnaire in general.

Date:
Place: Signature of Respondent

Appendix II

Department of Commerce
Manipur University,
Canchipur, Imphal-795003, Manipur

QUESTIONNAIRE FOR NGO/MFI/SHPI

1. Name of the NGO/MFI/SHPI..............................
2. Address of the organization.......................................
3. Year of establishment ....
4. Year of working Microfinance...............................
5. What are the objectives of your organization?
6. Functioning area in the field of microfinance.............
7. Does your organization have the bank linkage programme ? (Yes/No)
   (i) If no give the reasons
   (ii) If yes provide the column 4 of following table
8. Please supply the following information

Year	*No. of SHG/JLG formed*	*No. of SHG/JLG actively working*	*No. of SHG/JLG linked with bank*

9. Do you get any financial assistance for microfinance? (Yes/No) if yes give the detail.

Name of the funding agencies	*Amount*	*Rate of interest per month*	*Tenure of the loan*

10. What is the minimum and maximum loan amount given to the microfinance beneficiaries?

Type of loan	*Minimum*	*Maximum*	*Average*
Group			
Individual			

11. Please supply the following information regarding your microfinance loan:

Rate of interest	Methods
Mode of interest	(a) Flat (b) Reducing (c) Both
Mode of recovery	(a) Daily (b) Weekly (c) Fortnightly (d) Monthly
Tenure of the loan	

12. Does your organization give the forward and backward linkage to the beneficiaries? (yes/no)
13. Does your organization give the training to the microfinance beneficiaries? (yes/no)
    (i) If yes specify the training..................................
    (ii) If no give the reason...
14. Give suggestion or recommendation if you have regarding microfinance in the state.

Respondent

Appendix III

List of Micro Entrepreneurs with Address

Sl. No.	Name of Micro-entrepreneurs	Types of Enterprise	Address
1.	Pecha	Dry flower	Ningthoupham Senapati
2.	Khingken	Weaving	Kangpokpi Ward 1
3.	Rita Keishing	Cloth shop	Chatric khunou, Ukhrul
4.	Lilywon	Vegetable vendor	Chatric khunou, Ukhrul
5.	Soying	Piggery	Chatric khulen, Ukhrul
6.	RS Kanmila	Vegetable vendor	Ngaimo Village, Ukhrul
7.	Apei	Cloth shop	Lunghar, Ukhrul
8.	Ramtawon	Tea hotel	Phungludang, Ukhrul
9.	Tosil Tarao	Bamboo mat	Heikakpokpi, Tarao
10.	Sachui	Video CD. Parlour	Noney Bazar
11.	Sulomi	Pan shop	Noney Bazar
12.	Dorcart	Book store	Noney Bazar
13.	Kajaibonli	Vegetable vendor	Noney Bazar
14.	Margaret	Cement store	Noney Bazar
15.	Athiu Kamei	Garment shop	Noney Bazar
16.	N. Lakitabi Devi	Vegetable vendor	Kakyai Mamang Nambol
17.	M. Indumati Devi	Toy shop	Nambol
18.	Kh. Ibemcha Devi	Grocery	Nambol Awang Leikai
19.	N. Shakhitombi Devi	Betlenut leaf	Kongkham Nambol
20.	Radhamani	Jung jewellery	Kakching Khunjai
21.	Ashem Usha	Vegetable vendor	Kakching Lamkhai
22.	N.(o) Kiranbala Devi	Grocery	Kakching Indrani Manak
23.	Ongnam Ushakiran	Fruit vendor	Kakching Khunyai Leikai
24.	K.G. Agui	Hotel	Tarung Langol
25.	Anjali Bista	Grocery	Lamphel
26.	A(o). Baby Devi	Embroidery	Kumbi Bazar
27.	E(o). Henulata	Fish Firm	Kumbi Bazar
28.	L. Sulochana Devi	Grocery	Kumbi Bazar
29.	N. Ibungo	Hotel	Kumbi IB road
30.	Kumam Boby Singh	Jewellery	Turenban Leikai, Moirang
31.	Oinam Medha Singh	Oil seller	Kumbi Bazar
32.	K(o). Pramo	Garment shop	Moirang Bazar

Sl. No.	Name of Micro-entrepreneurs	Types of Enterprise	Address
33.	Ng(o). Promila Devi	Motors Parts	Moirang Bazar
34.	K(o). Jugita Devi	Moreh Dukan	Moirang Bazar
35.	K(o). Anitabi Devi	Embroidery	Moirang konjengbam
36.	L. Gobin Singh	Electronic shop	Moirang Bazar
37.	W. Sandhyarani Devi	Vegetable vendor	Thoubal Achouba
38.	W. Chandrajini Devi	Fire wood shop	Thoubal kshetri Leikai
39.	Surmangol	Variety Store	Thoubal kshetri leikai
40.	N. Nobin Singh	Nongin enterprises	Thoubal Okram
41.	Ak. Gyaneldro Singh	G.S. Electronics	Thoubal wangmataba
42.	W. Maimu Devi	Tea stall	Thoubal awang leikai
43.	Y. Dasumati Devi	Shoe vendor	Thoubal Bamon Leikai
44.	Kh. Sunita Devi	Cloth vendor	Thoubal Kshetri leikai
45.	N. Geetarani Devi	Cloth vendor	Thoubal achouba UBIoppt
46.	Indira Devi	Tea Hotel	Tuibung Bazar CCpur
47.	Kh. Surjit Singh	SS Hotel	Thoubal Melaground
48.	Akoijam Manileima	Variety store	Thoubal Nongakhong
49.	T. Ngulleinmang	Rising Star Medico	Kholmun vill. Ccpur
50.	Thoinu	Vegetable vendor	Tuibung forest gate ccpur
51.	Kimneichung	Grocery shop	Tuibung ccpur
52.	Lhaikim	Thangting agency	Khoimul ccpur
53.	Hanglem Nonibala	Food items	Sagolband tera lukram
54.	Bino Devi	Weaving	Awang maibam leikai
55.	Seram Prabha	Cloth vendor	-do-
56.	Oinam Muhini	Embroidery	Heirangoitong
57.	Oinam Roma	Embroidery	-do-
58.	Oinam Devala	Embroidery	Awang Maibam Leikai
59.	Loitam Lolini	Embroidery	-do-
60.	S. Ibeyaima Devi	Vegetable vendor	-do-
61.	S. Tharongoubi Devi	Weaving	-do-
62.	L. Swadhini Devi	Embroidery	-do-
63.	Th. Jamuna Chanu	Weaving	-do-
64.	Tharongou	Hotel	Maibam Leikai
65.	H. Romoni	Cosmetic items	-do-
66.	A. Romila	Weaving	-do-
67.	Th. Nganbi	Grocery shop	-do-
68.	Th. Pramodini	Bamboo shop	-do-

Sl. No.	*Name of Micro-entrepreneurs*	*Types of Enterprise*	*Address*
69.	Inaobi Devi	Cloth vendor	Heirangoithong
70.	S. Tombi Devi	Weaving	-do-
71.	Th Sobhasini	Grocery	-do-
72.	L. Chaobi Devi	Vegetable vendor	Malom Bazar
73.	Th Sunita Devi	Embroidery	Meitram Awang Leikai
74.	P. Sapana	Cloth vendor	Thangmeiband
75.	I Landhoni	Hotel	-do-
76.	Ch Premi	Embroidery	-do-
77.	Ch Asha Devi	Poultry	-do-
78.	Ph Rashi	-do-	-do-
79.	N. Premoda	Charcoal shop	-do-
80.	Kh Mema	Grocery shop	-do-
81.	N. Saroja	Poultry	-do-
82.	L. Itobi	Handloom	-do-
83.	Ok. Abe	Silk yarn	-do-
84.	Keisam Sajita	Making detergent	-do-
85.	W. Radhamani	Embroidery	-do-
86.	Ibemcha	Rice mill	-do-
87.	T. Joyshree	Embroidery	-do-
88.	Sandhyarani	Vegetable vendor	-do-
89.	Akebi	Silk yarn	-do-
90.	Ibesana	Pan shop	-do-
91.	Tampha naorem	Grocery	-do-
92.	Bijeshori	Chicken centre	-do-
93.	Meghabala	Weaving	-do-
94.	Tombi	Tailoring	-do-
95.	A. Manitombi	Grocery	-do-
96.	Y. Kunjarani	Hotel	-do-
97.	W. Debjani	Grocery Shop	-do-
98.	T. Ibeyaima Devi	Grocery shop	-do-
99.	Y. Ronita	Embroidery	-do-
100.	Sunolata	Silk yarn	-do-
101.	H. Devala Devi	Weaving	-do-
102.	I. Tombisana	Embroidery	-do-
103.	Ibeyaima	Hotel	-do-
104.	A. Abem	Grocery	Liwa Maning Leikai
105.	O. Takhel	Goldsmith	-do-

Sl. No.	Name of Micro-entrepreneurs	Types of Enterprise	Address
106.	L. Bala	Charcoal shop	-do-
107.	Th. Sabitri	Weaving	Naorem leikai
108.	L. Loli	Weaving	Liwa Oinam Leikai
109.	Thoibi	Weaving	-do-
110.	Landhoni	Weaving	-do-
111.	N. Pramodini	Vegetable vendor	Naorem Leikai
112.	Th Anan Devi	Fruit vendor	-do-
113.	L. Santibala Devi	Weaving	-do-
114.	N. Amusana	Chicken centre	-do-
115.	N. Bilasini	Grocery	-do-
116.	T. Shandhyarani	Cloth vendor	Liwa Maning
117.	N. Basanti Devi	Cloth vendor	Naorem Leikai
118.	S. Chandrakala	Hotel	-do-
119.	N. Indira Devi	Cloth vendor	-do-
120.	N. Sundari	Jewellery item	-do-
121.	Th Usharani Devi	Cloth vendor	-do-
122.	N. Kanon	Grocery shop	-do-
123.	Sunibala	Weaving	-do-
124.	L. Nirmala	Hotel	-do-
125.	T. Kumari	Weaving	-do-
126.	Y. Kumudini	Hotel	-do-
127.	N. Victory	Grocery	-do-
128.	N. Thoibi	Weaving	-do-
129.	Y. Jibanlata	Weaving	-do-
130.	N. Sangita	Weaving	-do-
131.	N. Ranjita	Weaving	-do-
132.	N. Muhini	Weaving	-do-
133.	N. Bindiya Devi	Embroidery	-do-
134.	L. Surbala	Cloth vendor	-do-
135.	L. Memton	Cloth vendor	-do-
136.	N. Tombi Devi	Silk product shop	-do-
137.	N. Nganbi Devi	Weaving	-do-
138.	Th. Romi Devi	Grocery	-do-
139.	S. Tamubi	Toy shop	Haobam marak
140.	L. Ibemcha	Grocery	-do-
141.	S. Radharani	Silk yarn	-do-
142.	L. Sobita	Embroidery	-do-

Sl. No.	*Name of Micro-entrepreneurs*	*Types of Enterprise*	*Address*
143.	L. Guneshori	Making dry food	-do-
144.	S. Sarina	Silk Yarn	-do-
145.	L. Jayenti Devi	Gift items	-do-
146.	Mema	Making Detergent	-do-
147.	S. Memtombi	Making Photo frame	-do-
148.	H. Prava Devi	Weaving	Pishum
149.	M. Nirmala Devi	Cloth vendor	Sagolband
150.	H. Lakshmi	Cloth vendor	-do-
151.	M. Priya Devi	Food items	-do-
152.	M. Umashini	Variety store	-do-
153.	H. Purnima	Grocery	-do-
154.	M. Sarju	Embroidery	-do-
155.	M. Rojina	Embroidery	-do-
156.	Th Ibethoi	Cloth vendor	-do-
157.	G. Satyapriya	Garment shop	-do-
158.	Sunolata	Embroidery	-do-
159.	M. Inaobi	Charcoal shop	-do-
160.	M. Naobi	Jewellery workshop	-do-
161.	G. Padmabati	Embroidery	-do-
162.	Kh. Yaima	Embroidery	-do-
163.	Th. Sujata	Charcoal shop	Waheng Leikai
164.	W. Guni	Fruit seller	-do-
165.	W. Memcha	Grocery shop	-do-
166.	Th Tombi	Grocery shop	-do-
167.	W. Dhaneshori	Hotel	Sagolband
168.	A. Bala	Clay shop	-do-
169.	M. Gomti	Fruit shop	-do-
170.	W. Indubala	Cloth shop	-do-
171.	L. Memtombi	Hotel	-do-
172.	M. Mema	Dry fish	-do-
173.	T. Babita Devi	Grocery	-do-
174.	S. Sanahanbi	Grocery	-do-
175.	Th Nganthoi	Dry fish	-do-
176.	S. Medha	Silk garment	-do-
177.	Ratna Jain	Garment	-do-
178.	L. Ibemcha	Charcoal	-do-
179.	Th Leena	Grocery	-do-

Sl. No.	*Name of Micro-entrepreneurs*	*Types of Enterprise*	*Address*
180.	M. Ibemhal	Fish shop	-do-
181.	Ibeyaima Devi	Hotel	-do-
182.	A. Sundari	Hotel	-do-
183.	M. Geeta Devi	Grocery	-do-
184.	A. Guni	Vegetable vendor	-do-
185.	A. Tombi	Vegetable vendor	-do-
186.	Th. Inakhunbi	Jewellery workshop	Wangkhei
187.	H. Mema	Hotel	-do-
188.	Th. Thoibi	Cloth vendor	-do-
189.	Th. Pati	Embroidery	-do-
190.	RK. Sunitibala	Poultry	-do-
191.	H. Babita	Cloth vendor	-do-
192.	H. Memtombi	Blacksmith	-do-
193.	Akashini Devi	Weaving	-do-
194.	Th. Rashi	Embroidery	-do-
195.	H. Ahem Devi	Textile shop	-do-
196.	H. Onita	Grocery	-do-
197.	H. Jibanlata	Pan shop	-do-
198.	L. Shanti	Grocery	Brahmapur Nahabam
199.	Tampha	Bakery	-do-
200.	K. Chandrajini	Grocery	-do-

Appendix IV

List of MFI with address

Sl. No.	*Name of MFI/NGO/SHPI*	*Address*	*Year of estbl.*
1.	Loyalam Bank Project	Lamsang	1992
2.	Youth Volunteer Union (YVU)	Thoubal	1996
3.	Self-Employment Volunteer Association (SEVA)	North Babupara	1996
4.	MACHA LEIMA	Palace compound, Imphal East	1997
5.	Friendship Centre Manipur	Khurai Lamlong	1997
6.	Educated and Self-Employed Women Society Service Associaton (ESWOSSA)	New Chekon	2000
7.	Development and Relief Dept. RNBA	Langol Tarung	2000
8.	Rural Aid Service (RAS)	Churachandpur	2001
9.	Human Development Agency	Uripok Cheirap Manang	2003
10.	Organisation for Rural Improvement (ORI)	Nambol Bazar	2003
11.	Women's and Child Welfare Association.	Kangpokpi, IT road	2004
12.	Human and Social Welfare Association (HASWA)	Nagamapal, Imphal	2004
13.	Diocesah Social Service Society	Mantripukhri Lamlongei	2005
14.	Urban and Rural Development Agency (URDA)	Malom Tuliyaima	2006
15.	Ukhrul District Women Institute of Micro Credit (UDWIN)	Viewland zone III Ukhrul, Manipur	2007
16.	Volunteers for Village Development Micro Finance	VVD, Ukhrul	2007
17.	Chanura Microfin, Manipur	Hodam Leirak Machin	2007
18.	RCN-REACH-M	Nungourok Pallel chandel	2008
19.	WWAGS (Leirik Microfinance)	Wangjing Bazar. S.K. Leikai	2010
20.	LEIMA MICROFIN (SRO)	Thoubal Ningombam	2010

Appendix V

Indigenous Institutions in the Northeast India

Box 3.1: Indigenous Institutions in the Northeast

- Namghars and Pujaghars which are prevalent in Assam. A compulsory deposit of a fixed amount by each household is made to the Namghar (prayer hall) in a religious institution. It is lent out at zero or lowers than market interest rates to address emergencies or extreme distress. Some amount is also used for common community needs, such as road construction.
- Marups in Manipur are Rotating Savings and Credit Associations (RoSCAs), groups of people who pool money weekly or monthly and then distribute it to the RoSCA members in turn. The turns are decided by mutual consent, lottery, and seniority within the group or bidding. The frequency of deposit in the pool depends on the occupation of members, and members all typically save the same amount (although some members may have multiple 'shares' and thus contribute double or triple the amount and thus receive two or three pay-outs). The tenure depends on the number of members in the group and typically varies from 20 to 30. No new memberships are allowed during the tenure, and the group may dissolve after the tenure.
- Sonchay, Somobay, Samiti, Got (in Assam) are Accumulating Savings and Credit Associations (ASCAs). These are savings based groups of generally 25-40 where members deposit monthly savings of a fixed amount into a central pool, from which money is lent out to members and non-members. ASCAs are usually purpose-based groups which run for 1-2 years, and often liquidate and provide pay-outs prior to festivals. Members earn interest in proportion to their savings amount. ASCAs are very common in the valleys of Assam, as well as in some parts of Meghalaya and Nagaland.
- Shinglups are prevalent in the Manipuri community of the valley region of Manipur. They are religious boards in each locality which take care of the expenditures incurred during death ceremonies.
- Mahari Associations which are welfare groups prevalent amongst the Garo clan in Meghalaya. Contributions are made by all households of the clan, the amount being fixed by the committee, headed by the Nokma (the village headman). Mahari fund is used for the general welfare of the clan, for marriages, death ceremonies, emergencies, etc.

Source: Micro Saves India Focus Note 13; "Saving Behaviour of Poor People in Northeast of India"; Madhurantika Moulik.

Appendix VI

Microfinance Bill 2012

MFI Bill-2012 As introduced in the Parliament

Preamble

A Bill to provide for development and regulation of the micro finance institutions for the purpose of facilitating access to credit, thrift and other microfinance services to the rural and urban poor and certain disadvantaged sections of the people and promoting financial inclusion through such institutions and for matters connected therewith or incidental thereto.

CHAPTER I: PRELIMINARY

Sec- 2(1)(a)

"annual percentage rate" means aggregate rate per annum in percentage consisting of interest, processing fees, service charges and any other charges or fees

Sec- 2(1)(b)

"client" means any member of the microfinance institution or self-help group or any other group availing the microfinance services from such institution or group

Sec- 2(1)(e)

"District Micro Finance Committee" means a Committee constituted by the Reserve Bank under Section 10;

Sec- 2(1)(f)

"margin" means the difference between the annual percentage rate charged by the microfinance institution and the cost of funds

raised in percentage by the microfinance institution for providing any micro-credit facilities;

Sec- 2(1)(g)

"***Member***" means a Member of the Micro Finance Development Council constituted under Section 3;

Sec- 2(1)(h)

"***micro credit facilities***" means any loan, advance, grant or any guarantee given or any other credit extended in cash or kind with or without security or guarantee

Sec- 2(1)(i)

"***microfinance institution***" means,—

(A) a society registered under the Societies Registration Act, 1860; or
(B) a company registered under Section 3 of the Companies Act, 1956; or
(C) a trust established under any law for the time being in force; or
(D) a body corporate; or
(E) any other organisation, as may be specified by the Reserve Bank, the object of which is to provide microfinance services in such manner as may be specified by regulations.

but does not include—

(i) a banking company, the State Bank of India including its subsidiary banks, a scheduled bank, a co-operative bank, Export and Import Bank, Reconstruction Bank, National Housing Bank, National Bank, a Regional Rural Bank and Small Industries Development Bank;
(ii) a co-operative society engaged primarily in agricultural operations or industrial activity or purchase or sale of any goods;

(iii) any individual carrying on the activity of money-lending and registered as a moneylender under the provision of any State law which regulates such activities;

Sec- 2(1)(j)

"***microfinance services***" means any one or more of the following financial services provided by any microfinance institution, namely:

(A) micro-credit facilities involving such amount, not exceeding in aggregate five lakh rupees for each individuals and for such special purposes, as may be specified by the Reserve Bank from time to time, such higher amount, not exceeding ten lakh rupees, as may be prescribed;

(B) collection of thrift;

(C) pension or insurance services;

(D) remittance of funds to individuals within India subject to prior approval of the Reserve Bank and such other terms and conditions, as may be specified by regulations.

Implications

Under Sec. 25 (2) The Reserve Bank has been entrusted with the powers to issue directions ceiling on amount of micro-credit facilities and the number of individual clients to whom such micro-credit facilities may be provided by any microfinance institution; Removed.

Sec- 2(1)(r)

"***thrift***" means money collected in any form other than in the form of current account or demand deposits, by a microfinance institution from members of self-help groups or any other group of individuals, by whatever name called, who are availing micro-finance services provided by such microfinance institution in accordance with the regulations made by the Reserve Bank in this behalf.

Chapter-2 Microfinance Development Council (MFDC)

Composition

Four officers, one each from the Ministry or the Department of the Central Government having the administrative control of Finance, Rural Development, Women and Child Development and Housing and Urban Poverty Alleviation, not below the rank of Joint Secretary to the Government of India, to be nominated by the Central Government—ex-officio Members not more than four persons, of whom at least two shall be women, to be nominated by the Central Government, in consultation with the Reserve Bank from amongst persons with experience in the field of banking, rural credit or microfinance or the representatives of microfinance institutions or scheduled banks or any other institution providing microfinance services—Members

Implication

Total members = 5
Ex Officio members = 8
Sector Representation limited to 4
Central Govenment Representation increased to 4

Chapter-III: State Microfinance Council

Sec- 2(1)(q)

In Addition to the functions already mentioned, shall Coordinate the activities of the District Micro Finance Committees in the State; shall submit a quarterly report to the Central Government on the implementation of the measures undertaken for the promotion and development of the microfinance institutions in the State.

Chapter IV: District Microfinance Committees

10. (1) The Reserve Bank may, constitute a District Microfinance Committee in each district, to be headed by the Collector or an officer not below the rank of Additional

Collector in that district in such manner as may be specified by regulations.

(2) The District Micro finance Committee shall meet at such time and place, as the Collector may direct, at least once in three months and shall observe such rules of procedure in regard to the transaction of business at its meetings, as may be specified by regulations: Provided that the representatives of the Lead Bank of the District, representative of the National Bank in the district, a representative of microfinance institutions operating in the district and beneficiaries of microfinance services shall be invited to the meetings of the District Microfinance Committees.

Explanation.—For the purposes of this section, "Lead Bank" of the District means a bank to which a district is assigned as per the Lead Bank Scheme of the Reserve Bank of India.

11. The District Micro Finance Committee shall discharge the following functions, namely:—
    (a) to review growth and development of microfinance activities in the district;
    (b) to monitor over-indebtedness, if any, caused by microfinance institutions in the district; and
    (c) to monitor whether methods of recovery used by micro-finance institutions are in accordance with the guidelines made by the Reserve Bank and to report to the Reserve Bank in respect of the violations, if any.
12. Every District Micro Finance Committee shall submit a quarterly report to the Reserve Bank in such form and manner as may be specified and forward its copy to the State Micro Finance Council.

Chapter V: Registration of Micro Finance Institutions

Microfinance institution, in existence at the commencement of this Act, engaged in providing microfinance services before such commencement, would have apply for registration to the Reserve Bank before the expiry of three months. Provided that they may continue to carry on its activity of providing microfinance services till the disposal of such application.

NOF-5 Lakh

"Net owned fund" shall have, *mutatis mutandis,* the same meaning as assigned to it in the Explanation to sub-Section (7) of Section 45-IA of the Reserve Bank of India Act, 1934.

Removed to Sec-28

Completely Removed

Chapter VI: Reserve, Accounts, Audit and Returns

Reserve Fund

Reserves to be created as prescribed.

Provided that nothing contained in this sub-section shall apply to a NBFCs Registered with RBI which is maintaining such reserve fund pursuant to any provisions of the RBI Act, 1934 or any directions or regulations issued thereunder.

Chapter VII: Functions and Powers of Reserve Bank

Sec 25(2)-RBI may issue directions on Ceiling on Amount of microcredit facilities and number of clients.

Chapter VIII: Micro Finance Development Fund

The Central Government may, after due appropriation made by Parliament by law in this behalf, grant such sum of money as that Government may think fit, to the Reserve Bank for being utilised for the purposes specified under sub-Section (3) of Section 32.

Chapter IX: Redressal Mechanism

Entrust the function of Grievance redressal to any Ombudsman established under any other scheme framed by the Reserve Bank for clients of banks, with powers to issue directions to microfinance institutions.

Chapter XI: Delegation of Powers

The Central Government, in consultation with the Reserve Bank may, by notification, delegate any of the powers of the Reserve Bank conferred under this Act, except under Sections 30, 37 and 49, to the National Bank or any agency under the control of the Central Government in respect of any microfinance institution or a class of microfinance institutions or microfinance institutions generally, subject to such conditions as it deems fit.

Chapter XII: Miscellaneous

Preference in repayment:

In the event of any microfinance institution making default in repayment of thrift to its members or clients who had made a contribution to thrift, all the workmen shall be paid their dues in priority to all others and thereafter all such members or clients of such microfinance institution shall have a preference in repayment, and shall have the first charge over the assets of the microfinance institution and specified unencumbered securities, if any, referred to in sub-section (3) of Section 18.

Sec-44: Power to Central Government to issue Direction to RBI, MFDC, SAC on matters of policy and implementation of Schemes

The provisions of this Act shall have effect, notwithstanding anything inconsistent therewith contained in any other law for the time being in force or any instrument having effect by virtue of any such law.

Explanation is removed.

Appendix VII

Malegam Committee Report

Some of the recommendation of Malegam Committee has been discussed as below:

Sl. No.	*Para No.*	*Recommendations*
1.	3.8	*The need for regulation:* A separate category be created for NBFCs operating in the Microfinance sector, such NBFCs being designated as NBFC-MFI
2.	4.2	*Definition*: A NBFC-MFI may be defined as "A company (other than a company licensed under Section 25 of the Companies Act, 1956) which provides financial services pre-dominantly to low-income borrowers with loans of small amounts, for short-terms, on unsecured basis, mainly for income-generating activities, with repayment schedules which are more frequent than those normally stipulated by commercial banks and which further conforms to the regulations specified in that behalf". Provision should be made in the regulations to further define each component of this definition.
3.	5.9	*Regulations to be specified* A NBFC classified as a NBFC-MFI should satisfy the following conditions: (a) Not less than 90 per cent of its total assets (other than cash and bank balances and money market instruments) are in the nature of "qualifying assets." (b) For the purpose of (a) above, a "qualifying asset" shall mean a loan which satisfies the following criteria:- (i) The loan is given to a borrower who is a member of a household whose annual income does not exceed ₹ 50,000;

Sl. No.	*Para No.*	*Recommendations*
		(ii) The amount of the loan does not exceed ₹ 25,000 and the total outstanding indebtedness of the borrower including this loan also does not exceed ₹ 25,000; (iii) The tenure of the loan is not less than 12 months where the loan amount does not exceed ₹ 15,000 and 24 months in other cases with a right to the borrower of prepayment without penalty in all cases; (iv) The loan is without collateral; (v) The aggregate amount of loans given for income generation purposes is not less than 75 per cent of the total loans given by the MFIs; (vi) The loan is repayable by weekly, fortnightly or monthly instalments at the choice of the borrower. (c) The income it derives from other services is in accordance with the regulation specified in that behalf.
4.	5.10	*Regulations to be specified:* A NBFC which does not qualify as a NBFC-MFI should not be permitted to give loans to the microfinance sector, which in the aggregate exceed 10 per cent of its total assets.
5.	7.11	*Pricing of Interest:* There should be a "margin cap" of 10 per cent in respect of MFIs which have an outstanding loan portfolio at the beginning of the year of ₹ 100 crores and a "margin cap" of 12 per cent in respect of MFIs which have an outstanding loan portfolio at the beginning of the year of an amount not exceeding ₹ 100 crores. There should also be a cap of 24 per cent on individual loans.
6.	8.7	*Transparency in Interest Charges:* (a) There should be only three components in the pricing of the loan, namely: (i) a processing fee, not exceeding 1 per cent of the gross loan amount, (ii) the interest charge, and (iii) the insurance premium.

Sl. No.	*Para No.*	*Recommendations*
		(b) Only the actual cost of insurance should be recovered and no administrative charges should be levied. (c) Every MFI should provide to the borrower a loan card which: (i) shows the effective rate of interest, (ii) the other terms and conditions attached to the loan, (iii) information which adequately identifies the borrower, and (iv) acknowledgements by the MFI of payments of instalments received and the final discharge. The Card should show this information in the local language understood by the borrower. (d) The effective rate of interest charged by the MFI should be prominently displayed in all its offices and in the literature issued by it and on its website. (e) There should be adequate regulations regarding the manner in which insurance premium is computed and collected and policy proceeds disposed of. (f) There should not be any recovery of security deposit. Security deposits already collected should be returned. (g) There should be a standard form of loan agreement.
7.	9.7	*Multiple-lending, Over-borrowing and Ghost-borrowers:* (a) MFIs should lend to an individual borrower only as a member of a JLG and should have the responsibility of ensuring that the borrower is not a member of another JLG. (b) a borrower cannot be a member of more than one SHG/JLG. (c) not more than two MFIs should lend to the same borrower. (d) there must be a minimum period of

Sl. No.	*Para No.*	*Recommendations*
		moratorium between the grant of the loan and the commencement of its repayment. (e) recovery of loan given in violation of the regulations should be deferred till all prior existing loans are fully repaid.
8.	9.12	*Multiple-lending, Over-borrowing and Ghost-borrowers:* All sanctioning and disbursement of loans should be done only at a central location and more than one individual should be involved in this function. In addition, there should be close supervision of the disbursement function.
9.	10.5	*Credit Information Bureau:* (a) One or more Credit Information Bureaus should be established and be operational as soon as possible and all MFIs be required to become members of such bureau. (b) In the meantime, the responsibility to obtain information from potential borrowers regarding existing borrowings should be on the MFI.
10.	11.12	*Coercive Methods of Recovery:* (a) The responsibility to ensure that coercive methods of recovery are not used should rest with the MFIs and they and their managements should be subject to severe penalties if such methods are used. (b) The regulator should monitor whether MFIs have a proper Code of Conduct and proper systems for recruitment, training and supervision of field staff to ensure the prevention of coercive methods of recovery. (c) Field staff should not be allowed to make recovery at the place of residence or work of the borrower and all individual loans.
11.	15.3	*Corporate Size All:* NBFC-MFIs should have a minimum Net Worth of Rs.15 crore.
12.	16.3	*Corporate Governance:* Every MFI should be required to have a system of Corporate Governance in accordance with rules to be specified by the Regulator.

Sl. No.	Para No.	Recommendations
13.	17.3	*Maintenance of Solvency:* Provisioning for loans should not be maintained for individual loans but an MFI snould be required to maintain at all times an aggregate provision for loan losses which shall be the higher of: (i) 1 per cent of the outstanding loan portfolio or (ii) 50 per cent of the aggregate loan instalments which are overdue for more than 90 days and less than 180 days and 100 per cent of the aggregate loan instalments which are overdue for 180 days or more.
14.	17.5	*Maintenance of Solvency*: NBFC-MFIs should be required to maintain Capital Adequacy Ratio of 15 per cent and subject to recommendation 21 below, all of the Net Owned Funds should be in the form of Tier I Capital.
15	18.10	*Need for Competition*: Bank lending to the Microfinance sector both through the SHG-Bank Linkage programme and directly should be significantly increased and this should result in a reduction in the lending interest rates.
16.	19.5	*Priority Sector Status:* Bank advances to MFIs shall continue to enjoy "priority sector lending" status. However, advances to MFIs which do not comply with the regulation should be denied "priority sector lending" status. It may also be necessary for the Reserve Bank to revisit its existing guidelines for lending to the priority sector in the context of the Committee's recommendations.
17.	20.5	*Assignment and Securitisation:* (a) Disclosure is made in the financial statements of MFIs of the outstanding loan portfolio which has been assigned or securitised and the MFI continues as an agent for collection. The amounts assigned and securitised must be shown separately. (b) Where the assignment or securitisation is with recourse, the full value of the outstanding loan

Sl. No.	*Para No.*	*Recommendations*
		portfolio assigned or securitised should be considered as risk-based assets for calculation of Capital Adequacy. (c) Where the assignment or securitisation is without recourse but credit enhancement has been given, the value of the credit enhancement should be deducted from the Net Owned Funds for the purpose of calculation of Capital Adequacy. (d) Before acquiring assigned or securitised loans, banks should ensure that the loans have been made in accordance with the terms of the specified regulations.
18.	21.4	*Funding of MFIs:* (a) The creation of one or more "Domestic Social Capital Funds" may be examined in consultation with SEBI. (b) MFIs should be encouraged to issue preference capital with a ceiling on the coupon rate and this can be treated as part of Tier II capital subject to capital adequacy norms.
19.	22.7	*Monitoring of Compliance:* (a) The primary responsibility for ensuring compliance with the regulations should rest with the MFI itself and it and its management must be penalized in the event of non-compliance (b) Industry associations must ensure compliance through the implementation of the Code of Conduct with penalties for non-compliance. (c) Banks also must play a part in compliance by surveillance of MFIs through their branches. (d) The Reserve Bank should have the responsibility for off-site and on-site supervision of MFIs but the on-site supervision may be confined to the larger MFIs and be restricted to the functioning of the organizational arrangements and systems with some supervision of branches. It should also include supervision of the industry associations in so far as their

Sl. No.	Para No.	Recommendations
		compliance mechanism is concerned. Reserve Bank should also explore the use of outside agencies for inspection. (e) The Reserve Bank should have the power to remove from office the CEO and/or a director in the event of persistent violation of the regulations quite apart from the power to deregister an MFI and prevent it from operating in the microfinance sector. (f) The Reserve Bank should considerably enhance its existing supervisory organisation dealing with NBFC-MFIs.
20.	23.4	*Moneylenders Acts:* NBFC-MFIs should be exempted from the provisions of the Money-Lending Acts, especially as we are recommending interest margin caps and increased regulation.
21.	24.7	*The Micro Finance (Development and Regulation) Bill 2010*: Subject to Smt. Rajagopalan's reservations as expressed in para 24.6 above, we would, therefore, recommend the following: (a) The proposed Act should provide for all entities covered by the Act to be registered with the Regulator. However, entities where aggregate loan portfolio (including the portfolio of associated entities) does not exceed ₹ 10 crore may be exempted from registration. (b) If NABARD is designated as the regulator under the proposed Act, there must be close co-ordination between NABARD and Reserve Bank in the formulation of the regulations applicable to the regulated entities. (c) The microfinance entities governed by the proposed Act should not be allowed to do the business of providing thrift services.
22.	25.7	*The Andhra Pradesh Micro Finance Institutions (Regulation of Money Lending) Act :* If the Committee's recommendations are accepted, the

Sl. No.	*Para No.*	*Recommendations*
		need for a separate Andhra Pradesh Micro Finance Institutions (Regulation of Money Lending) Act will not survive.
23.	26.2	*Transitory Provisions :* (a) 1st April 2011 may be considered as a cut-off date by which time our recommendations, if accepted, must be implemented. In particular, the recommendations as to the rate of interest must, in any case, be made effective to all loans given by an MFI after 31st March 2011. (b) As regards other arrangements, Reserve Bank may grant such extension of time as it considers appropriate in the circumstances. In particular, this extension may become necessary for entities which currently have activities other than microfinance lending and which may need to form separate entities confined to microfinance activities.

Bibliography

Books

Aghion Beatriz Armendariz de and Morduch Jonathan (2005). *The Economics of Microfinance.* Massachusetts London, England: The MIT Press Cambridge.

Agrawall, A.N. (1997). *Indian Economy-Problems of Development and Planning.* New Delhi, India: Wishwa Prakashan.

Ahmed, Rais (2009). *Micro-Finance and Women Empowerment*, New Delhi, India: Mittal Publications (Vol. I, II & III).

Anita, Gill (2000). *Rural Credit Markets, Financial Sector Reforms and the Informal Lenders*, India: Deep & Deep Publications Pvt. Ltd., Rajouri Garden New Delhi-27.

Asian Development Bank (1997). *Microenterprise Development: Not By Credit Alone.*

Banerji, Sumeeta and Kumar Sachin (2007). *Poverty Microfinance Community.* Hyderabad, India: Survarna Gandham, Maanveeya Holdings and Investment (P) Ltd.

Dichter Thomas and Harper Malcolm (Ed.). (2007). *What's wrong with Microfinance.* UK, England: Intermediate Technology Publications Ltd.

Gareth, A. Jones and Kavita Datta (1999). *Housing and Finance in Developing Countries.* London and New York: Routledge.

Ghate, Prabhu (2008). *Indian Microfinance: The challenges of rapid growth.* New Delhi, India: Sage Publications India Pvt Ltd.

Henry, Carla *et al.* (2003). *Microfinance Poverty Assessment Tool.* CGAP/The World Bank, Washington DC: www.cgap.org.

Hulme, David and Arun Thankom (Ed.). (2009). *Microfinance – a reader.* London and New York: Routledge Taylor and Francis Group (e-book).

Kamdar, Sangita (Ed). (2007). *Microfinance Self-Employment and Poverty Alleviation.* Mumbai, India: Himalaya Publishing House Pvt. Ltd.

Karmakar, K.G. (Ed.). (2008). *Microfinance in India.* New Delhi, India: Sage Publications India Pvt Ltd.

Lazar, Daniel and Malabika Deo (2009). *Micro Finance, Performance Evaluation and Enterprise Development.* Chennai-02, India: Allied Publishers Pvt. Ltd.

Lazar, Daniel and Palanichamy, P. (Ed). (2008). *Microfinance and Poverty Eradication - Indian and Global Experiences.* New Delhi, India: New Century Publications.

Lazar, Daniel, Aravanan S. and Deo Malabika (Ed.). (2011). *Embodiment of Empowerment SELF-HELP GROUP.* Chennai, India: Vijay Nicole Imprints Pvt. Ltd.

Lazar, Daniel, P. Natarajan and Malabika Deo (2010). *Microfinance Enabling Empowerment.* Ram Nagar South Chennai-91, India: Vijay Nicole Imprints Pvt. Ltd.

Ledgerwood, Joanna and White Victoria (2006). *Transforming Microfinance Institutions – Providing full financial services to the poor.* The World Bank, 1818 H Street NW, Washington, DC 20433.

Misra, Indira (2005). *Micro-credit for Macro Impact on Poverty.* New Delhi, India: National Publishing House.

Navajas, Sergio and Tejerina Luis (2006, Nov.). *Microfinance in Latin America and the Caribbean: How Large Is The Market.* Inter-American Development Bank. Retrived from http://www.iadb.org/sds/mic

Ohanyan, Anna (2008). *NGOs, IGOs and The Network Mechanisms of Post-Conflict Global Governance in Microfinance.* New York, NY 10010: Palgrave Macmillan.

Ready, Reckoner on Microfinance, year 2010, UNDP, India

Reddy, C.R. (1987). *Rural Banking in India.* Coimbatore, India: Rainbow Publications,

Robinson, Marguerite S. (2001). *The Microfinance Revolution, Sustainable Finance for the Poor.* California. Communications Development Incorporated, Washington DC & San Francisco.

Rutherford, Stuart (2009). *The Pledge – ASA, Peasant Politics, and Microfinance in the Development of Bangladesh.* USA: Oxford University Press.

Shivamaggi, H.B. (1998). *Banking and Rural Development.* New Delhi, India: Mittal Publications.

Singh, Ravishankar Kumar (Ed.). (2005). *Poverty and Sustainable Development – third world perspectives.* Delhi, India: Abhijeet Publications.

Srinivasan, N. (2009). *Microfinance India – State of the Sector Report 2009.* New Delhi, India: Sage Publications India Pvt Ltd.

Sundaresan, Suresh (Ed.). (2008). *Microfinance–Emerging Trends and Challenges.* USA: Edward Elgar Publishing Limited.

Torre, Mario La and Vento Gianfranco A. (2006). *Microfinance.* New York: Palgrave Macmillan.

Journals, Proceedings and Publications

ACCESS. *Annual Report.* 2008-09.

ACCION International. *Annual Report.* 2008.

ADB. (2008). *MIX Asia 100 – Ranking of microfinance institutions.* April 2008.

Badatya, K.C. *et al.* (2006). Microfinance for Microenterprises, An Impact Evaluation Study of Self-Help Groups. Hyderabad. *NABARD, Andhra Pradesh Regional Office.*

Banking Finance. Vol. XX, No. 10. October 2007.

Banking Finance, Vol. XXII, March 2009. pp. 10-12.

BANIJA. Vol.1, No.1. July 2008.

Credit and Development Forum (CDF). (2006). *Bangladesh Microfinance Country Profile,* January 2006.

CRISIL. (2009). *India Top 50 Microfinance Institutions – A Financial Awareness Initiative of CRISIL.* October, 2009.

Directorate and Statistics Government of Manipur. *Economy Survey Manipur-2010-11.*

DGCCS'S Journal of Commerce. Vol. VII, No.1, 2010.

Final Report (2007). Functioning and Performance of Swashakhi and Swayamsiddha Projects In India, Solidarity of the Nation Society, U.P. Sponsored by Planning Commission Government of India, New Delhi.

FWWB. *Annual Report.* 2008-09.

Human Development Report. 2005.

International Journal of Microfinance. Vol. 1, No. 1. January – June 2011.

Indian Journal of Marketing. Vol-XXXVIII, No.3. March 2008.

Indian Journal of Marketing. Vol. XXXIX. June 2009.

Journal of Commerce and Management Thought. Volume I, No. 2. April 2010

Kurukshetra. Vol. 57, No. 2, December, 2008.

Latiffee, H.I. and Kulkarni, B.N. (2007). *Microcredit in India–Grameen International Conference on Micro Credit in India: Conference Report,* 1-2 February, 2007. India: Mumbai.

MYRADA. *An Agency Profile Past, Present and Future.* Jan., 2010, p. 1.

NABARD. *Annual Report.* 2003-04 to 2010-11.

NABARD. *Microfinance – an insight into the world of microfinance.* April-June 2009.

NEDFi. *Annual Report.* 2010-11.

Pondicherry University (2011). *International Journal of Microfinance, a Biannual Journal I (I).*

Providing Financial Supports for Micro Enterprise Development, Small and Medium Enterprises Ministerial Meeting Chiang Mai, Thailand 7-8 August 2003.

Report of the Committee on India Vision 2020. Chairman Dr. S.P. Gupta, Planning Commission Government of India, New Delhi, December, 2002.

Report (2007). The Steering Committee On Micro-Finance and Poverty Alleviation. New Delhi. *The Eleventh Five Year Plan* (2007-08–2011-12) Development Policy Division Planning Commission.

Reserve Bank of India. (2006-07). *Report on Trend and Progress of Banking in India.* pp. 152-156.

Report on Trend and Progress of Banking in India 2008-09, Reserve Bank of India.

RGVN. *Annual Report.* 2009.

SKS Microfinance. *Annual Report.* 2009.

Statistical Tables Relating to Banks in India 2011-2012 by Reserve Bank of India.

Status of Micro Finance in India 2009-10, NABARD

Status of Microfinance in India, 2011-12, Taking Rural India. Forward, NABARD.

The Financial Sector, Planning Commission *Vision 2020 for India.*

The Indian Journal of Commerce. Vol. 61, No. 3. July-September 2008.

The Management Accountant (2008). *The Institute of Cost and Works Accountants of India,* Volume 43, No. 11.

World Bank, India: Development Policy Review: "Sustaining Reform, Reducing Poverty". Washington DC. World Bank, 2003.

World Bank, Improving Access To Finance In Brazil. Washington DC: World Bank., 2003a.

World Bank, Microfinance in India: Issues, Challenges and Policy Options. Washington DC: World Bank, 2003.

World Bank. (2005). "Microfinance can be the biggest instrument in the fight against poverty." Error! Hyperlink reference not valid. (accessed Feb 23, 2006).

Yojana. Vol. 52, January 2008.

Research Papers and Articles

Agrawal, Monca (2009, April-June). Micro-insurance Market in India. *Microfinance World, NABARD,* 9.

Ahirrao, Jitendra (2009, Feb.). Rural Women Empowerment through Microfinance. *Kurukshetra,* 57(4), 23-25.

Allen, Hugh (2007). Finance begins with savings, not loans. In Dichter Thomas & Harper Malcolm (Ed.), *What's wrong with Microfinance?* (pp. 49-59). U.K., England: Intermediate Technology Publications Ltd.

Badatya, K.C.; B.B. Wadavi and Ananthi, S. (2006) Microfinance for Microenterprises, an impact Evaluation study of Help Groups. Evaluation study series, Andhra Pradesh No. 13. National Bank for Agriculture and Rural Development Andhra Pradesh Regional Office, Hyderabad

Chakraborty, Dipanjan. (2010). The Role of Micro Finance in Developing Rural Entrepreneurship in Assam. *DGCCS's Journal of Commerce,* VII (1), 121-130.

Chaudhuri, Ranjan, Sushil and Patil Pravin. (2009, June). Conceptualizing Microfinance Initiatives in India Using SAP-LAP Model: A New

Paradigm in Marketing Engineering. *Indian Journal of Marketing*, XXXIX, 23-29.

Das, Sanjay Kanti. (2010). Microfinance and North Eastern Region – A Review. *DGCCS's Journal of Commerce*, VII (1), 106-120.

Gupta, M.S. (2008, July-September). Microfinance through Self-Help Groups – an emerging horizon for rural development. *The Indian Journal of Commerce*, 61(3), 36-47.

Impact of Self-Help Groups (Group Process) on the social/empowerment status of women members in southern India by Myrada, 25th and 26th November 2002.

Indian school of microfinance for women Ahmedabad, Integrated course on Microfinance for development 2nd to 21st February 2009.

James, C. Brau and Gary, M. Woller (2004). Microfinance: A Comprehensive Review of the Existing Literature. *Journal of Entrepreneurial Finance and Business Ventures*, Vol. 9, Issue I, pp. 1-26.

Koul, Divy Ninad and Mohan Giresh. Women's Self-Help Groups and Microfinance. *Kurukshetra*, 57(4), 13-15.

Kumar, A. Ramesh (2007). SBI and Its Role in The Microfinance Movement. In Kamdar Sangita (Ed.), *Microfinance Self-Employment and Poverty Alleviation* (pp. 74-78). New Delhi: Himalaya Publishing House.

Mangala, A. Sabadra. (2010, April). Microfinance – A Tool for Poverty Eradication. *Journal of Commerce and Management Thought*, I (2).

Meitei Surjit and Singh Rajmani, (2011), Microfinance and Women's Socio-Economy, *DGCCS's Journal of Commerce*, VIII (I) page 60-68.

Microfinance and the Rural Poor: Impact Assessment Based on Field work in Madhya Pradesh, India, Niranjan Sarangi, 26th January 2007.

Micro Save, Market-led solutions for financial services, Savings- an Essential Service for the Poor, optimising performance and efficiency series.

Ministry of Development of North Eastern Region, Minutes of the Meeting chaired by Shri Pranab Mukherjee, Hon'ble Minister of External Affairs, to discuss issues relating to "Look East Policy *vis-à-vis*. North Eastern region" venue-vigyanbhawan, New Delhi, 31st October 2007.

Pandey, Manas. (2008, July-September). Micro Financing: A Blessing for the Poor. *The Indian Journal of Commerce*, 61(3), 48-52.

Pangannavar, Arjun Y. (2008, Dec.). Self-Help Groups and Rural Poverty. *Kurukshetra*, 57(2), 12-16.

Rajkumar, K Prabakkar. (2006, September). Refinancing Support of NABARD to Self-Help Groups (SHGs) in Tamil Nadu during 1996-97 to 2001-02. *Banking Finance*, 7-15.

Rangarajan, C. (2005) Microfinance and its future directions, New Delhi, *Keynote Address during High Level Policy Conference on Microfinance in India*- May 3.

Rao, K Srinivasa. (2008, December). Financial Inclusion: Taking Banking Services to the Bottom of the Pyramid. *Banking Finance*, 5-12.

Sharma, B. Ashok. (2009, April-June). The Success of Microfinance in India. *Microfinance World, NABARD,* 4-6.

Sharma, Puspa Raj (2005). Millennium Development Goals and International Year of Microfinance in Nepal. *The Journal of Nepalese Business Studies II* (1) Dec.

Shiralashetti, A.S. and S.S. Hugar (2008, January). Micro Finance – A study of Self-Help Groups and Bank Linkage. *The Journal of Business Studies,* 5(9), 31-37.

Singh, Gurmeet. (2009, Feb). Microfinance—An Innovation in Rural Credit System. *Kurukshetra,* 3-6.

Singh, Rajmani. (2008). Micro Finance for Micro Enterprise Development – A Panacea to Poverty Alleviation. *DGCCS's Journal of Commerce,* V(1), 142-150.

Singh, Rajmani (2012) Microfinance for Micro-entrepreneurs:Boon or Bane. Published in edited volume of Inclusive Financial Structure, Edited by Rudra P. Pradhan, Bloomsbury New Delhi-70 pp. 268-275

Sinha, Frances (2007). SHGs in India: Numbers, poverty outreach and empowerment, partially. In Dichter Thomas & Harper Malcolm (Eds.), *What's wrong with MICROFINANCE?* (pp. 73-82). UK, England: Intermediate Technology Publications Ltd.

Sriram, S.M. (2008, January). Commercialisation of Microfinance. *Yojana,* 52, 33-35.

Srivastava, Swami Prakash (2009). Micro-Credit and Its Role In Poverty Alleviation and Rural Development of India. In Ahmed Rais (Ed.), *Micro-Finance and Women Empowerment* (pp. 653-671). New Delhi, India: Mittal Publications.

The Future of Microfinance: Visioning the who, what, when, where, why, and How of Microfinance Expansion over the Next 10 years, H.I. Latifee, Managing Director Grameen Trust Bangladesh.

Thekkekara, T.F. (2007). The SHG Movement in South Asia – A perspective on empowerment of women. In Kamdar Sangita (Ed.), *Microfinance Self-Employment and Poverty Alleviation* (pp. 111-155). New Delhi: Himalaya Publishing House.

Thorat, Y.S.P. (2005) Theme Paper at the High Level Policy Conference on Microfinance in India, New Delhi, 03 to 05 May, Microfinance In India: Sectoral Issues And Challenges.

Thorat, Usha (2007, June 19). Taking Banking Services to the Common Man– Financial Inclusion. *MT-DFID Financial Inclusion Conference 2007.* Whitehall Place, London, UK.

Understanding the Clients of Microfinance: A Household Level Study in Manipur. Friends of Women's World Banking, India.

Vyas, V.S. (2007). The Microfinance Movement: An Assessment. In Sangita Kamdar (Ed.), *Microfinance Self-Employment and Poverty Alleviation* (pp. 1-13). New Delhi: Himalaya Publishing House.

Index